The Spirit That Moves Us

A Literature-Based Resource Guide:
Teaching About Diversity, Prejudice, Human Rights,
and the Holocaust

Volume I, Grades Kindergarten through Four

Laura R. Petovello, J.D.
Revised by Donna Taranko and Sharon Nichols, 1998

In association with The Holocaust Human Rights Center of Maine

Tilbury House, Publishers
Gardiner, Maine

Tilbury House, Publishers
132 Water Street
Gardiner, Maine 04345

First printing, revised edition: October, 1998.

10 9 8 7 6 5 4 3 2 1

Library of Congress Cataloging-in-Publication Data

Cover Photos: Copyright ©1998 Robert I. Katz
Layout: Nina Medina, Basil Hill Graphics, Somerville, ME
Editing and Production: Jennifer Elliott, Judith Robbins, Barbara Diamond
Printing and Binding: InterCity Press, Rockland, MA

This resource guide is dedicated to Gerda Haas,
educator, author, survivor, and the spirit
behind "the spirit that moves us."

Contents

Introduction
Objectives of *The Spirit That Moves Us*   7
Children's Literature as a Vehicle for Achieving Objectives   8
An Overview of *The Spirit That Moves Us*   8
Internet Resources   9
About The Holocaust Human Rights Center of Maine   10

CHAPTER I *Celebrating Diversity*   11
Introduction   11
Diversity within the Human Family   11
The Power of Naming   12
Race versus Ethnicity   13
Lesson Plans
    Everybody Cooks Rice   14
    Ben's Trumpet   20
    How My Parents Learned to Eat   24
    My Buddy   30
Additional Recommended Children's Books on Diversity   33

CHAPTER II *Learning from Many Cultures*   37
Introduction   37
Guidelines for Choosing Multicultural Literature   38
Teaching about Native Americans   39
A Message to Teachers   39
Lesson Plans
    Why Mosquitoes Buzz in People's Ears   40
    Gluskabe and the Four Wishes   44
    Brother Rabbit: A Cambodian Tale   48
    The Woman Who Outshone the Sun   52
Additional Recommended Children's Books on Diverse Cultures   56

CHAPTER III *Creating Community*   63
Introduction   63
Meaning of Community   63
Making Communities Competent   64
Human Rights as Expressions of Community Values   65
    History of Human Rights   65
    The Nature of Human Rights   65
    The United Nations and Human Rights   67
    Community, Human Rights, and Citizenship   68
Lesson Plans
    The Mitten   69
    Sam Johnson and the Blue Ribbon Quilt   74
    Blueberries for Sal   78
    Uncle Willie and the Soup Kitchen   82
Additional Recommended Children's Books on Community   87

CHAPTER IV *Confronting Prejudice*   91
   Introduction   91
   Key Concepts   91
   Definitions for Children   92
   Challenging Prejudice in the Schools   92
   Using Children's Books to Confront Prejudice   93
   Lesson Plans
     Amazing Grace   94
     Tar Beach   99
     Angel Child, Dragon Child   103
     The Hundred Dresses   108
     White Wash   113
   Additional Recommended Children's Books on Prejudice   116

CHAPTER V *Beginning Holocaust Studies*   119
   Introduction   119
   Definitions   119
   Topics and Lessons   120
   Teacher Preparation   121
   Student Preparation   122
   Teaching the Books   122
   Themes in Holocaust Children's Literature   123
   Lesson Plans
     Terrible Things   124
     Best Friends   129
     The Lily Cupboard: A Story of the Holocaust   133
     The Number on My Grandfather's Arm   136
     Child of the Warsaw Ghetto   139
     Passage to Freedon: The Sugihara Story   144
   Additional Recommended Children's Books on the Holocaust   148
   References for Teachers and Students   148

APPENDIX A *Articles for Teachers*   152
   Introduction   152
   Why Do People Hate, by Herbert Buschbaum   152
   The Holocaust: An Historical Summary, United States Holocaust Memorial Museum   154
   Children in the Holocaust   159
   Guidelines for Teaching About the Holocaust, United States Holocaust Memorial Museum   162
   The United Nations Declaration on the Rights of the Child, 1959   172

APPENDIX B *Resources for Teachers*   173
   Introduction   173
   Resources for Teachers: Bibliography   173
     Part 1: Ethnic Studies   173
     Part 2: Prejudice and Discrimination   180
     Part 3: Human Rights   181
     Part 4: The Holocaust   181
     Part 5: Ecology   184
     Part 6: Teaching Strategies   185
     Part 7: Videography   185
   Resources for Teachers: Holocaust and Human Rights Resource Organizations   189
   Resources for Teachers: Recommended Children's Books   189

Acknowledgments

Many people—teachers, librarians, curricular consultants, members of the Holocaust Human Rights Center and Education Institute boards, and secretarial staff—assisted with the planning, review, evaluation, and preparation of *The Spirit That Moves Us.* The author would like to thank Nancy Andrews, Esther Glusker, Shirley Helfrich, Rita Kissen, Peg Stewart, Robert Katz, Roberta Gordon, John Mizner, Sharon Jackiw, Tony Brinkley, Ragnhild Baade, Yvon Labbé, Rhea Côté Robbins, Herbert Martin, Gerry Morin, William Baker, Gerda Haas, George Lyons, Merle Nelson, Gary Nichols, Sharon Nichols, Nancy Schatz, William Small, Landon Summers, Steve Black, Walter Taranko, Maizie Argondizza, Mary Robinson, Paula Dunfee, Beth Lyons, Anne Pooler, Donna Taranko, Deborah Ullman, Winnie McPhedran, Selma Black, Ari Levy, Richard Riley, Joyce Spinelli, Pam Marschall, Brandon Bayne, Chris Nichols, Angela Thibodeau, Sheila Wilensky-Lanford, Jennifer Elliott, and Dawn C. Cormier.

The author especially thanks the teachers and librarians at the schools that piloted the Guide—Belgrade Elementary School, Canaan Christian School, Levey Hebrew Day School, Manchester Elementary School, and Reiche Elementary School—for their review and comments. Finally, we are grateful to the Maine State Library staff, without whose unstinting assistance the Guide could not have been completed.

A special acknowledgment goes to the 1997–1998 third grade class at Wayne Elementary School for their assistance in selecting the books for the revised edition. Our deepest appreciation to Winnie McPhedran for reviewing the revised edition.

Introduction

*The hearts of little children are pure, and
therefore, the Great Spirit may show to them
many things which older people miss.*
—Black Elk

The Holocaust began over fifty years ago. This is ancient history for today's students. What possible connection exists between the Holocaust and education for the youngest students? What can elementary students learn from understanding some of the context in which the Holocaust occurred? Why should teachers want to prepare children for Holocaust studies?

The Holocaust was conceived and perpetrated by educated members of Christian, Western developed nations. In an open letter to teachers, a Holocaust survivor gives the best, and really the only necessary, reason for *The Spirit That Moves Us*.

> Dear Teacher:
>   I am a survivor of a concentration camp. My eyes saw what no man should witness:
>   Gas chambers built by LEARNED engineers; Children poisoned by EDUCATED physicians; Infants killed by TRAINED nurses; Women and babies shot and burned by HIGH SCHOOL and COLLEGE graduates.
>   So I am suspicious of education.
>   My request is: Help your students become human. Your efforts must never produce learned monsters, skilled psychopaths, educated Eichmanns.
>   Reading, writing, and arithmetic are important only if they serve to make our children more humane."
>
>   —Haim Ginott[1]

Social psychologists tell us that children learn prejudice early in their lives. But just as prejudice and hate can be taught, so can their opposite values: tolerance, acceptance, love. The "spirit" in the title of this Guide refers to those attitudes and values which lead people to do good deeds; when confronted with moral choices, to do what is right. The Holocaust Human Rights Center of Maine believes that schools are one of the best hopes for instilling this spirit in young students, thus reducing the possibility of future genocides.

OBJECTIVES OF *THE SPIRIT THAT MOVES US*

Through the reading of children's literature, *The Spirit That Moves Us* hopes to inspire in early elementary students:

- an understanding of the concepts of diversity, culture, community, prejudice, and human rights;
- a vision of a world where people are embraced for their similarities and appreciated for their differences;
- an understanding of the harm caused by prejudice and an ability to confront prejudice individually and as part of a community;
- an ability to think critically about human behavior;
- a desire to act morally.

[1] Haim Ginott, *Teacher and Child* (New York: MacMillan, 1972), p. 317.

CHILDREN'S LITERATURE AS A VEHICLE FOR ACHIEVING THE OBJECTIVES

Telling stories is an ancient tradition. The books in *The Spirit That Moves Us* tell stories about different people in many different situations. Intuitively, it makes sense that stories not only entertain but also teach. The experience of numerous educators bears out this supposition.

Dealing with Diversity through Multicultural Fiction, by Lauri Johnson and Sally Smith, describes a successful project to help students develop critical reading skills and confront prejudice by reading and discussing fiction. Summarizing their experience, the authors believe this works because:
* children read differently when they read for pleasure than when they read to gain information;
* children need access to a variety of books that address their developmental needs;
* children can identify with characters like themselves;
* children can develop empathy with characters whose life experiences are different from their own;
* children's books transmit values and perceptions of the world.[2]

The Spirit That Moves Us uses literature as a springboard for teaching concepts, critical thinking skills, and values. Accomplishing this by reading interesting, moving, and beautiful books is a pleasurable approach for children and teachers.

AN OVERVIEW OF *THE SPIRIT THAT MOVES US*

The Spirit That Moves Us is a resource guide rather than a curriculum. It is not intended to be read as a book. Teachers are not only encouraged, but are expected, to choose the books that best fit their teaching goals and to develop their own curricular approaches.

Children in grades kindergarten through four have significant differences in interests and reading abilities. The author has indicated an appropriate grade level for each book, but only as a suggestion. Teachers are the best judge of books appropriate for their classrooms.

This introduction and chapters one through five begin with an introduction offering background information useful to teaching the books. Next, lesson plans summarize the featured books, identify concepts, give discussion questions that move from comprehension to analysis, and suggest multidisciplinary activities to reinforce the concepts. The concluding section of these chapters annotates additional children's books to supplement or to use instead of the books with lesson plans. Teachers should also note the additional resources listed in Appendix B, arranged by subjects relevant to the suggested lessons.

The activities are specific to the book for which the lesson plan was developed. Many of the activities, however, are transferable to other books in the Guide. The majority of activities is most suitable for children in grades two through four, but are adaptable for younger students. It is not necessary to use all of the activities in each plan to teach the concepts. For most books, several of the suggested activities will be sufficient.

Appendix A, "Articles for Teachers," provides material on the concepts and historical events portrayed in the children's literature. Appendix B, "Resources for Teachers," has an extensive annotated bibliography of resource materials, a videography, a list of organizations where teachers can obtain additional information or classroom speakers, and a list by author of the children's books annotated in *The Spirit That Moves Us*.

---

[2] Lauri Johnson and Sally Smith, *Dealing with Diversity through Multicultural Fiction* (Chicago: American Library Association, 1993), pp. 35-37.

INTERNET RESOURCES

The Internet can provide a variety of resources that are of use to both teachers and students. However, it also contains misinformation, personal diatribes, and other material inappropriate for students. Particularly when searching for information about the Holocaust, students are apt to stumble onto "Holocaust revisionists" (deniers), Neo-Nazi propaganda, and other material created by hate groups. Teachers are advised to work with students when using the Internet, to make the process of finding information interactive between student and teacher, not just student and computer.

The following web sites contain information that may be used in conjunction with the lesson plans in this guide. The sites included here are only those created and maintained by legitimate organizations. While some information created by individuals may be useful to students, individual web sites are not included here due to the uncertainty about the quality and content of the information they contain. Legitimate, responsible organizations such as those included here should contain links to other reliable web sites that may be used by supervised students.

Because information on the Internet is always changing, it is possible that some of these sites may no longer exist when students and teachers try to access them. In that case, use one of the search engines to search for key words, such as "Holocaust," "human rights," or "social activism" to find similar sites that may be useful. Teachers are advised to check the validity of the resources accessed by such a search before exploring them with students.

1. Teaching Tolerance
   http://www.splcenter.org

   Teaching Tolerance is a national education project dedicated to helping teachers foster equity, respect and understanding in the classroom and beyond. There are many free curriculum resources listed.

2. Multicultural Pavilion at the University of Virginia
   http://curry.edschool.virginia.edu/go/multicultural/teachers.html

   This site contains articles for teachers on multicultural issues and philosophy, paths to other sites, a Multicultural Song Database, and a Teacher's Corner, which provides online exchange and networking opportunities for teachers and their students.

3. The United States Holocaust Memorial Museum
   http://www.ushmm.org/index.html

   This site contains a complete description of the museum, as well as information for teachers on teaching about the Holocaust and for students on learning about the Holocaust.

4. The Simon Wiesenthal Center and the Museum of Tolerance
   http://www.wiesenthal.com

   The museum of tolerance focuses on the dynamics of racism and prejudice in America and the history of the Holocaust. This web site includes an on-line tour of the museum, as well as lists of events and resources, and information designed especially for kids. Included in this site is "The Children of the Holocaust," which contains different biographies of children who lived through or died in the Holocaust.

5. Anti-Defamation League
    http://www.adl.org/

    This site contains information on the Anti-Defamation League's *A Classroom of Difference*, diversity training programs, and much more.

6. Skipping Stones Magazine
    http://www.nonviolence.org/skipping/

    This site provides teaching resources and information on videos and multicultural books.

7. The Holocaust Human Rights Center of Maine
    http://www.state.me.us/msl/hhrc/htm

    This site includes information on the Center's activities, traveling exhibits, and resource guides.

ABOUT THE HOLOCAUST HUMAN RIGHTS CENTER OF MAINE

The Holocaust Human Rights Center (HHRC) grew out of a seminar, "Teaching about the Nazi Holocaust in Maine Schools," held at Bowdoin College in 1984. The participants found the seminar to be a powerful and compelling commentary on the fragility of democracy. Under the leadership of Gerda Haas, a Holocaust survivor and author of a book on the Holocaust, they formed the Holocaust Human Rights Center of Maine. Incorporated in May 1985, the Center's mission is to educate about the Holocaust, to advocate for human rights and dignity, and to celebrate diversity.

The HHRC sponsors educational programs, distributes information about speakers and resources, helps educators develop local programs and curricula, and contributes books and videos to the Holocaust collection at the Maine State Library.

CHAPTER 1

Celebrating Diversity

And I look forward to a world which will be safe, not only for democracy and diversity, but also for personal distinction.
—John F. Kennedy

INTRODUCTION

As our world grows smaller, and our need to get along with each other grows larger, understanding and appreciating human diversity become ever more important. In the United States, with our great "cultural mosaic," teachers have a unique opportunity to demonstrate the benefits of celebrating differences.

Few educators would argue with teaching the democratic ideals of tolerance and equality. We need only look to Nazi Germany to find a chilling example of the power of education to pervert democracy by teaching the physical, intellectual, and moral superiority of one group over all others.

In the acclaimed film *Europa, Europa*, the lead character, a Jewish teenager, finds himself masquerading as a German in an elite school for Nazi youth. A professor visits the class to teach the "science" of racial purity. He selects the boy for an experiment, using calipers to measure his forehead, nose, chin, and ears, comparing the measurements to the standards for Aryan purity. When his experiment is complete, he tells the class that while the boy is not of the very highest level, presumably because he has dark hair and eyes, he is nevertheless, scientifically, one-hundred-percent Aryan. The inescapable conclusion: the boy is one of us, not one of them.

This scene is terrifying for the poor boy, who expects his charade (and attempt to survive) to be discovered at any moment. It could be amusing to watch the pompous professor make a fool of himself, except that the audience knows the Nazi and his impressionable students believed this "science."

Using difference to define minority groups as "other," somehow less human and worthy than the majority, did not begin with anti-Semitism or end with the Holocaust. All one has to do is open a newspaper to see examples of hatred in our schools and communities, based on fear of diversity.

Two educational movements—teaching tolerance for diversity and teaching multiculturally—have been advanced by theorists and practitioners alike as methods for countering intolerance and hatred. In this and the next chapter, *The Spirit That Moves Us* introduces children's literature featuring concepts central to these movements.

This chapter, "Celebrating Diversity," focuses on diversity told through stories of contemporary children and families in the United States. Chapter Three, "Learning From Many Cultures," uses creation stories, folktales, legends, histories, and contemporary stories from various cultures to celebrate diversity. Because information in both introductions is relevant to both chapters, teachers may want to read them as one unit on teaching diversity through multicultural children's literature.

DIVERSITY WITHIN THE HUMAN FAMILY

Understanding that people, regardless of perceived or real differences, are fundamentally alike is the first step to seeing diversity as a source of wealth. Through children's literature, children can discover that all people are biologically similar, grow up in families of some sort, have talents and aspirations for the future, and have cultures created by shared history, language, traditions, spirituality, and environment.

Analysis of commonalities sets the stage for recognizing individual, familial, and cultural differences. For example, all people have similar facial characteristics differentiating them from other species, but within this commonality lies great diversity. Everywhere children grow up in families, but families may be nuclear, tribal, institutional, or of some other structure.

Although much of the diversity portrayed in children's literature is cultural, a wide variety of diversity is available for analysis. In the Guide's books, children can discover diversity in:
• physical appearance;
• gender;
• skills and talents;
• likes and dislikes;
• emotions and reactions to different situations;
• family structure;
• affectional and sexual preferences;
• language;
• customs, traditions, and other aspects of culture;
• life experiences.

When children conceptualize that diversity complements our common humanness, teachers can help children understand why all people should be treated fairly, equally, and with kindness. Because diversity is part of our humanity, celebrating diversity means we can learn from each other, delighting in what our individual, familial, and cultural differences have to say about being human.

Patricia Beilke and Frank Sciara suggest that teaching young children about diversity leads to the following results:
• recognizing differences in others and considering these differences in a positive light;
• including "left out" children in the "in" group;
• recognizing and respecting the rights and privileges of others;
• motivating children to think about themselves and others and their influence upon one another;
• considering and respecting the feelings of others;
• learning that nonacceptance of others harms both the name-caller and the one verbally attacked;
• learning about children of different ethnic groups and socio-economic backgrounds.[1]

When children see themselves mirrored in the books valued by their teachers, children develop self-esteem. When children see their teachers value people who are perceptibly different, children develop empathy for those they might otherwise fear or hate. By giving children the knowledge, critical thinking skills, and values to understand diversity, teachers lay the groundwork for children to create community and respond to prejudice.

THE POWER OF NAMING

Names define who we are. For minority groups that historically have been discriminated against, naming is especially important. Names can connote authority, status, and value, or they can be used to denigrate and dehumanize.

Naming is also an act of personal and group power. In the United States, many minority groups have been labeled by the majority with inaccurate or pejorative names. Insisting upon a valued, accurate name often has been the first step in a group's movement for human rights.

The act of self-definition is dynamic, changing as group consciousness changes. For example, prior to the civil rights movement, African Americans were named "colored" or "Negro," defined by the white majority according to race or an inaccurate reference to skin color. In the 1960's African Americans embraced the name "Black," renaming themselves with pride. In the 1990's African Americans have insisted on another change, this time naming themselves according to their ancestry and status as Americans, rather than skin color.

Other groups—such as Franco-Americans, people with disabilities, gays and lesbians, and Latino people—are engaged in a similar process. Because this process is fluid, not all group members may be satisfied with the same name. The safest course to pursue is to ask, and use, the name a group or indi-

[1] Beilke, P. and F. Sciara, *Selecting Materials for and about Hispanic and East Asian Children and Young People.* Hamden, CA: Library Professional Publications, 1986.

vidual prefers. For example, some Native Americans prefer to be called Indians, others native peoples, still others Native Americans, and some by their tribal designation. Using the preferred name shows respect for self-definition and autonomy.

When referring to a particular book, I have kept the names used by the author. For non-Native groups living in the United States, I have appended "American" to the group's ancestry or ethnicity to denote United States residence and/or citizenship. For example, Asians are people living in Asia; Asian Americans are people of Asian ancestry living in the United States.

Because cultures vary within regions of the world, I also have been as specific as possible when referring to a group. For example, the Abenaki, Lakota Sioux, and Navajo are all Native Americans with cultural and historical similarities, but also with many differences. People from eastern Asia have commonalities, but also significant cultural distinctions. Accordingly, we use Chinese American, Japanese American, Vietnamese American, etc., when referring to specific Asian American ethnic groups.

Finally, unless a word is pejorative, we have kept the terms used within the books themselves. Some books refer to Cambodia, others to Kampuchea. Some refer to the great creator of the Wabanaki as Glooskap, others as Koluscap or Gluskabe. Some of the Holocaust books use the German names for concentration camps, others use the name given by the country in which the camp was located. Rather than attempt uniformity, we have retained the author's choices.

RACE VERSUS ETHNICITY

Because "race" is such a loaded word, one that is widely misunderstood and misapplied, we recommend that teachers not explain diversity in racial terms. For example, Nazi Germany defined Jews as a separate racial group, but there is no Jewish race.

As John Langone explains in *Spreading Poison*, race is a social construct used to classify human beings into groups. Anthropologists recognize three human races: Caucasoid, or white; Negroid, or black; and Mongoloid, or yellow. All people can be assigned to a race or subgroup within a race based on their physical appearance, but really this serves no purpose. Anthropologists also have established that all races originated from common ancestors who were black. Human physical differences resulted over time from adaptations to different environments. At best, racial classification provides a gross method for subdividing the one human race. At worst, it fosters racism through the incorrect and unsubstantiated belief that different races have different inherited characteristics such as athletic ability, intelligence, or criminality.

A more useful way to categorize people is by their ethnicity or ancestry. In *Teaching Strategies for Ethnic Studies*, James Banks defines an *ethnic group* as people who share a sense of group identification, a common set of values, political and economic issues, and other cultural elements. Ethnicity does not necessarily denote a minority. For example, people of English ancestry might be the single largest reported ethnic group in a particular state. They are the majority, but also an ethnic group.

Banks defines a *minority ethnic group* as one with unique physical and/or cultural characteristics that enable people who belong to the majority group to identify minorities easily and to discriminate if so inclined. For example, he says that Jews are properly characterized as an ethnic group with unique cultural and religious characteristics. In Israel, Jews are the majority group. In the United States, Jewish Americans are a minority ethnic group. Similarly, Native Americans have unique physical and cultural characteristics based on ancestry and history. In post-colonized America, Native Americans are a minority ethnic group. Emphasizing racial differences ultimately leads to a dead end. It separates people arbitrarily, telling us nothing about their language, culture, history, or values. Presenting cultural diversity free of stereotypes based on race is one way to teach children about the similarities and differences among groups of people.

Sources

Banks, James A. *Teaching Strategies for Ethnic Studies.* 5th ed. Boston: Allyn & Bacon, 1991.

Beilke, Patricia F. and Frank J. Sciara. *Selecting Materials for and about Hispanic and East Asian Children and Young* People. Hamden, CT: Library Professional Publications, 1986.

Langone, John. *Spreading Poison: A Book about Racism and Prejudice.* Boston: Little, Brown and Companuy, Inc., 1993.

United States Department of Commerce. Economic and Statistics Administration, Bureau of the Census. *Statistical Abstract of the United States* 1993. Washington, DC: GPO, 1993.

LESSON PLAN FOR:
Everybody Cooks Rice,
**by Norah Dooley. Minneapolis: Carolrhoda Books, 1991.
Grades K-4**

Story Summary

Carrie's younger brother Anthony is late for dinner. She knows if he is not outside playing, he is probably at a neighbor's house mooching food. At Mrs. D's, who is from Barbados, the family is sitting down to a dinner of black-eyed peas and rice. Carrie does not find Anthony, but she does have a taste of their dinner. She next tries the Diazes', from Puerto Rico, who are making rice and pigeon peas colored yellow by turmeric. As Carrie searches among her neighbors, she also samples rice flavored with fish sauce from Vietnam, biryani from India, steamed rice with tofu and vegetables from China, and creole-style rice from Haiti. When she arrives home, she finds her brother already there, waiting for dinner. Carrie, though, is too full to eat the Italian *risi e bisi,* rice and peas, cooked by her mother.

Concepts Summary

While emphasizing people's basic similarity, Carrie's story shows children how much cultural and ethnic diversity can exist in one United States neighborhood. She and Anthony have welcomed the immigrant families into their community, learning from and enjoying the different peoples inhabiting their immediate world.

Objectives

The student should be able to:
- identify the different peoples, places from which they emigrated, cultures, and family structures in the story;
- analyze the similarities shared by the story's characters;
- understand the concepts of ethnicity and immigration;

- recognize that the United States is a pluralistic country composed of many Native and ethnic groups;
- recognize how diversity enhances the protagonists' lives and analyze how diversity can enhance the student's life.

Materials

Books: *Everybody Cooks Rice*, by Norah Dooley; *Corn is Maize*, by Aliki
Art Supplies: Paper, markers, crayons, colored pencils, pastels, prints, clay, papier-mâché, art pictures
Music: Recordings of symphonic, jazz, rap, rock and roll, folk, salsa or other kinds of music
Equipment: Measuring spoons and cups; world map; apples and oranges; different types of rice; lined sand box, dirt; costumes

CONCEPT: *MEANING OF DIVERSITY*

Discussion Questions
- Why did Anthony like to visit so many houses in his neighborhood?
- What is a "moocher"?
- How do Carrie and her neighbors look different? How do they look alike?
- How is Carrie's family different from and the same as her neighbors'?
- How do you think Carrie's daily life is different from and the same as her neighbors'?
- Why do you think people from so many different countries eat rice?
- Did Carrie like all of the rice dishes? Which ones did she seem to like best?
- Do you eat rice in your home? How is it prepared? Do you like it?

Activities

Art

- Show children several different drawing and painting supplies. Have them make a picture of their family, using each type of supply. Have children discuss how each supply was the same, different, and whether it was fun to use different types of art supplies.
- Divide children into groups, having each group analyze a different illustration. As a class, have each group present its findings, and then decide what is different and similar among the characters, their homes, and their meals.

Language Arts

- Using the illustrations to see what is similar and different among the characters, have children write their own definitions of different, same, and similar. Children can test the validity of their definitions by applying them to different aspects of the story.
- Have children choose one of the families, and tell or write a story about how their family is different from or similar to the one they chose.
- Older children can analyze the story's plot, discussing how the author uses the plot to explore the differences and similarities among the neighborhood residents.

Geography

- Help children locate each of the geographical settings in the story (Barbados, Puerto Rico, Vietnam, India, China, Haiti, Italy, United States) on a world map. Have children draw their own map of one of the chosen areas. Older children can identify the continent of each area.
- From the information given by the map, have older children analyze the area's differences and similarities; for example, some are islands, some are peninsulas, some border different oceans on the same continent, and some are relatively

bigger or smaller. Lead a discussion on the information that can be discovered from maps.

Social Studies

- For younger children, have them analyze what one cultural aspect, food, tells about cultural similarities and differences. For example, people from many cultures like rice, but also like to cook their rice with different flavorings and foods.
- Extend the lesson for older children by having them identify all the cultural aspects shown in the story. Make a list of what they identify. Then lead a discussion on cultural aspects of the children's lives, such as holidays, heroes, history, language, and traditions. Return to the first list, having children analyze what is missing. Discuss different ways children can learn about cultures, and what they would need to know to make accurate judgments about cultural differences and similarities.
- Show children different types of rice (white, brown, long and short grain, basmati, etc.). Have children examine each carefully, noting similarities and differences such as size, color, shape, and smell.
- Discuss the origin of rice as a food staple, how and where it grows, the different types of rice, its nutritional value, and how it can be combined with other foods to make a nutritionally complete meal. Have children cook and eat some of the rice recipes from the book.

Math

- For younger children, use the common exercise of adding and subtracting dissimilar objects to explain the concepts of difference and similarity.
- Use the recipes to teach weights and measures, e.g., the number of teaspoons in a tablespoon, the number of cups in a quart.
- Use the recipes to teach fractions. For example, in the biryani recipe, children can add the total number of teaspoons and the total number of cups of food used in the recipe.

Science

- Children can build a small rice paddy, perhaps in a sandbox, and attempt to grow rice. Have children draw, describe, and explain each stage of the growth process.

CONCEPT: *VALUE OF DIVERSITY*

Discussion Questions
- Do you think Carrie liked visiting her neighbors? Why?
- What did she learn from each family?
- If each family had cooked rice exactly the same way, do you think Carrie would have liked tasting each dish? Why or why not?

- Would you like to live in a neighborhood with people from many different cultures?
- Would it be scary? Why or why not?
- Would it be fun? Why or why not?

Activities

Art

- Have children draw a picture of an object, using their imaginations and different art supplies to create whatever they want. Tack the pictures on the wall. Now, draw a picture on the blackboard, telling children to draw exactly the same picture. Tack these pictures up too. Lead a discussion on which picture was more interesting to draw, having children analyze the value of diversity in art.
- Extend the lesson by showing children pictures of paintings using different cultural and artistic styles. Have them analyze how the styles are different, what pictures they personally like, and what it would be like if all artists could only paint in one style. Have children paint a picture in the style of their choice.

Music

- Using the same approach as in the art activity, have children listen to excerpts of culturally different types of music, analyze what they like, and speculate on what it would be like if all music were the same. Have children beat out typical rhythms from different types of music on percussion instruments.

Language Arts

- Have children tell or write a story about visiting two families: a fictional family that is just like theirs and their best friend's family. Have them analyze which family they would like to visit and why.

Social Studies

- Have children interview family members about their ethnic background, customs, and skills. Have each child report to the class. Have children identify the differences just within their own classroom, analyzing how knowing about differences and similarities benefits them.

Science

- Use multicultural examples to demonstrate the scientific and technological contributions of different cultures. For example, discuss how canoes and snowshoes were as integral to Native American peoples as sailing ships and skis were to Europeans. Have children analyze how science and technology from different cultures benefit them today.

CONCEPT: *PLURALISTIC SOCIETY*

Discussion Questions

- Why do you think people from so many different countries move to the United States?
- What are some other countries from which people have immigrated to the United States?
- Why does Carrie's mother speak English, while Mrs. Hua is just learning the language?
- When the first groups of Europeans moved to the United States, did they find people already living here? Who were those people?
- Do Native Americans still live in the United States? Where?
- Are there neighborhoods in your town where people from different countries live? Where are they from?

Activities

Art

- Have children create an art work in the medium of their choice showing an aspect of their family, ways they celebrate holidays, a clay sculpture of an important family artifact, or a collage. Ask them to discuss why these symbols are important to them.

Drama

- Using the characters in the story, have children tell or write a play about all the families at a neighborhood event, such as a picnic. Have children brainstorm on what kinds of foods they might bring, what they might have in common to talk about, and how the characters just learning English might communicate. If desired, have children act out the play.

Language Arts

- Have children identify the cultural aspects of the story: language, country of origin, foods. Have children apply the concept of cultural diversity to the story's plot.
- Extend the lesson for older children by identifying words from Native American and other non-English languages that are in common use. Lead a discussion on how words from different cultures become part of a common language.

Geography

- Using the world map, identify the languages typically spoken in each family's country of origin. By discussing why people in Haiti and Vietnam often speak French, why Puerto Ricans speak Spanish and English, and why many people in India speak English, introduce the concept of cross-cultural influences through colonization and other means.

Social Studies

- The story introduces cultural diversity by showing the country of origin for different languages and foods. Extend the lesson by having children identify additional countries they want to know about, offering similar information on immigrants from these countries. Older children can do this as a research project.
- For older children, have them generate a list of questions they would like answered about some of their state's ethnic groups. Enlist the school librarian in a research project to help each child answer one of the questions and report to the class. Invite an immigrant or a foreign visitor to class to lead the discussion.

Science

- Compare and contrast growing methods, cooking methods, and the nutritional value of rice with the native American grain maize. See *Corn is Maize* for information about corn's origin and uses. Have children experiment with different ways to cook rice and cornmeal.

Community Resources

Use this book as a springboard for an oral history project. With their parents' assistance, have children interview people on their street to discover their ethnic background. Children can ask their neighbors where their family originated, what stories they brought with them, and what recipes are passed generationally.

Other Recommended Children's Books
Transcultural studies:
Talking Walls, by Margy Burns Knight
People, by Peter Spier
How My Family Lives in America, by Susan Kuklin

Books featuring ethnic foods:
How My Parents Learned to Eat, by Ina R. Friedman
Angel Child, Dragon Child, by Michele Maria Surat
Tar Beach, by Faith Ringgold
Toby Belfer Never Had a Christmas Tree, by Gloria Teles Pushker
Mrs. Katz and Tush, by Patricia Polacco

Resources for Teachers
Banks, James A. *Teaching Strategies for Ethnic Studies*. 5th ed. Boston: Allyn & Bacon, 1991.
Banks, James A. and Cherry A. McGee Banks. *Multicultural Education: Issues and Perspectives*, 3rd ed. Seattle: University of Washington, 1997.
Gollnick, Donna M. and Philip C. Chinn. *Multicultural Education in a Pluralistic Society*. 2nd ed. Columbus, OH: Merrill Publishing, 1986.
Gomez, Ray. *Teaching with a Multicultural Pespective*. ED339548 91. 1992. http./www.ed.gov/databases/ERIC_Digests/ed339548.html, (2 July, 1998).
Miller-Lachmann, Lyn, ed. *Our Family, Our Friends, Our World: An Annotated Guide to Significant Multicultural Books for Children and Teenagers*. New Providence, NJ: R.R. Bowker, 1992.

Sine, Pat. *Multicultural Education Resources*. Oct. 8, 1997 http.//www.udel.edu/sine/educ/multcult.htm
    (2 July, 1998).

Resources for the Classroom

Blackaby, Susan. *One World: Multicultural Projects and Activities*. Mahwah, NJ: Troll Associates, 1992.
Hayden, Carla D., ed. *Venture into Cultures*. Chicago: American Library Association, 1992.
Heltshe, Mary Ann and Audrey Burie Kirchner. *Multicultural Explorations*. Englewood, CO: Teacher
    Idea Press, 1991.

Supplemental Children's Books

Aliki, *Corn is Maize: The Gift of the Indians*. New York: Crowell, 1976.
Brown, Ruth. *Alphabet Times Four*. New York: Dutton Children's Books, 1991.
Chermayeff, Ivan and Jane Clark. *First Words*. New York: Harry N. Abrams, Inc. 1990.

LESSSON PLAN FOR:

Ben's Trumpet, by Rachel Isadora. New York: Mulberry Books, 1979. Grades K-4

Story Summary

Ben, growing up in the 1920s, loves to hear the Zig Zag Club musicians play, filling the air with the sounds and rhythms of jazz. The trumpet is his favorite instrument. Ben plays an imaginary trumpet for hours at a time, until his friends laugh at him. Ben has a chance to realize his dreams, though, when the Zig Zag Club trumpet player shows Ben how to play a real trumpet.

Concepts Summary

Ben's story demonstrates how his individual interests and talents make him different in some ways from his friends. The story also implies the cultural influences on Ben's choice of instrument and music. His dream seems out of reach until Ben's desire and talent are recognized by an adult who had a similar dream, and who starts Ben on his path to self-expression.

Objectives

The student should be able to:

• recognize how Ben is different from and similar to other children, generalizing this to differences and similarities among all children;
• identify and analyze the historical and cultural influences forming Ben's dream;
• understand how the arts can express the self;
• learn about African American culture.

Materials

Books: *Ben's Trumpet*, by Rachel Isadora

Children of Promise: African-American Literature and Art for Young People, by Charles Sullivan

The People Could Fly: American Black Folktales, by Virginia Hamilton

The Knee-High Man and Other Tales, by Julius Lester

Art Supplies: Paper, markers, paints, clay

Music: Recordings of jazz, gospel, blues, rap, and orchestral music

Equipment: Materials for making percussion instruments, water glasses, spoons

CONCEPT: *INDIVIDUAL DIVERSITY*

Discussion Questions

- Is Ben playing a real trumpet? How do you play an imaginary trumpet?
- Why do you think Ben plays an imaginary trumpet? What does this tell you about Ben?
- Why does Ben stop playing his trumpet when teased by the other boys?
- What makes Ben different from his friends? How is he the same? How is Ben different from you? How is he the same?
- Do you think there are many ways people can be different? What are some of the ways?
- Do you want to be the same as everyone you know? Why or why not?
- Do you think it is possible for everyone to be the same? Why or why not?
- What are some ways you are different and special? Do you like these parts of yourself? Why?
- Do you like music? Why? How does music make you feel inside?
- If you played an instrument, what would it be? Why? What would your choice tell about you?
- What is Ben's special dream for himself?
- What does the behavior of Ben's friends and family tell you about their belief in Ben's dream?
- Who helps Ben learn to play the trumpet?
- Why do you think the trumpet player does this? What does he see in Ben that is similar to himself?
- Do you think Ben will grow up to be a jazz musician? Why or why not?
- Do you have a special dream? What is it? What can you do to make it come true?

Activities

Art

- Describe different forms of art, such as music, painting, clothes design, dance, and writing. Brainstorm about how art is self-expression. Have children prepare an original art work in a medium of their choice expressing a dream for their future.

Music

- Identify and explain the different instruments in the book. Bring examples of different instruments to the class. Show how to use them and have children make sounds on each instrument.

Language Arts

- Have children identify examples of artistic imagination and creativity. Have them analyze what makes a work creative. See if children can develop their own definitions of imagination and creativity, applying them to situations in the story and their own lives.
- Have students read a story and write their own story, discussing how the two activities require different kinds of imagination.
- Have children guess the meaning of "cat's meow." Identify other examples of slang expressions from the 1920s and compare them with current slang. For older children, lead a discussion on how slang enters language.

Math

- Demonstrate the connections between math and music. For example, using a keyboard, have children count the number of notes in a scale or the number of beats in a measure.
- For older children learning about fractions, have them analyze the similarities between fractions and rhythmic notations in music.

Science

- Have children experiment with ways objects can make sounds, and depending on the size and type of the objects, how the sounds are different. To explore how acoustics affect sound, have children use the objects in rooms of varying sizes.
- Have children make simple instruments—such as drums, cymbals, bells, and a xylophone out of filled glasses of water. Explore how and why each makes sounds. The materials used can be contrasted with materials that will not work; for example, cymbals made of wood will not "clang" as cymbals should.

CONCEPT: *CULTURAL INFLUENCE*

Discussion Questions

- From the pictures in the story, do you think Ben lived in the past? Why?
- What do the cars and clothes in the story tell about the era in which Ben lived?
- What does Ben look like? What do his appearance and place where he lives tell you about Ben's ethnic group?
- What is jazz? What is a jazz club?
- Have you ever been to a party or holiday celebration where music was played? What kind of music did you hear?
- Why do you think music is important when people gather to celebrate or have fun?
- What kinds of music do you like? Why?
- How do you think people get ideas for making different instruments? What kind of instrument could you make?
- Besides music, what are some other things you enjoy? How did you learn about these activities?

Activities

Art

- Identify how the clothing and cars in the book are different from those we see today. Children can draw different styles from the past, or can imagine and draw what they think clothes and cars will look like in the future.
- Show some of the artwork in *Children of Promise: African-American Literature and Art for Young People*. Lead a discussion on what the art tells about African-American culture and history. Have children create an art work showing African-American people.

Music

- Explore the difference between jazz and orchestral music by listening to examples of each. If possible, use examples of the same piece of music recorded in the different styles.
- Listen to examples of different music originating in African-American culture, such as gospel, jazz, blues, and rap. Teach children a gospel song. Have children discuss how each musical style makes them feel.
- For older children, discuss connections between African-American history and music. Have children analyze how music from an ethnic minority culture can become part of mainstream culture.

Language Arts

- Read several African-American folktales. Children may tell or write an original story based on a traditional folktale character.
- Help older children analyze the allegories in African-American folktales. Have children speculate whether Ben might have heard these stories, and what they would have told him about his history, culture, and values.
- Choose a culture represented in your state. Read a story from the culture, having children analyze what information and values are transmitted by the story.

History

- Prepare a lesson on basic African-American history. Help children analyze how this history might have influenced where Ben lived and his dream to be a musician.

Community Resources

Ask a musician, ideally a trumpet player, to visit the class and demonstrate different styles of music. Ask an African American to visit the class to talk about contemporary African-American culture.

Other Recommended Children's Books
Individual diversity:
Black Is Brown Is Tan, by Arnold Adoff
A Country Far Away, by Nigel Gray
Where's Chimpy? by Berniece Rabe
Why Am I Different? by Norma Simon
Owliver, by Robert Kraus
Tar Beach, by Faith Ringgold

American culture:
Amazing Grace: The Story Behind the Song, by Jim Haskins
Follow the Drinking Gourd, by Jeanette Winter

Resources For Teachers

Banks, James A. *Teaching Strategies for Ethnic Studies.* 5th ed. Boston: Allyn and Bacon, 1991.
Banks, James A. and Cherry A. McGee Banks, *Multicultural Education: Issues and Perspectives,* 3rd. ed.
    Seattle: University of Washington, 1997
Perry, Theresa and James W. Fraser, eds. *Freedom's Plow.* New York: Routledge, 1993.

Resources for the Classroom

Blackaby, Susan. *One World: Multicultural Projects and Activities.* Mahwah, NH: Troll Associates, 1992.
Hayden, Carla D., ed. *Venture into Cultures.* Chicago: American Library Association, 1992.
Skipping Stones: A Multicultural Children's Magazine, Eugene, OR.

LESSON PLAN FOR:
How My Parents Learned to Eat, by
**Ina R. Friedman. Boston:
Houghton Mifflin, 1984.
Grades K–4**

Story Summary

A young girl explains how her family eats
dinner. Her father and mother, John and Aiko,
met when John was a sailor stationed in
Yokohama where Aiko was a school girl. Every
day, they went for walks in the park. They
wanted to date, but were afraid to eat together
because John did not know how to use chopsticks and Aiko did not know how to use a
knife and fork. As they grew to like each other
more and more, they secretly found ways to
learn each other's customs. John was taught to
use chopsticks by a kind waiter in a Japanese
family-style restaurant. Aiko was taught to eat with a knife and fork by an uncle who knew Western
customs. In their home now, some days they eat with chopsticks and some days with knives and forks.

Concepts Summary

While explaining how John and Aiko learned each other's customs, the book explores the differences
between two cultures. Children can learn why it is important that people know and respect each
other's cultures, and how different customs and cultures can be combined in a family.

Objectives

The student should be able to:
• identify diverse family structures;

- identify differences and similarities between customs in Japan and the United States;
- learn about Japanese culture;
- understand how appreciation of and respect for different cultures and customs benefit everyone.

Materials

Books: *How My Parents Learned To Eat*, by Ina R. Friedman
Why Am I Different? by Linda Pellegrini
Long Is a Dragon, by Peggy Goldstein

Art Supplies: Paper, markers, water colors, paper for *origami*, black ink

Foods: Soybeans, *tofu*

Equipment: Map of Asia, abacus

CONCEPT: *FAMILY DIVERSITY*

Discussion Questions

- From clues in the story, how do you know John and Aiko married and started a family?
- Do all families have a mother, father, daughter, and uncle?
- What are some other members who might be part of a family?
- Who makes up your family? What family members do you live with? Who else is part of your family?
- How is the family in the story like your family? How is it different?
- Do you know any families with parents from different countries? Do they have different skin colors? Speak different languages? Have different religions?
- What do you think about seemingly different adults who marry and have a family? What might be positive? What might be difficult?
- What are some ways children may come to live in a family?
- Were you adopted, or was anyone you know adopted?
- Do you think all families should be alike? Why or why not?

Activities

Art

- Have children draw a picture of their family.

Language Arts

- Read *Why Am I Different?* Define adoption. Have children compare the differences and similarities among the family in this story, the family in *How My Parents Learned to Eat*, and their own families.
- Have children imagine that a long-lost relative has appeared at a family gathering. Have children tell or write a story about this family member's past and how he or she affects the family.

Social Studies

- Have children prepare a family tree and show their family drawing and family tree to the class, explaining the family structure and one thing they like about their family. Tack the drawings and trees on the wall, having children analyze the ways their and their classmates' families are similar and different, and what different family structures have to offer.
- As an alternative, adopted and foster children can develop a family tree based on their current living situation, noting the traits they have in common with non-biological family members and drawing conclusions about how similarities and differences exist in non-biologically related families.

Math

- For older children, have them extend their family trees into the future, adding children, relatives by marriage, and so on. Have children write a story problem requiring multiplication skills to illustrate the concept of geometrical expansion.

CONCEPT: *CULTURAL DIVERSITY*

Discussion Questions

- What do you think John and Aiko liked about each other?
- What customs did John and Aiko have in common? What customs were different?
- What values did John and Aiko have in common? What values were different?
- Why were John and Aiko scared to try different ways to eat?
- Why do you think people in some countries use chopsticks and people in other countries use knives and forks?
- Why did Aiko's uncle teach her to use a knife and fork?
- Why did the waiter help John learn to use chopsticks?
- What are some advantages of knowing how to eat with both chopsticks and knives and forks?
- What other customs are different in America and Japan?
- If you were to visit Japan, how would you learn Japanese customs?
- If a new friend had recently arrived in the United States, what customs do you think he or she might want to learn? How could you help teach them?
- Can you think of any customs it would be useful to know about in your state? How about eating a lobster? Walking with snowshoes? Building a fire in a woodstove?
- When you read the story, did you enjoy learning about Japan? Why, or why not?
- Have you ever traveled to a new city? State? Country? How were these places different from and the same as your hometown?
- What would it be like if every place you went and everyone you met were the same? Would you like this? Why or why not?

Activities

Art

- Look at examples of Japanese-style paintings and Western-style paintings. Discuss how they are different in style and use of color. Have children draw or paint a picture in a Japanese style.
- Introduce a Japanese art, such as *origami* or *ikebana* (flower arranging). Have children make original works of art using the new technique.

Language Arts

- Have children list the Japanese words used in the book (e.g., *sukiyaki*, *tofu*, *kimono*). Explain what each word means.
- The signs in the story are in Japanese. Have children compare Japanese and English writing.
- Using *Long is a Dragon*, teach children to draw Chinese characters. (There are three ways to write Japanese, one of which is based on Chinese.) Have children learn to write a word or sentence in Chinese. Discuss the differences and similarities between writing based on stylized pictures that form a concept and letters that combine to form a word.
- For older children, extend the lesson by showing different forms of written letters, such as in Greek, Arabic, or Hebrew alphabets. Have them learn to write some of the letters, comparing them to English ones.

Geography

- Using a map of Asia, have children locate Japan and Yokohama. Ask children to speculate why a sailor might be more likely to visit Yokohama than a city in the interior.
- Have children identify prominent geographical features of Japan. Have children compare features of Japan and the geography of their state.
- Identify other eastern Asian countries.

Social Studies

- Using the map of Asia, introduce similarities and differences among two or more eastern Asian countries, such as Japan, Vietnam, Kampuchea, Korea, and China.
- For older children, extend the lesson by having them analyze how history and geographical proximity can result in important similarities but also major differences in cultures that may appear alike on the surface. Children could also use this lesson to analyze regional differences within the United States.

Math

- Teach children to count, add, and subtract on an abacus. If older children become adept, hold a competition to see if an abacus and calculator are equally fast computational tools. Have children explore which kinds of computations can most easily be done with an abacus and which with a calculator.

Science

- Bring soybeans and *tofu* to class. Discuss the origins of *tofu* and how it is made. List other foods made from soybeans, and discuss how one food source can become so many different types of foods. Have children make a food, such as soy milk, from the soybeans.

CONCEPT: RESPECT FOR DIVERSITY

Discussion Questions

- In the story, why does the family use chopsticks some days and knives and forks on others?
- Why do you think they decided to do this? What might have happened if Aiko insisted the family always use chopsticks, or if John said they must all use forks and knives?
- What other customs might John and Aiko combine in their family? Do you think accommodating different customs is a good idea? Why or why not?
- What kinds of dinner customs does your family follow?
- If people from another culture visited your family, how would you feel if they made fun of your family's customs? Why would you feel this way?
- How do you think people from another culture would feel if you made fun of or refused to learn their customs? What could you do so this would not happen?
- What are some things you might learn from Japanese culture other than how to eat with chopsticks? Why might it be a good idea to understand Japanese culture?
- What are some things you have already learned from other cultures? How about playing hockey or paddling a canoe? What other things might you learn?

Activities

Language Arts

- Discuss what is meant by "foreign ways." Have children identify the different "foreign" customs in the book and explain what makes them foreign to John and to Aiko.
- Have children analyze how a "foreign" custom can become a natural part of life. Have children develop a definition of "foreign" and brainstorm words other than "foreign" to describe different customs.

Social Studies

- Have children collect examples of their family traditions. Ask them to describe where their traditions came from and why their family follows them. Children with parents from different cultures or traditions can explore how their families accommodated their different traditions; for example, eating vegetarian and non-vegetarian meals, celebrating both Hanukkah and Christmas.
- For older children, divide the class into several groups. Have each group study one or two customs, common to their state. Have each group report what they learned to the class, explaining the customs and how they could participate respectfully in them.
- For older children, have them imagine they are going to open a business in northern Japan to build their favorite snow sleds. Have children brainstorm on what they would need to know and how they would need to behave to have a

successful business. For example, have children learn several courtesy phrases in Japanese or practice eating with chopsticks. Ask children to consider what might happen if they did not take the time to learn this and act respectfully.

Community Resources
- Ask a person of Asian descent to describe a typical meal in his or her culture, how he or she eats in America, and what he or she likes about American food and Asian food. If the person is an immigrant, ask how he or she learned American customs.
- Extend this by asking the guest to describe and/or demonstrate customs other than those concerning food.

Other Recommended Children's Books
Family diversity:
Families Are Different, by Nina Pellegrini
Black Is Brown Is Tan, by Arnold Adoff
An Mei's Strange and Wondrous Journey, by Stephan Molnar-Fenton
I Have a Sister—My Sister Is Deaf, by Jeanne Whitehouse Peterson
At Daddy's on Saturdays, by Linda Walvoord Girard
POWWOW, by George Ancona
One Dad, Two Dads, Brown Dad, Blue Dad, by Johnny Valentine

Japanese culture:
Little Oh, by Laura Krauss Melmed and Jim Lamarche
Tree of Cranes, by Allen Say

Other Asian cultures:
Brother Rabbit: A Cambodian Tale, by Minfong Ho, Saphan Ros, Jennifer Hewetson
The Three Little Fawns, by Veasna Kem and Vech Pra
Judge Rabbit and the Tree Spirits, by Linda Mao Wall and Cathy Spagnoli
Angel Child, Dragon Child, by Michele Maria Surat

Transcultural studies:
The Way to Start a Day, by Byrd Baylor
Talking Walls, by Margy Burns Knight
How My Family Lives in America, by Susan Kuklin
People, by Peter Spier

Resources for Teachers
Perry, Theresa and James W. Fraser, eds. *Freedom's Plow.* New York: Routledge, 1993.

Resources for the Classroom
Blackaby, Susan. *One World: Multicultural Projects and Activities.* Mahwah, NJ: Troll Associates, 1992.
Hayden, Carla D., ed. *Venture into Cultures.* Chicago: American Library Association, 1992.
Heinz, Elgin. *Stepping Stones: Teaching About Japan in Elementary Grades.* Mill Valley, CA: The U.S.-Japan Education Group, 1991.
Li, Marjorie H. and Peter Li, eds. *Understanding Asian Americans: A Curriculum Resource Guide.* New York: Neal-Schuman Publishers, Inc., 1990.

LESSON PLAN FOR:
My Buddy, by Audrey Osofsky.
Illustrated by Ted Rand.
New York: Henry Holt, 1992.
Grades K-4

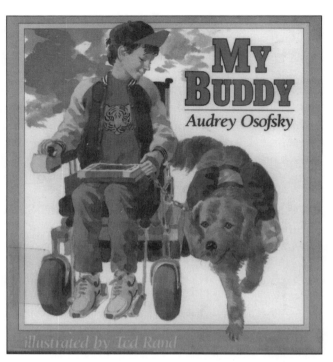

Story Summary

The narrator is a boy who has muscular dystrophy and who uses a wheelchair for transportation. His parents and friends help him, but he wants to do more for himself. Through a service dog program he learns to work with Buddy, a golden retriever. Buddy turns lights on and off, picks up the telephone, opens the door, and helps his master run errands in town. Buddy also goes to school, where he becomes an accepted member of the class.

Concepts Summary

The story challenges children to explore how people with disabilities are essentially the same as people without disabilities. It demonstrates how accommodation can minimize the effects of a disability. The story also shows how children struggle to establish identity and independence, thus becoming unique individuals.

Objectives

The student should be able to:
• identify the boy's disability and learn about different physical and mental abilities;
• analyze how people with disabilities are the same as everyone else;
• learn how environmental and technological adaptation minimize disability;
• understand and empathize with the boy's quest for independence.

Materials

Books: *My Buddy*, by Audrey Osofsky
        We Can Do It! by Laura Dwight
Art Supplies: Paper and markers
Equipment: Ramp and heavy ball or other object

CONCEPT: *DIFFERENT ABILITIES*

Discussion Questions

• Have you ever used a wheelchair? Do you know anyone who does?
• What are some of the things the boy can't do? What are some of the things he can do? With Buddy's help?
• Do you like the boy in the story? Why or why not? If he were a classmate, would you want to be his friend? What do you think you could learn from him?

- What is most important for us to know about the boy? Is it that he has a disability? Is it that he likes and wants to do the same things as his friends?
- How would you describe the boy to a friend who had not met him? How do you think he would describe himself?
- Do you know any children or adults who have a disability? How would you describe them to a friend?
- Do you have friends who can run faster or jump farther than you can? Does this mean you have a disability? Why or why not?

Activities

Art

- Have children draw a picture of how they see themselves physically.
- Pair children, having each draw a picture showing a physical ability or other talent of their classmate. Show the drawings to the class, having them analyze what the drawings say about the different abilities of their classmates.

Language Arts

- Have children make a list of three things they do well and three things they would like to be able to do but can't. Use this exercise to lead a discussion on the relativity of the terms ability and disability.
- People with disabilities are sensitive to the language used to describe them. Introduce the concept of "people first." Have children analyze why it is important to refer to people with disabilities as people first, people who happen to have a disability. Have children think of examples showing how labelling people by their physical condition is nonsensical, such as calling someone a "cold" or a "limp" when what they have is a cold or a limp.
- If it would not harm children in the class, have children make a list of stereotyping words, such as "retard" and "crippled," and discuss why these words hurt. Discuss respectful terms and methods for describing people with different disabilities.
- Have children imagine they have lost the ability to do something they take for granted, and tell or write a story about a day in their life. Children could describe some of the problems they might confront, or how they would want to be treated in school and in the community.
- Read *We Can Do It!* Have children explore how the children in this story are the same as everyone else.

Social Studies

- Ask children to describe how their self-identity might be changed if they had muscular dystrophy. Discuss whether they might feel different because of who they were, or because of how they were treated by others. Make a list of the ways they would like to be treated. (Other disabilities could be substituted or used to supplement the discussion.)
- Have children analyze ways other than physical abilities that people can be different, such as the country they live in, their religion, or their language. Have them discuss whether these differences make people good or bad, or whether they matter at all in terms of individual worth. Have children apply this analysis to people with various disabilities.

CONCEPTS: *ACCOMMODATION AND INDEPENDENCE*

Discussion Questions

- Why does the boy want to do more things on his own?
- What is important for you to be able to do on your own? Why?
- What do you do when you want to do something on your own, but don't know how?
- What does it mean when the boy said he had to learn to be a leader?
- What would you think about having a Service Dog accompany one of your classmates to school?
- Can you think of any barriers in your school or town that might make it difficult to use a wheelchair? What could be changed to make it easier to use a wheelchair?
- Can you think of other situations where a person might need assistance to be independent?
- What about a child who is lost on her first day in a new school? What might she need?
- What about a child who has moved to your school from another country and doesn't speak English? What might he need?
- What about a child with a broken leg? Who can't hear? Who can't see? Who has experienced the death of a loved family member or friend? What might they need?
- How would you want to be treated if you needed special assistance?

Activities

Language Arts

- Have children describe how the boy is both dependent and independent. Help children develop definitions of these terms and apply them to their own lives.
- Older children can contrast independence in the story's context with other meanings of independence, such as how the United States is an independent country.
- Have children list the ways the boy became more independent, even though he was not "cured," after he learned to work with Buddy.

Science

- Explain muscular dystrophy and how it and other disabilities are caused.
- List common disabilities, such as blindness, deafness, mental retardation, cerebral palsy, learning disabilities, and muscular dystrophy, explaining the limitations caused by each. Have children brainstorm methods for accommodating these disabilities so as to increase independence. Introduce technology of which children might be unaware, such as Braille or computer voice synthesizers. Have children experiment with these technologies, learning their basic use.
- Conduct an experiment on building a wheelchair ramp for a building that has steps. Have children experiment by rolling heavy objects up a ramp, steepening the incline until it is difficult to keep the object from rolling backwards. Have children speculate what would happen to a person using a wheelchair if a ramp were too steep.
- Have children survey their classroom and school for accessibility. For example, are there stairs to the school, the lunch room, the library? If there is an elevator, are the buttons labeled in Braille? Are there obstacles in the hallways that might trip someone with a visual impairment? If the school is completely accessible, have children survey the accommodations, such as curb cuts and ramps.
- When the survey is complete, have children brainstorm about ways to remove or accommodate barriers. Children can present their ideas to their principal.

Community Resources

- Ask adults with a disability to visit the classroom and discuss some of the barriers they faced and how they achieved independence.
- Ask someone from an independent living center to help plan the building survey and brainstorm about accommodations. Have them demonstrate different technological accommodations.

Other Recommended Children's Books

Disability:

Where's Chimpy? by Berniece Rabe
I Have A Sister—My Sister Is Deaf, by Jeanne Whitehouse Peterson
Mandy, by Barbara Booth

Differences and similarities:

Why Am I Different? by Norma Simon
The Day of Ahmed's Secret, by Florence Parry Heide and Judith Heide Gilliland
The Woman Who Outshone the Sun, by Alejandro Cruz Martinez
When Clay Sings, by Byrd Baylor

Independence:

The Paper Bag Princess, by Robert Munsch
Miss Rumphius, by Barbara Cooney

Resources for Teachers

Biklen, Douglas, Diane Ferguson and Alison Ford, eds. *Schooling and Disability*. Chicago: The National Society for the Study of Education, 1989.

> The following free resources are available from Teaching Tolerance, PO Box 548, Montgomery, AL 36101-0548:
>
> Order Fax: 334-264-7310
> Editorial fax: 334-264-3121
> Phone: 334-264-0286
>
> *Teaching Tolerance*, a semiannual magazine
> *Starting Small: Teaching Tolerance in Preschool and the Early Grades*, a video and text
> *The Shadow of Hate: A History of Intolerance in America*, video and text

Resources for the Classroom

ACTION Office of Equal Opportunity. *Handicap Accessibility: A Self-Evaluation Guidebook for ACTION and its Grantees*. Washington, D.C.: U.S. Government Printing Office, 1992.
Matiella, Ana Consuelo. *Positively Different: Creating a Bias-Free Environment for Young Children*. Santa Cruz, CA: ETR Associates, 1991.
Sygall, Susan and Cindy Lewis. *Global Perspectives on Disability: A Curriculum*. Eugene, OR: Mobility International USA, 1992.

Additional Recommended Children's Books on Diversity

Family Diversity

Adoff, Arnold. *Black Is Brown Is Tan*. New York: Harper Trophy, 1973. (Grades K–2)
    This book, in the form of a poem, tells of Momma, the color of chocolate milk, and of Daddy,

white, whose face turns tomato red when he puffs and yells the children into bed. In this family, children and grandparents, aunts and uncles, are all the colors of the human race.

Bloom, Suzanne. *A Family for Jamie.* New York: Clarkson Potter publications, 1991. (Grades K–2)
Molly and Dan live in the country, where they enjoy making all kinds of things. But they cannot make a baby, so they decide to adopt. The book describes the adoption process: visiting an adoption counselor, dreaming about what they will do with their child, preparing for the baby, accepting the help and gifts of family and friends, and welcoming Jamie into their home.

Girard, Linda Walvoord. *At Daddy's on Saturdays.* Morton Grove, IL: Albert Whitman & Co., 1987. (Grades 1–4)
Katie's dad moves out of the house when he and her mom are divorced. Katie is angry, sad, and afraid her dad will never come back. Katie's dad explains he is not getting divorced from her. He will always be her daddy. Katie's mom explains Katie did not make her dad go away; divorce is never a child's fault. Katie helps her dad learn to cook, and continues to share daily life with her mom. Katie learns that although divorce is sad, there are still things she can count on.

Pellegrini, Nina. *Families Are Different.* New York: Holiday House, 1991. (Grades K–4)
Nico is six. Because Nico and her sister were born in Korea, they look alike, but not like their parents. Nico feels sad and angry about this, until her mother tells her that there are different kinds of families. Nico looks around, seeing children living with one parent, two parents, or grandparents. There are families with stepsisters, or with parents who do not look like their biological children. Nico realizes she is like everyone else because she is different.

Ethnic and Physical Diversity

Baylor, Byrd. *Hawk, I'm Your Brother.* New York: Aladdin Books, 1976. (Grades K–4)
Rudy Soto, a Native American boy, dreams of flying like a hawk. He tries to find someone to teach him to fly, but people only smile when he asks for help. Rudy steals a young hawk, whom he hopes can teach him. Instead, the hawk screams and fights to escape the string tied to his leg. Rudy waits, wanting the hawk to be content with his life. When he sees this will never happen, Rudy realizes if he truly loves the hawk, he must release him to join the other hawks in the sky. Free now, the hawk flies, but he returns every day to call to Rudy. Rudy's people recognize he has become the hawk's brother, able to fly in his mind.

Baylor, Byrd. *When Clay Sings.* New York: Charles Scribner's Sons, 1972. (Grades K–4)
Through examples of Native American pottery from the American Southwest, Baylor explains how Native American children today make a game of searching for bits of clay that were the utensils of their ancient ancestors. Parents remind children that every piece of clay is a piece of someone's life, so it must be respected. For example, women must have sung special songs as they made the clay into bowls, mugs, and cooking pots. Sometimes children find pieces they can fit together and thus see the design. They recognize the symbols, still familiar to their culture.

Bonners, Susan. *The Wooden Doll.* New York: Lothrop, Lee & Shepard, 1991. (Grades K–4)
Stephanie visits her grandparents by herself for the first time. She longs to play with her Grandpa's wooden doll, but is told she is too young. When everyone else is asleep, however, she discovers two secrets. Her grandpa's special name for her, Stefania, is written on the bottom, and a whole family of dolls is nestled inside. That evening, Grandpa tells her the doll's story. It was his mother's doll, given to her by her father when Grandpa was born. Grandpa's mother gave him the doll when he left Poland to travel to America. Stephanie is named after her great grandmother, which is why her name is on the doll. Grandpa gives Stephanie the doll, but she decides to leave it at his house so he will not be lonely.

Bunting, Eve. *How Many Days to America?* New York: Clarion Books, 1988. (Grades K–4)
Subtitled "A Thanksgiving Story" and set in the Caribbean, Bunting's book puts a different slant on traditional Thanksgiving tales. A family decides they must leave after soldiers invade their village. Taking only money and a change of clothes, they flee to a small fishing boat crowded with other refugees. The trip is terrifying. The motor quickly breaks, their food and water run out, and many are sick. Thieves in a motorboat steal their few possessions. They find land, but soldiers will not allow them to come ashore. They sight land again. This time, the people on the dock call, "Welcome, welcome to America." For the refugees, it is not only "coming-to-America" day, it is their first Thanksgiving.

Gray, Nigel. *A Country Far Away*. New York: Orchard Books, 1988. (Grades K–4)
Everyday experiences—doing chores, going to school, riding bikes and playing soccer, celebrating the birth of a baby—are shown through the eyes of two young boys who live in two different countries and cultures. The illustrations demonstrate how the boys experience the same events. At the end, they dream of visiting a country far away and of making new friends.

Kuklin, Susan. *How My Family Lives in America*. New York: Bradbury Press, 1992. (Grades K–4)
Sanu, Eric, and April are American children who have at least one parent not born in America but born in Senegal, Puerto Rico, and China. The text and accompanying photographs show the children with their families. The true stories emphasize the everyday ways heritage is transmitted through songs, games, language, stories, and special occasions.

Russo, Marisabina. *A Visit to Oma*. New York: Greenwillow Books, 1991. (Grades K–4)
Celeste spends Sunday afternoons with her great grandmother, Oma, an immigrant who never learned to speak English. While Oma talks, Celeste imagines the story she thinks Oma is telling. This week, the story is about Oma's arranged marriage to a man she does not love, her courage in leaving, and her happiness when she finds Leo, her true love. The gentleness and creativity in their relationship allows them to overcome the language barrier.

Simon, Norma. *Why Am I Different?* Niles, IL: Albert Whitman & Co., 1976. (Grades K–2)
Simon portrays everyday situations in which children see themselves as "different." She explores differences related to physical appearance; abilities and preferences; home and neighborhood experiences; family life; ethnic, religious, and cultural backgrounds; parental occupations; and special circumstances, such as adoption. The book celebrates the virtues of self-respect, respect for others, diversity, and individual contributions.

Children with Disabilities

Booth, Barbara D. *Mandy*. New York: Lothrop, Lee & Shepard, 1991. (Grades 1–4)
Mandy's disability is never named; rather, as she and her grandmother bake cookies, dance, and walk in the woods, how Mandy lives with her deafness is revealed. During their walk, Mandy's grandmother loses a precious pin given to her by her husband. Mandy confronts her fear of the dark to find the pin and return it to her surprised and delighted grandmother.

Peterson, Jeanne Whitehouse. *I Have A Sister–My Sister Is Deaf*. New York: Harper Trophy, 1977. (Grades K–4)
The narrator has a younger sister who is deaf. She explains that her sister can say some words and can express herself eloquently with her face and shoulders. Her sister cannot do some things. She cannot sing, hear a shouted warning, or listen to the sounds of a wind chime. But other things she does very well indeed: play the piano, watch for quick movements in the grass, and climb to the top of the monkey bars.

Rabe, Berniece. *Where's Chimpy?* Niles, IL: Albert Whitman & Co., 1988. (Grades K–2)
  Misty has Down's syndrome, but that does not slow her down. It is bedtime, but Misty cannot go
  to sleep without Chimpy, her toy monkey. Misty and her father look everywhere Misty has
  played during the day. They find many other toys, but no Chimpy. Finally, Misty remembers she
  took a bath before bedtime. She finds Chimpy in the bathroom, covered by a towel. When Misty
  and her father settle down to read, her father's glasses are missing. Misty remembers where he
  put them, and they read their bedtime story.

Gender and Jobs

Munsch, Robert. *The Paper Bag Princess.* Toronto: Annick Press, Ltd., 1980. (Grades K–4)
  In a reversal of the usual prince and princess story, Prince Ronald is kidnapped by a fire-breath-
  ing dragon, who also destroys the castle and all of Princess Elizabeth's clothes. Undeterred,
  Princess Elizabeth puts on a paper bag and goes off to find her prince. After using her wits to put
  the dragon to sleep, she rescues Ronald. Ronald, however, does not want Elizabeth until she
  again looks like a princess. Elizabeth tells Ronald he may look nice but he is a bum, and she
  throws him out.

Schwartz, Amy. *Bea and Mr. Jones.* New York: Puffin Books, 1982. (Grades K–2)
  Bea is tired of kindergarten, and Mr. Jones is tired of his advertising job. So one day father and
  daughter switch places. As it turns out, Bea is brilliant at advertising, and Mr. Jones excels at
  kindergarten. They each have found their proper niche in the world.

CHAPTER 2
Learning From Many Cultures

We are the creature of questions and consciousness, and the creature of storytelling, the creature who addresses other creatures with words, with stories... And this is true universally. Every place I've been on this planet, children ask fundamentally the same questions. They want to know where did we come from, where are we, and where are we going?
—Robert Coles

INTRODUCTION

Just as Nazi Germany attempted to eradicate individual diversity, it also attempted to glorify one cultural heritage above all others, doing its best to destroy Jewish culture in the process. Books were banned, synagogues destroyed, and traditional ways of life, especially in Eastern Europe, obliterated. The Nazis attempted to destroy Judaism, but even the murder of millions of Jews failed to accomplish this. We must be grateful that their attempt to impose cultural uniformity was unsuccessful, and let it serve today as a reminder to value cultural diversity.

Cultural diversity is important for the same reason that individual diversity is important. *Webster's Tenth Collegiate Dictionary* defines culture as, "The integrated pattern of human knowledge, belief, and behavior that depends upon [human] capacity for learning and transmitting knowledge to succeeding generations." Just as unique individuals make unique contributions to the common good, unique cultures teach unique knowledge, ways to act in the world, and lessons about values that address the questions heard by Robert Coles. It is as if the world were a giant laboratory, with different groups continuously experimenting with and defining humanness. Learning about many cultures makes this vast repository of evolving knowledge and wisdom available to all who enter multicultural study.

Anthropologists have shown that every culture has its explanation for how its people were created. Every culture has stories, legends, and folktales conveying the history, traditions, and values of its people. Studying these and contemporary stories from many cultures can help children understand not only other peoples, but themselves. By analyzing themes common to their own and other cultures, children gain a deeper understanding of what it means to be human, and of how diverse peoples conceptualize a common world.

While we believe that learning from many cultures is essential to an appreciation of diversity and ultimately essential to the pursuit of peace, we also believe it is important to apply universal moral values to multicultural education. Indeed, one of the lessons of multicultural study is that there are bedrock, basic beliefs which can be called universal. In our modern world, these are best expressed in the United Nations Universal Declaration of Human Rights, discussed in the next chapter. The values so eloquently stated in that document flow throughout the ancient and modern tales told in the children's literature here.

So, this chapter's books convey universal moral lessons or highlight traditions that value life and goodness. One of the pleasures of reading the books is the discovery that extraordinarily different cultures hold remarkably similar beliefs about goodness. It is just as wrong to be greedy in the Miskito Indian culture of Nicaragua as it is in the Danish culture of Europe. Bravery and loyalty are as valued in China as they are in Iran.

At the same time, people do not always act according to their culture's best traditions. Teachers must take care not to extol cultural diversity in such a way that children do not learn how to discriminate between those cultural beliefs that safeguard life and those that harm life. The Nazis promoted Jew hatred, a destructive part of German and other cultures. That Jew hatred was a cultural belief did not make it good. Although early elementary students may be too young to analyze and make judgments about internal cultural contradictions, teachers must be able to do this. And to do it well, teachers must know their own stereotypes and biases.

In other words, educators need sufficient personal insight and cultural knowledge to teach about cultural diversity accurately and in perspective. For example, teaching the graciousness of pre-Civil War Southern culture while ignoring its racism does children a disservice. This same analysis can be applied to many other situations. Exploration of the moral complexity of various cultures, including our own, can be genuinely beneficial for young students, provided they are ready to tackle ambiguity and contradiction. Confronting these issues head-on is one way teachers can help children develop critical thinking skills and moral values.

GUIDELINES FOR CHOOSING MULTICULTURAL LITERATURE

Teachers who take care to recognize their biases and to educate themselves about different cultures still face a common problem in teaching multicultural literature: finding books that accurately and respectfully portray the traditions and values of a particular culture. Many American children's books are filled with stereotypes and the imposition of Eurocentric values and emotions on non-European peoples. A number of the books in Appendix B offer guidelines for evaluating multicultural stories. We particularly recommend *Promoting World Understanding through Literature, K-8,* by Mary C. Austin and Esther C. Jenkins; *Our Family, Our Friends, Our World,* by Lyn Miller-Lachmann; and *Through Indian Eyes: The Native Experience in Books for Children,* by Beverly Slapin and Doris Seule.

The following is a condensed list of criteria from these and other books for beginning reference.

Accuracy All facts should be accurate. The thoughts, emotions, perspectives, and values of the characters should be culturally accurate. Artificially happy endings should be avoided. Whether the material is historic, folkloric, or contemporary, fiction should be clearly identified. Sources for material should be given.

Authenticity The author's perspective is critical. Look at sources to see whether the author is a member or participant of the group portrayed or whether the author is an outsider looking in. Avoid books with Western values and emotions that have been imposed on non-Western characters.

Audience The books should be sensitive to children's developmental levels. They should engage the reader's empathy, so that children are transported deeply into the culture and see the story through the characters' eyes.

Plot Ethnic characters should be strong, shown in settings and having experiences with which children can identify and which are culturally accurate. The characters should have clear ethnic attributes but face universal problems and issues. Cultural information should be integrated so that it flows with the story and does not stop the story line. The plot should not exaggerate the exotic but rather show typical life experiences within the culture.

Illustrations Illustrations should be accurate, ethnically sensitive, and technically well done. Ethnic features should not be exaggerated; neither should characters be homogenized by giving characters a Caucasian appearance with dark coloring. Characters within the story should appear different, with distinct individual characteristics.

Stereotypes Books should be totally free of prejudicial concepts, words, phrases, and clichés. Characters should show diversity and individuality. Roles and environments should show a range of living conditions and lifestyles, avoiding generalizations such as "all Africans live in rural villages." The plot should avoid stereotypical situations, such as ones where all problems are solved by white people. Language should be accurate, with dialect used to show authenticity, not to ridicule. Racial and ethnic epithets should not be used if they will hurt or humiliate young children.

TEACHING ABOUT NATIVE AMERICANS

Teaching appropriately about Native Americans presents unique issues. While Native Americans are one ethnic minority among many in the United States, their history and culture make them different from every other group. These differences should be taught, so that children clearly understand the differences and similarities among Native peoples and immigrant ethnic groups.

One difference is that Native peoples were the original settlers of what European colonists termed the "New World." Native peoples did not have an immigration experience at all similar to other ethnic groups who now live in the United States. A second difference is that the United States government historically pursued a policy aimed at destroying Native culture. Native peoples have experienced dispossession of their land, decimation in their numbers, and in some instances attempted genocide by the government and white settlers. Accordingly, it is essential for children to learn that Native peoples and their culture continue to exist, and that Native peoples are working everywhere to keep their culture alive and healthy.

Books about Native Americans should be reviewed according to the criteria for all multicultural literature. In addition, Barbara Kuipers, in *American Indian Reference Books for Children and Young Adults*, suggests that teachers evaluate books about Native Americans for these additional qualities:

- Is Native American culture evaluated from the perspective of Native American values and attitudes rather than from those of another culture?
- Does the literature discuss the contributions of Native Americans to western civilization?
- Does the author recognize diversity among nations, tribes, cultures, and lifestyles?
- Are Native Americans portrayed accurately as individuals?
- Does the literature recognize Native American people as an enduring minority group, not as vanished or assimilated?
- Are Native American languages and dialects respectfully portrayed?
- Does the literature give realistic descriptions of Native American life?
- Does the literature portray realistic roles for Native American characters?

This chapter includes several books about Native American creation stories, legends, and folktales. To forestall the impression that Native Americans exist only in the past, we recommend that these stories be used in conjunction with books with contemporary Native American characters. Teachers can locate such books in Chapters 1, 3, and 4.

A MESSAGE TO TEACHERS

In teaching cultural diversity or multiculturalism, proceed with caution!

Think of yourself as a living laboratory for your students and as a culturally based member of an ethnic group. Judging how deeply or how unattached you are to your own cultural self is a good place to start. Begin with yourself, learn who you are culturally, and build a sound foundation on which to base your lessons before you ask your students to learn about themselves and others.

Culture is a relationship. Before entering the classroom we need to know our own biases, affirmations and rejections. Self-awareness is the essential first step to understanding what it means to belong to another cultural group. Our own examined cultural experiences can enhance the depth and meaning of what is taught, or our unexamined biases and inaccuracies can be transmitted to our students. Enthusiasm for, and celebration of, a culture are only a part of the examination of culture; deeper knowing comes when there is a dialogue—sometimes a difficult dialogue—about what it means to be a part of that particular culture. Students sense when the material presented to them is inauthentic. If you do not know enough to teach about a culture, ask for dialogue and assistance from members of that culture.

What cultural groups are present in your state? Why is there a large concentration of some cultural groups but not others? What diversities are present within a cultural group? What gender differences are present? Are ethnic jokes relevant?

How connected are your students to their own culture? What do you want them to know about their culture? The culture of other groups? Celebrations, recipes, and costumes are only a small part of what it means to belong to a cultural group. The teacher, as interpreter of the culture, needs to teach what has been made invisible in addition to the well-known. What is not obvious about a particular cultural group is as important as what is obvious.

In order to make a difference in children's lives, we, as educators, must be self-aware. We must alert children to their own biases, affirmations, rejections, and subscription in their cultural group. We must teach knowledgeably and sensitively about minority cultures.

The challenge in teaching cultural diversity lies not only in the complexity of the culture but also in the lack of materials readily at hand. *The Spirit That Moves Us* is a beginning step to bring together materials about cultures and members' experiences as majority or minority groups. But it is only a beginning. Much remains to be learned and written about cultural diversity and discrimination. As you teach the books recommended in this Guide, I hope your own explorations will add to the body of knowledge and to a deeper understanding of diversity and multiculturalism.

—Rhea J. Côté Robbins

[Rhea J. Côté Robbins is a Franco-American, parent, teacher, and staff member at the Franco-American Center in Orono, Maine.]

LESSON PLAN FOR:
WHY MOSQUITOES BUZZ IN PEOPLE'S EARS, **by Verna Aardema. Illustrations by Leo and Diane Dillon. New York: Dial Books for Young Readers, 1975. Grades 4-K**

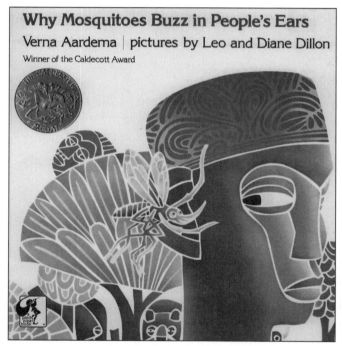

Story Summary

In this humorous story set in Western Africa, a mosquito lies to an iguana, setting off a chain reaction among the animals that culminates when a monkey accidentally kills an owlet. The mother owl, grief-stricken, does not wake the sun, so night lasts endlessly. As the night stretches on, King Lion calls a meeting of the animals. They investigate, judging the mosquito to be at fault. The mother owl, satisfied, wakes up the sun. Meanwhile, the guilty mosquito buzzes in people's ears to ask if everyone is still angry. People, of course, exact punishment by swatting at, and with luck, squashing the guilty mosquito.

Concepts Summary

Through the common folkloric device of animal stories, this tale demonstrates how people use entertaining stories to transmit cultural values and explain natural phenomena. It also introduces the concepts of community and justice.

Objectives

The student should be able to:
- recognize the story's cultural context;
- recognize the plot's use of a "chain of events" to advance the story;
- understand how justice is delivered to the offender;
- identify some common folklore themes.

Materials

Books: *Why Mosquitoes Buzz in People's Ears*, by Verna Aardema
Raccoon, Koluskap, and his Relatives, by the Wabnaki Bilingual Education Project
The Knee-High Man and Other Tales, by Julius Lester
Resource Guide: Amoaku, W. K. *African Songs and Rhythms for Children*. New York: Schott Music, 1971.
Art Supplies: Papier-mâché, puppets, magazines for collages, paper and markers, pictures of sub-Saharan African art
Equipment: Percussion instruments, map of Africa

CONCEPT: CULTURAL VALUES

Discussion Questions

- What did the mosquito do to start the events that led to the owlet's death?
- What was the crow's job? Can you think of animals in your town who give warning signals?
- Do you think that the monkey meant to kill the owlet?
- Why did the animals decide it was the mosquito who should be punished?
- Why was Mother Owl satisfied by the decision to punish the mosquito?
- At the beginning of the story, do you think the mosquito told a lie? How do you feel when someone tells you a lie?
- Was the mosquito brought before the council? Why not?
- What was the mosquito's punishment? Do you think this was fair?
- What is a guilty conscience?
- Can you think of a time you had a guilty conscience? What did you do about it?
- Do you think the story might have ended differently if the mosquito had admitted what she had done?
- What does this story teach about telling a lie and telling the truth?
- Did you like the story? Do you agree with its moral? Why?

Activities

Art

- Have children make papier-mâché figures of some of the animals in the story.

Drama

- Have children write a play based on the story, and using the papier-mâché figures or puppets, act it out.

Language Arts

- Have children identify the moral values and the lesson conveyed by the story. Help children develop their own definitions of "moral" and "value."
- Have children tell or write their own folktale that has "a moral of the story."
- The story uses the device of repetition to explain the chain of events. Discuss why this is effective storytelling, especially when stories are transmitted orally rather than in writing. Have children tell or write a brief story using this device.

Social Studies

- Have children brainstorm a list of moral values important to their friendships with their classmates and the conduct of their classroom. (Older children can include moral values important to a democratic society.)
- Have children identify from whom and how they are learning their moral values and the lessons attached to the values. For example, children could develop statements such as "it is important to tell the truth because otherwise a friend might be hurt." Children might identify their parents, teacher, church, books, or personal experiences as sources for values and their lessons.

CONCEPT: *CULTURAL CONTEXT*

Discussion Questions

- From the clues in the story and the illustrations, where do you think this story takes place?
- Who do you think made up this story?
- Do you slap at mosquitoes that buzz in your ears?
- Do you think the people who made up the story do the same thing with buzzing mosquitoes? Why?
- If there were no mosquitoes, pythons, and lions where the people lived who made up the story, do you think the story would be different? Why? How might it be different?
- Although there are no people in the story, does it still tell you something about the people who made it up? What ideas might you have about the story's authors?

Activities

Art

- Children can cut out pictures of animals that live in West Africa and make a collage.
- Have children illustrate the folktale they told or wrote for the language arts activity in the previous section.
- Bring examples or pictures of sub-Saharan African art to the class. Help children analyze how this art is similar to and different from western art, and what it tells them about West African culture.
- Have children make a mask or other traditional sub-Saharan work of art.

Music

- Using percussion and other simple instruments, demonstrate musical styles native to sub-Saharan Africa. *African Songs and Rhythms for Children* can be used to teach children an example of African music.

Language Arts

- Have children brainstorm about how folktales may originate, why folktales are important, and why they like folktales.
- The story can be used to demonstrate how people make up folktales based on the world where they live. For example, stories of the Passamaquoddy, featuring a raccoon and a turtle, can be compared to this story. Similarly, African American folktales can be introduced to emphasize this point.

Geography

- Identify West African countries on a map. Older children can research the geographic environments and animals native to these countries.

Social Studies

- Introduce a unit on West African culture, rural and urban. Cultural aspects such as religion and social organization can be tied to the values conveyed by the story.

Science

- The story presents animals native to West Africa. Some of these are native to North America as well, such as owls, rabbits, and mosquitoes; others are not, such as lions, iguanas, and monkeys. Explain how animals can originate on one continent and travel to others, and how some animals adapt to more than one environment and climate, while others do not.

Community Resources
Contact a local college or group for speakers to visit the class and demonstrate examples of contemporary African culture.

Other Recommended Children's Books

Animal-based folktales:
Bringing the Rain to Kapiti Plain, by Verna Aardema
The Cat's Purr, by Ashley Bryan
The Wind Eagle and Other Abenaki Stories, by Joseph Bruchac
The Three Little Fawns, by Veasna Kem and Vech Pra

Folktales with a moral:
Louhi, Witch of North Farm, by Toni De Gerez
The Talking Pot, by Virginia Haviland
The Invisible Hunters, by Harriet Rohmer

Sub-Saharan African culture:
Mufaro's Beautiful Daughters, by John Steptoe
A Country Far Away, by Nigel Gray
Talking Walls, by Margy Burns Knight
Galimoto, by Karen Lynn Williams

Resources for Teachers

Murphy, E. Jefferson and Harry Stein. *Teaching Africa Today: A Handbook for Teachers and Curriculum Planners*. New York: Citation Press, 1973.

Resources for the Classroom

Heltshe, Mary Ann and Audrey Burie Kirchner. *Multicultural Explorations*. Englewood, CO: Teacher Idea Press, 1991.

Knight, Margy Burns and Thomas V. Chan. *Talking Walls Teacher's Guide*. Gardiner, ME: Tilbury House, 1992.

LESSON PLAN FOR:
GLUSKABE AND THE FOUR WISHES, retold by Joseph Bruchac. Illustrated by Nyburg Shrader. New York: Cobblehill Books, Dutton, 1988, 1995. Grades 2-4

Story Summary

Gluskabe, helper of the Great Spirit, did many things to make the world right and then went to a far-off island. He let it be known that he would grant one wish to anyone who came to him.

And so, four Abenaki men seeking wishes from Gluskabe set out on a great and dangerous journey to this island. On the way they faced fierce storms and turbulent seas, but eventually they reached Gluskabe. The four men each had a different wish—one for great height, one for long life, one for many possessions, and one for the ability to hunt well to feed his people. Each man was given a pouch with instructions not to open it until he reached home.

Concepts Summary

This legend, retold by storyteller Joseph Bruchac, is representative of traditional Native American teaching stories which are entertaining but also carry a lesson. It teaches important values: connections between the natural world and people, respect for living things, the need for self-improvement, honest self-assessment, why people should help others, and the need for patience.

Objectives

The student should be able to:
- learn how the Abenaki explain creation and occurrences in nature;
- understand the importance, purpose, and universality of tales and stories to the Abenaki and other cultures;
- recognize Abenaki values about nature, human beings, and animals;
- learn about Abenaki culture.

Materials

Books: *Gluskabe and the Four Wishes*, retold by Joseph Bruchac
The Invisible Hunters, by Harriet Rohmer
The People Shall Continue, by Simon Ortiz
Resource Guide:
The Wabanakis of Maine and the Maritimes, by the American Friends Service Committee

CONCEPT: *ABENAKI VALUES*

Discussion Questions

- What are the difficulties the four men must overcome?
- How do they solve each one? What did each man contribute to the journey?
- What things do you think are important in the Abenaki culture? What things do they respect?
- How do they feel about animals?
- Why do you think the animals were delighted when they saw the humans Gluskabe made?
- What did the animals mean when they said Gluskabe had a great sense of humor?
- Do you think animals have opinions about people? If yes, what might those opinions be?
- Do you have opinions about animals? What are they? Where do you think your opinions come from?
- If you like animals, how do you treat them? Is this the same as or different from how they are treated in the story?
- If you like people, how do you treat them? Is this the same as or different from how they are treated by Gluskabe in the story?
- Do you think all people today respect animals and people? What evidence might tell you yes? What evidence might tell you no?
- What do you think about the four wishes? Which one would you have made? Or would you have chosen something different?
- Why did the fourth man get his wish?

Activities

Art

- Show the illustrations in *The Invisible Hunters*, a native peoples' folktale from Nicaragua. Using just the pictures, have children analyze the characteristics and values this culture attributes to the three hunters. Then read the story, having children compare their assumptions to the values in the story.

Language Arts

- Have children identify several legends from United States history, such as Betsy Ross sewing the American flag or George Washington cutting down the cherry tree. Have children analyze what these legends tell about values in the United States. Lead a discussion on why people use legend and myth to explain who and what they are, and to transmit values to future generations.
- Have children imagine and write a legend explaining the importance of one of their cultural values.

CONCEPT: *ABENAKI AND OTHER WABANAKI CULTURES*

Discussion Questions

- What clues does the story give about Gluskabe? Where does Gluskabe live?
- Do you think Gluskabe is a human being? If not, what is Gluskabe?
- Does the story explain fog? What does it say about the height of the pine trees?
- Why do you think tales like this were told by Native Americans?
- How did we get these stories?

Activities

Art

- Bring examples of Wabanaki art and crafts, such as baskets or decorative clothing, to the class. Have children examine closely the quality and beauty of the work. Lead a discussion on what this says about Wabanaki values. To better understand the skills involved in weaving, have children make their own baskets.
- Make a Native American "talking stick." Pass the stick from child to child around a circle as they retell the story, each child adding another part of the story in order. While holding the stick, only that child may speak.

Language Arts

- Read the Russian tale *The Fisherman and the Goldfish* by A. Pushkin and compare the fisherman's wishes to those of the four Abenaki men.
- Read the Russian tale *The Firebird* and compare/discuss the values of the three brothers with those of the four Abenaki men, especially around following directions.
- Read *The Cat That Went to Heaven* by Elizabeth Coatsworth and compare the feelings of and about animals in the Buddhist tradition with those feelings in the Abenaki tradition.

Geography

- Using a map of North America, identify where the Wabanaki lived before colonization of Canada and the United States and the principal areas where they live today. Have children analyze the effect of the imposition of nation states on Wabanaki lands.

History

- Read *The People Shall Continue*, a children's history of Native North Americans. Expand the lesson by introducing Wabanaki history within the context of Native North American history.

Social Studies

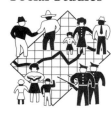

- Explore the social organizations of Native American nations by introducing the groups comprising the Wabanaki people—the Abenaki, Passamaquoddy, Penobscot, Micmac, and Maliseet. Help children analyze the differences and similarities between Native American social organizations and the groups comprising their own community.

Science

- Bring several examples of traditional Abenaki technology to class, such as snowshoes, bows and arrows, traps, and tools. To the extent possible, have children experiment with their use. Help children analyze why many of these technologies continue to be used by Native and non-Native Americans alike.

Community Resources

Ask a member of any Native American tribe/nation to visit your class to discuss their values, culture, and technology. Or invite a member of a Native American tribe/nation to come and share a value tale.

Other Recommended Children's Books

The Abenaki:
The Wind Eagle and Other Abenaki Stories, by Joseph Bruchac

Native American folktales:
The Legend of the Bluebonnet, by Tomie DePaola
A Promise Is a Promise, by Robert Munsch and Michael Kusugak
The Story of Jumping Mouse, by John Steptoe

Native American children:
Hawk, I'm Your Brother, by Byrd Baylor

Ceremony—In the Circle of Life, by White Deer of Autumn.
POWWOW, by George Ancona
When Clay Sings, by Byrd Baylor

Resources for Teachers
Slapin, Beverly and Doris Seale, eds. *Through Indian Eyes: The Native Experience in Books for Children.*
      3rd ed. Philadelphia: New Society Publishers, 1992.
Smith, Carter, ed. *Native Americans of the West: A Source Book on the American West.* Brookfield, CT:
      The Millbrook Press, Inc., 1992.

Resources for the Classroom
Anderson, William M. *Teaching Music with a Multicultural Approach.* Reston, VA: Music Educators
      National Conference, 1991.
Hayden, Carla D., ed. *Venture into Cultures.* Chicago: American Library Association, 1992.
Blood, Charles L. *American Indian Games and Crafts.* New York: Franklin Watts, 1981.
Caduto, Michael J. and Joseph Bruchac. *Keepers of the Earth: Native American Stories and Environmental
      Activities for Children.* Golden, CO: Fulcrum Publishing, 1989.
_____. *Keepers of the Animals: Native American Stories and Wildlife Activities for Children.* Golden, CO:
      Fulcrum Publishing, 1991.
Harvey, Karen D., Lisa D. Harjo and Jane K. Jackson. *Teaching About Native Americans.* Washington,
      DC: National Council for the Social Studies, 1990.

Supplemental Children's Books
Watson, Jane Werner. *The First Americans.* New York: Pantheon Books, 1990.
Whitehead, Ruth Holmes and Harold McGee. *The Micmac: How Their Ancestors Lived Five Hundred
      Years Ago.* Halifax, N.S., Canada: Nimbus Publishing, 1983.

LESSON PLAN FOR:
**Brother Rabbit: A Cambodian Tale,
by Minfong Ho and Saphan Ros.
New York: Lothrop, Lee &
Shepard Books, 1997. Grades 1-4.**

Story Summary
Brother Rabbit wants to get across the river
to sample some tender rice seedlings. He
compliments a crocodile and tells him he can
cure him of having such rough skin if the
crocodile will give him a ride across the river.
When Brother Rabbit can't keep his promise,
the crocodile is angry and vows to trick the
rabbit. Brother Rabbit then outwits a woman
and an elephant in addition to tricking the
crocodile again. Finally the furious crocodile
plays dead and Brother Rabbit is gulped

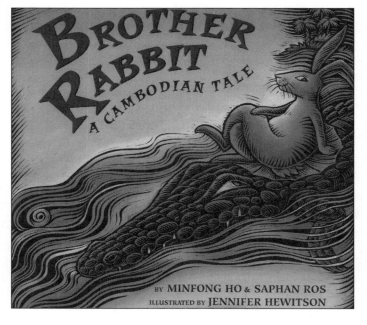

down. But Brother Rabbit's wit and persistence don't miss a beat, and he threatens to eat the crocodile's guts. The frightened crocodile lets him out of his stomach, gives him a ride back across the river, and promises never to trick Brother Rabbit again.

Concepts Summary

A favorite theme in Cambodian folktales involves a small but clever animal getting the better of someone stronger and meaner but not as bright. This reflects the potential power of the farmers and villagers over their mighty landlords and kings, thus their delight in stories such as these. It also introduces the concept of how folktales may be connected to the political, social, and economic realities of a country's geography and history.

Objectives

The student should be able to:
* identify the cultural setting of the story;
* identify a common theme in Cambodian folklore;
* recognize the role quick wit, cleverness, and resilience may play in getting through difficult situations;
* understand how a folktale may be connected to the political/social/economic reality in a community.

Materials

Books: *Brother Rabbit: A Cambodian Tale*, by Minfong Ho and Saphan Ros
Equipment and Supplies: Dictionaries, globe, world map, computer with Internet access

CONCEPTS: *QUICK WIT AND CLEVERNESS*

Discussion Questions

* Why did Bother Rabbit need the crocodile's help? Why wasn't he afraid of the crocodile? What trick did Brother Rabbit use to get the help he needed?
* Why was the crocodile willing to help him without eating him?
* What did Bother Rabbit do that made the crocodile angry?
* Was the crocodile the only one to get tricked by Brother Rabbit?
* How did the crocodile try to trick Brother Rabbit the first time? Did it work? Why not?
* What other problem did Brother Rabbit have in addition to crossing the river? How did he solve it?
* How did Brother Rabbit get back home? What other trick did the crocodile play? Did it work?
* Why do you think the elephant didn't eat Brother Rabbit? Would Brother Rabbit really have eaten the crocodile's guts? What didn't the crocodile know about a rabbit's diet?
* Do you agree with the ways Brother Rabbit solved his problems? Did he ever give up? Was there anything about the way Brother Rabbit acted that you did not like?

Activities

Science

* Have children find all the natural phenomena that occur in real life in this tale; i.e., an elephant not eating meat, a crocodile floating down the river, etc.

Language Arts

• Use the dictionary to look up the word resilience. Talk about its meaning and discuss it in relation to the story. Recall the ways Brother Rabbit lied in the story to get what he wanted. Have the children discuss if they think there are any times when lying is acceptable and/or necessary.

Social Studies

• Discuss famous people and/or other folktale characters who are known for their cleverness, intelligence or persistence.

CONCEPTS: *CULTURAL AND POLITICAL CONTEXT*

Discussion Questions

• From looking at the illustrations only, where do you think this story takes place? What clues are given?
• What do you already know about Cambodia from the story?
• Do you think Brother Rabbit is ever afraid in this story?
• Why was Brother Rabbit's small size not a problem? Why were the larger animals and people not able to trick Brother Rabbit?
• Why do you think Cambodian folktales often have the smaller character outwitting the larger one? What groups of people might need to think about outsmarting a more powerful group?

Activities

Language Arts

• Discuss the concept this story shows of larger vs. smaller with the smaller "winning." Brainstorm other opposites and find stories that match, such as slow vs. fast in the tortoise and the hare.

Geography

• Locate Cambodia on the map and on the globe. Note the neighboring countries, oceans, mountains and any other major geographical features. Use the Internet for more information.

History

- For older students, research the history of Cambodia to find out more about the difficulties among the peasants, the kings, and the landlords. Cambodia's recent history may also be of interest to some of the students.

Social Studies

- Read (or paraphrase for younger children) the information on the page directly preceding the beginning of the story. Research Cambodia to discover more about its culture and food. The Internet may provide more information.

Science

- Research other animals that are native to Cambodia.

Community Resources

Invite a person of Cambodian heritage or a Cambodian immigrant to visit and share with the class other Cambodian folktales or cultural information.

Other Recommended Children's Books

The Two Brothers, by Minfong Ho, Saphan Ros, Jean Tseng, Mao-Sien Tseng, Mou-Sien Tseng
Judge Rabbit and the Tree Spirit: A Folktale from Cambodia/Bilingual in English and Khmer, by Cathy Spagnoli, Lina Mao Wall, and Nancy Hom, Illustrator
Cambodia (Enchantment of the World), by Miriam Greenblatt

LESSON PLAN FOR:

The Woman Who Outshone the Sun, by Alejandro Cruz Martinez, et al. Pictures by Fernando Olivera; story by Rosalma Zubizarreta, Harriet Rohmer, and David Schecter. San Francisco: Children's Book Press, 1991. Grades K-4.

Story Summary

When Lucia Zenteno arrived in the village, she was so beautiful she outshone the sun. But Lucia was different. The river, with its water, fish, and otters, flowed into her hair when she bathed, leaving only when she combed her hair. The village elders said Lucia should be respected even if she was different. Others, however, were afraid and drove her away. Lucia stopped to bathe a last time, but this time the river did not leave her hair. The villagers suffered greatly from the drought, finally deciding to ask Lucia for forgiveness. Lucia said she would return the river if the villagers always treated everyone with kindness and respect. The villagers agreed, rejoicing when Lucia combed the river out of her hair. Although Lucia no longer lived among them, she was always there, helping the villagers to live with understanding in their hearts.

Concepts Summary

This legend, written in Spanish and English, is part of the oral history of the Zapotec Indians of Mexico. The legend teaches important values: connections between the natural world and quality of life, why people should be accepted for who they are, and the power of love and respect. It also teaches what can happen when a community becomes afraid and intolerant of those who are different, demonstrating how children can help to heal the effects of intolerance.

Objectives

The student should be able to:
• identify the values and moral lesson taught by the story;
• analyze how the story's lesson is conveyed by a magical legend;
• understand why the story's values are universal, and be able to apply them to contemporary situations;
• learn about Zapotec culture.

Materials

Books: *The Woman Who Outshone the Sun,* by Alejandro Cruz Martinez, et. al.
          The People Shall Continue, by Simon Ortiz
Art Supplies: Paper and markers, water colors, poster board, clay, pictures of murals by Diego Rivera
Equipment: Dance costumes, map of North America, map of Mexico and Central America, calendars

CONCEPTS: *UNIVERSAL VALUES*

Discussion Questions

- What makes Lucia Zenteno beautiful? Is she beautiful only because of how she looks?
- Would you like Lucia to live in your community and be your friend? Why?
- How was Lucia different from the other villagers? How was she the same?
- Why do you think the river loved Lucia?
- How did the villagers treat Lucia? Why do you think some were cruel to her?
- What did the village elders say about Lucia? Who disagreed? Why?
- What happened to the villagers after the river left with Lucia?
- Who asked Lucia for forgiveness? Why do you think the children could do this when the adults were silent?
- What did the villagers learn from their cruelty to Lucia and then from her forgiveness?
- What did you learn from this story?
- Can you think of a time you were treated cruelly? How did you feel?
- Can you think of a time you teased or treated someone else cruelly? How do you think that person felt? After reading this story, what could you do about such situations?

Activities

Art

- Have children draw their own pictures of Lucia, showing what makes her beautiful to them.
- Have children create an art work in the medium of their choice that shows their feelings when Lucia was driven from the village.

Language Arts

- Have children identify the words used to define the story's moral values, linking each word to an action from the story.
- The story was written by several authors based on a poem by Alejandro Cruz Martinez (also listed as an author). Have children write their own poem about an aspect of the story.

Social Studies

- Have children imagine they have traveled to a new place where they know no one and where they are a little different from the rest of the people. (Older children can choose a location, researching what it looks like, how people dress, and what language is spoken.) Have children imagine how they would want to be treated in this new place, comparing their ideas with the values represented by Lucia.
- Choose a contemporary example of intolerance in a community in your state. Explain the situation, helping children to analyze why the intolerance occurred, the values that are the antithesis of the intolerance, and what the children could do if this happened in their community.
- Have children prepare a wall poster showing what they learned from the story about accepting new people in their school. Have children share this with other classrooms.

Drama or Dance

• The story's text and illustrations have great flow and movement. Have children create a dance demonstrating the movement of the river, or write a play about the villagers' decision to ask Lucia for forgiveness.

CONCEPT: *ZAPOTEC CULTURE*

Discussion Questions

• Why was the river important to the villagers? If you live near a river, lake, or the ocean, is the water important to you? Why?

• When you are swimming, does the water ever feel as if it's part of you? Could this be what Lucia experienced, and perhaps the villagers as well?

• What does the landscape look like?

• How do the people look? What kinds of clothes do they wear? What language do they speak?

• What do the people's homes and buildings look like? What do you think they are made of?

• What kinds of plants are in the village?

• What animals are important to the villagers? Which of these animals also live in your state? Which do not?

• In many of the pictures, what objects or people appear in the sky? Why do you think they are there? What do they tell you about the Zapotec people?

• Like Lucia in the story, do you believe someone watches over you to keep you protected? Who? Why do you believe this?

• Can you think of other cultures where a person or being with special powers watches over the people? Which ones? Why do you think people from different cultures have this belief?

• By the end of the story, what have you learned about the Zapotec people? Would you like to meet Zapotecs? If you did, what are some questions you could ask about their lives and culture today?

Activities

Art

• The answers to many of the discussion questions are in the book's illustrations. As an alternative activity to the questions, divide the class into groups, assigning each group several pages of the illustrations. Have the groups note everything they see that tells them about Zapotec life and culture. Have each group report to the class, helping the class to re-create the culture shown in the story.

• Have children make models of the buildings and animals shown in the story. The illustrations rely on bold colors and lines to depict life in Central Mexico. Show children examples of similar work by other artists, such as the murals of Diego Rivera. Choosing subjects of their own, have children paint a picture in this style.

Language Arts

• Explain the concept of oral history. Have children suggest what it would be like to learn about their world through stories passed from generation to generation. Help children analyze modern instances of oral history.

• Ask children to tell the story to their family, explaining that this is a way to pass a tradition of the Zapotec to people in their state. The next day, have children discuss their experiences.

• From the perspective of a village child, have children tell or write a story about the river's meaning and usefulness to the plants, animals, individual villagers, and community in the story.

Geography

- Using a map of North America, locate Oaxaca, Mexico. Show the location of major groups of Native North Americans from Canada, the United States, and Mexico, helping children grasp the number and diversity of Native peoples who inhabit North America.

History

- Read *The People Shall Continue*, a picture book history of Native North Americans. Introduce a lesson on several of the Native American civilizations in Mexico and Central America, placing the Zapotec people in historical context.

Social Studies

- Extend the geography lesson by having children study the geographical features of Central Mexico. The book's illustrations contain many clues. Have children analyze how environment influences the architecture, dress, language, and other cultural aspects of the Zapotec.
- The book presents an interesting blend of cultures. For example, the people and the folktale itself are clearly Native American, yet the story is written in Spanish and English and the Mexican flag flies from one of the buildings.
- Help children analyze the influence of post-Columbian culture on the Zapotec, demonstrating that Native peoples retain aspects of their culture within the context of culture imposed by colonization.

Science

- The sun is one of the story's major symbols. Introduce children to the concept of a calendar, explaining how and why people divide time into different periods. Introduce a lesson on the sophisticated astronomy of pre-Columbian Mexican and Central American civilizations, teaching how these peoples developed calendars and the ability to predict astronomical phenomena. Have children make their own calendar, perhaps illustrating it in the style of the book.

Other Recommended Children's Books
Native American folktales:
The Invisible Hunters, by Harriet Rohmer
Mother Scorpion Country, by Harriet Rohmer
The Wind Eagle and Other Abenaki Stories, by Joseph Bruchac
North American Indian Stories, by Gretchen Mayo

Stories with a moral:
Hawk, I'm Your Brother, by Byrd Baylor

Brother Eagle, Sister Sky, by Chief Seattle
Judge Rabbit and the Tree Spirit, by Lina Mao Wall and Cathy Spagnoli

Transcultural stories:
The Way to Start a Day, by Byrd Baylor
 How My Parents Learned to Eat, by Ina Friedman
Talking Walls, by Margy Burns Knight
How My Family Lives in America, by Susan Kuklin

Resources for Teachers

Miller-Lachmann, Lyn, ed. *Our Family, Our Friends, Our World: An Annotated Guide to Significant Multicultural Books for Children and Teenagers*. New Providence, NJ: R.R. Bowker, 1992.

Resources for the Classroom

Anderson, William M. *Teaching Music with a Multicultural Approach*. Reston, VA: Music Educators National Conference, 1991.

Blackaby, Susan. *One World: Multicultural Projects and Activities*. Mahwah, NJ: Troll Associates, 1992.

Civilizations of the Americas. Austin, TX: Raintree/Steck-Vaughn, Publishers, 1992.

Forbes, Jack D. and Carolyn Johnson. *Handbook for the Development of Native American Studies*. Davis, CA: Native American Studies Tecumseh Center, 1972.

Harvey, Karen D., Lisa D. Harjo and Jane K. Jackson. *Teaching About Native Americans*. Washington, DC: National Council for the Social Studies, 1990, new edition, 1997.

Hayden, Carla D., ed. *Venture into Cultures*. Chicago: American Library Association, 1992.

Knight, Margy Burns and Thomas V. Chan. *Talking Walls Teacher's Guide*. Gardiner, ME: Tilbury House, 1992. Also, *Talking Walls: The Stories Continue Teacher's Guide*, 1995.

Supplemental Children's Books

Chermayeff, Ivan and Jane Clark. *First Words*. New York: Harry N. Abrams, Inc., 1990.
    Watson, Jane Werner. *The First Americans*. New York: Pantheon Books, 1990.

Additional Recommended Children's Books on Diverse Cultures
Transcultural Studies

Baylor, Byrd. *The Way to Start a Day*. New York: Charles Scribner's Sons, 1977. (Grades K–4)
    Every day, in different parts of the world, people rise to greet the sun and welcome a new day. Through simple verse, this book describes different ways people start their day, why it is important to respect each new sunrise, and how to experience the magic of a new day.

Knight, Margy Burns. *Talking Walls*. Gardiner, ME: Tilbury House, 1992. Also *Talking Walls: The Stories Continue*, 1995. (Grades K–4)
    These two books introduce children to different cultures by exploring walls around the world. The books show the impact of walls on the people who build and are divided or unified by them. The walls described in each book range from the Great Wall of China, to the wall of an Egyptian house with pictures showing the family's pilgrimage to Mecca, to the Vietnam Veterans' Memorial in Washington. Other walls are in places as diverse as Zimbabwe, Jerusalem, India, and Cuzco, Peru. (For information on the accompanying Teacher's Guides, see the annotations in Appendix B.)

Spier, Peter. *People*. New York: Delacorte Press, 1980. (Grades 1–4)
This non-fiction book, with colorful and detailed illustrations, shows how people around the world are different. Among other topics the book explains differences in physical appearance, play, pets, homes, holidays, food, religion, and languages. It ends with the idea that the world would be dreadfully dull if everyone were the same, so we should celebrate our uniqueness and differences.

Africa

Aardema, Verna. *Bringing the Rain to Kapiti Plain*. New York: Dial Books for Young Readers, 1981. (Grades K–2)
Aardema retells a tale from the Nandi, in Kenya. Ki-pat, while tending his herd, shoots an eagle feather into the dark cloud hanging over the plain, creating rain that makes the grass green and feeds the cows. The story uses a cumulative nursery rhyme reminiscent of European stories.

Steptoe, John. *Mufaro's Beautiful Daughters*. New York: Lothrop, Lee & Shephard Books, 1987. (Grades 1–4)
Mufaro's two daughters are very beautiful. Nyasha is kind and considerate, but everyone except Mufaro knows Manyara is selfish and bad-tempered. When the king wants to marry, Mufaro decides that only a king can choose between his daughters. Manyara leaves for the city on her own, determined to be the first to see the king. On the way, she ignores a hungry boy and the advice of an old woman. At the palace, she sees only a monster snake. Nyasha, who leaves the next morning accompanied by others from her village, feeds the boy and pays respect to the old woman. When she arrives, she discovers that the monster is a friendly snake. The snake turns into the king, who had also been the hungry boy and the old woman. He had learned that Nyasha is worthy as well as beautiful, so they marry. Manyara lives in the palace, but as a servant to the queen, her sister.

Williams, Karen Lynn. *Galimoto*. New York: Mulberry Books, 1990. (Grades K–3)
In a story set in a contemporary African village, Kondi is determined to make a *galimoto*, a push toy made of wires. His brother laughs at the idea, saying a boy seven years old cannot make such a complicated toy. All day, Kondi goes about gathering the wire he needs: from his friends, the village shop, the mill where the maize is ground, and the trash heap. Finally, he has enough, and he makes his *galimoto*, an intricate car fashioned of wire and bamboo.

African American

Hamilton, Virginia. *The People Could Fly: American Black Folktales*. New York: Alfred A. Knopf, Inc., 1985. (Grades K–4)
This collection of twenty-eight folktales is divided into four sections: animal tales; tales of the real, extravagant, and fanciful; tales of the supernatural; and slave tales of freedom. As the author explains in the introduction, slaves created a body of folktales about their experiences. After the Civil War, some of these tales were transformed into stories about people who outwitted the slave owners and won their freedom. Other stories were based on true tales of escape from slavery, or on tales of magic and fantasy. "These folktales were once a creative way for an oppressed people to express their hopes and fears to one another. As part of our tradition and history, they also belong to all of us."

Lester, Julius. *The Knee-High Man and Other Tales*. New York: Dial Books for Young Readers, 1972, new edition, 1992, Dutton. (Grades K–4)
These six stories from the tradition of African American folk literature were originally told

among the slaves. Slaves made up stories, many of which were actually about relations between the slaves and owners, as a form of resistance and as a way to transmit their culture and values from generation to generation. Here are the adventures of the knee-high man; the dog and the cat; Mr. Snake; Mrs. Wind and Mrs. Water; and two favorite characters of African American literature, Mr. Rabbit and Mr. Bear.

Asia

Bond, Ruskin. *Cherry Tree.* Honesdale, PA: Caroline House, 1988. (Grades K–4)
Rakhi returns from the bazaar in Mussoorie, India, with bright red cherries. After she eats the last one, her grandfather suggests she plant the seed in a corner of their garden. There are few fruit trees in the Himalayan foothills where she lives, so she is joyful when the tree grows. The tree survives monsoons, wagon carts, and caterpillars, returning to life each time it is damaged. After four years, Rakhi is rewarded by the first cherry blossom. As the tree and Rakhi continue to thrive, Rakhi looks forward to telling her children how she and her grandfather planted the tree many years ago.

Rose, Deborah Lee. *The People Who Hugged the Trees.* Niwot, CO: Roberts Rinehart, Publishers, 1990. (Grades K–4)
As a girl, Amrita loved the forest that stood at one end of her village in India. The trees provided shade from the desert sun and protection from sandstorms. When she grew to adulthood, she took her own children to the forest to teach them her love for the trees. One day, the maharajah's soldiers arrive to cut down the trees for a new fortress. Amrita runs to her village and rouses the other villagers, who rush to save the forest. The soldiers, frustrated, return to the maharajah, who brings even more soldiers to demolish the forest. Before they cut down the trees, a fierce sandstorm drives villagers and soldiers alike to the protection of the forest. After the sandstorm passes, the maharajah recognizes the villagers' wisdom and bravery, declaring that the forest will always remain a green place in the desert.

Say, Allen. *Tree of Cranes.* Boston: Houghton Mifflin Co., 1991. (Grades K–4)
A young boy in Japan celebrates Christmas in this book about the blending of family and cultural traditions. The boy disobeys his mother by playing at the neighbor's pond. When he comes home ill, she puts him to bed while she finishes making origami cranes. After a long time, the boy opens the window, where he sees his mother digging up a bonsai tree. She decorates the tree with the cranes and with candles, telling him about her childhood in California and about a special day of love and peace. The next day, he finds a samurai kite under the tree, and he and his father build a snowman. Looking back, the man who was the boy remembers that day of peace, his first Christmas.

Wall, Lina Mao and Cathy Spagnoli. *Judge Rabbit and the Tree Spirit.* San Francisco: Children's Book Press, 1991. (Grades K–4)
Judge Rabbit stories are part of the Cambodian folktale tradition. In this story, told in English and Khmer, a young man is called by his king to go to war. Hearing the man lament the loss of his loving wife and peaceful home, a tree spirit decides to investigate. Liking what he sees, he assumes the man's shape. After many months, the real husband returns home. The wife is dumbfounded to see them both, but cannot tell her husband from the tree spirit. In despair, the husband asks Judge Rabbit for help. Judge Rabbit tricks the tree spirit into revealing his true nature, proving that wisdom can fool even spirits.

Young, Ed. *Lon Po Po.* New York: Philomel Books, 1989. (Grades 1–4)
The Chinese tale of Lon Po Po, "Granny Wolf," similar to the European story of "The Wolf and the Seven Little Kids," comes from ancient Chinese tradition. In the story, the mother goes

to visit her mother, leaving her three daughters for the night. She warns her children to keep the door closed tight. That night, a wolf disguised as their grandmother comes to the door and convinces the children to let him in. They do, until the oldest discovers that their Po Po is really a wolf. She rescues herself and her sisters by tricking the wolf into climbing a ginkgo tree to get the delectable nuts.

Caribbean

Bryan, Ashley. *The Cat's Purr*. New York: Atheneum, 1985. (Grades K–2)
> Cat and Rat are best friends. Cat's uncle visits, bringing him a tiny drum. This drum is special; when stroked, it makes a soft "purrum purrum" sound. Cat is entranced. When he plays it for Rat, so is Rat. Rat wants to play the drum himself, so he tricks Cat into thinking he, Rat, is sick. Cat leaves to work in the fields, but Rat stays behind. When Cat hears the drum, he returns from the fields to catch Rat. To escape, Rat throws the drum into Cat's open mouth. Cats and rats are no longer friends, but cats now purr when gently stroked.

Bryan, Ashley. *The Dancing Granny*. New York: Aladdin Books, 1977. (Grades K–4)
> This book, a retelling of a West Indian folktale, explains how Granny loves to dance more than anything in the world. She beats out a rhythm as she plants and harvests her vegetables. Her crops seem to leap from the earth. Spider Ananse wants some of that delicious food, so he starts to sing a dancing song. Granny cannot help herself. She cartwheels out of the garden and dances until she is miles away. Meanwhile, Spider steals her vegetables. Granny finally gets even. She catches Spider around the waist with her hoe, making him her dancing partner. Together, they dance farther than Granny ever had alone.

Europe

De Gerez, Toni. *Louhi, Witch of North Farm*. New York: Puffin Books, 1986. (Grades K–4)
> In this folktale from an epic Finnish poem, Louhi decides to make trouble. While listening to Vainamoinen, the Great Knower, make beautiful music on his harp, she turns into an eagle, stealing the sun and moon. She locks them in her storeroom, so that the land is plunged into terrible darkness. Vainamoinen asks Seppo, a blacksmith, to make a new sun and moon. He tries, but there still is no light. Seppo, now very angry, makes an iron collar and chains to wrap around Louhi's neck. When Louhi hears of this, she returns light and the seasons to the world.

Geras, Adele. *My Grandmother's Stories*. New York: Alfred A. Knopf, Inc., 1990. (Grades 3–4)
> The text weaves ten traditional Jewish folktales with the story of a young girl visiting her grandmother. As they prepare for the Sabbath, clean the house, cook, and do laundry, the grandmother tells stories from her Russian Jewish heritage. The stories range widely, from ancient Jerusalem, where King Solomon teaches a miser to be generous; to the Russian countryside, where a clever peasant outwits the Czar; to a small village, where a Rabbi's wife gives wise advice.

Haviland, Virginia. *The Talking Pot*. Boston: Little, Brown and Co., 1971. (Grades K–4)
> Filled with details faithful to Danish traditions, this folktale explains how a poor family triumphs over the village miser. The family decides it must sell its only cow, but on the way to the market, the father trades the cow for a three-legged pot. This pot, however, is special because it can talk and walk. Once home, the pot makes several trips: to the rich miser's kitchen, where it is filled with pudding; then to the barn, where it is filled with wheat; and finally to the miser's house, where it is filled with gold coins. Each time, it returns the treasure to the poor family. The pot makes one last trip to the miser, who grabs for it. The pot skips away with the miser in pursuit. The family, poor no longer, often thinks of the pot, but it is never seen again.

Mani-Leib. *Yingl Tsingl Khvat.* Mt. Kisco, NY: Moyer Bell, 1918, 1986. (Grades 1–4)
   Originally published in Yiddish by the poet Mani-Leib, who lived in a *shtetl* as a youth, this
   edition presents the original Yiddish poem and illustrations with English translation. Yingl
   Tsingl, a child's name occasionally appearing in Yiddish, and Khvat, meaning plucky, lives in a
   village where snow does not fall during winter. The whole village is mired in mud. Yingl Tsingl
   Khvat meets a nobleman, who is so impressed by Yingl Tsingl's pluck that he gives him his horse
   and a magic ring. Yingl Tsingl uses the ring to make the snowfall, and then rides away on his
   horse. Every year, with the advent of winter and snow, the villagers remember the work of Yingl
   Tsingl Khvat.

Middle East

Early, Margaret. *Ali Baba and the Forty Thieves.* New York: Harry N. Abrams, Inc., 1989. (Grades 2–4)
   In this, one of the most popular tales from *The Thousand and One Nights*, Ali Baba, a poor but
   honorable man, finds a cave filled with treasure. The treasure is stolen by forty thieves. Ali Baba's
   older brother, rich but greedy, discovers the secret. He is murdered by the thieves, who decide
   they must kill whoever knows of their cave. They locate Ali Baba's home, but are outwitted by
   Morgiana, Ali Baba's foster daughter, who kills the thieves. Ali Baba's son and Morgiana marry.
   Ali Baba tells his son about the treasures, which they share wisely and generously. The family is
   blessed by Allah and loved by their city for many generations.

Heide, Florence Parry and Judith Heide Gilliland. *The Day of Ahmed's Secret.* New York: Lothrop, Lee
& Shepard Books, 1990. (Grades K–4)
   Tonight, Ahmed will tell his secret to his family, but first he has work to do. Traveling in his
   donkey cart through Cairo, he delivers heavy bottles of fuel to his customers. Ahmed enjoys the
   sights and sounds of Cairo, the mighty river and desert that border the city, and the people he
   meets along the way. When finally home, he proudly tells his secret—he has learned to write his
   name.

Native Central America

Rohmer, Harriet, Octavio Chow and Morris Vidaure. *The Invisible Hunters.* San Francisco: Children's
Book Press, 1987. (Grades 1–4)
   Told in Spanish and English, this legend of Nicaragua's Miskito Indians relates what happens
   when three brothers find a special vine, the Dar. The brothers promise the Dar, who can make
   them invisible, that they will never sell the meat of the *wari*, a delicious wild pig, or hunt with
   anything but sticks. On these conditions, the Dar allows them to take pieces of the vine on their
   hunts. The brothers become famous hunters. When European traders find the brothers, they
   convince them to sell the *wari* and hunt with guns. The brothers become greedy; the people go
   hungry, for their food is sold. As punishment, the Dar refuses to allow the brothers to become
   visible. The brothers beg the Dar and the village elders for another chance, but they are not
   forgiven.

Rohmer, Harriet and Dorminster Wilson. *Mother Scorpion Country.* San Francisco: Children's Book
Press, 1987. (Grades 1–4)
   In another legend from the Miskito Indians, Kati and her husband Nakili are very much in love.
   When Kati dies, Nakili refuses to be separated from her, convincing his relatives to bury them
   together. Nakili persuades Kati to take him with her to Mother Scorpion Country. Although
   Kati finds Mother Scorpion Country to be beautiful, Nakili does not, for he is still alive. Kati
   helps him return to his own land, where he tells his story to his relatives. When his tale is

finished, Nakili reaches for the beads given him by Kati. The beads turn into a poisonous snake, biting him and sending Nakili back to Kati in Mother Scorpion Country.

Volkmer, Jane Anne. *Song of the Chirimia*. Minneapolis: Carolrhoda Books, 1990. (Grades K–4)
This Guatemalan folktale, written in English and Spanish, retells a story of the ancient Maya. Clear Night, the king, has a daughter, Moonlight. They are happy until Moonlight grows up. It is time for Moonlight to marry, so the king orders all of the young unmarried men to the central plaza. Many bring beautiful gifts, but Moonlight is most impressed by a young man, Black Feather, who sings a joyful song. She tells him that if he can learn to sing like the birds, she will marry him. Black Feather goes deep into the woods to learn, but is unable to duplicate bird song. He is discouraged until the Great Spirit of the Woods appears and makes him a special pipe, a *chirimia*. Black Feather quickly learns to play such beautiful music that even the birds stop to listen. He returns to Moonlight, who is enchanted by his music, and they are married.

Native North America

Bruchac, Joseph. *The Wind Eagle and Other Abenaki Stories*. Greenfield Center, NY: Bowman Books, 1985. (Grades 1–4).
Bruchac says that in many history books, the Abenaki are reported as no longer present in large portions of their native homeland. In reality, many Abenaki went "underground," continuing to live throughout northern New England. The six stories gathered here, about Gluskabe and the wise advice of Grandmother Woodchuck, say much about what it means to be an Abenaki. Rather than physical punishment, Bruchac relates that Abenaki adults use the old stories which contain a lesson to correct their children's misdeeds. "A good story can stay with one for the rest of their life and continue to teach them—at least that is what Indian people believe."

Chief Seattle. *Brother Eagle, Sister Sky*. New York: Dial Books, 1991. (Grades K–4)
Original paintings illustrate the words of Chief Seattle, written or spoken in the 1850's to the federal government which sought to purchase his people's land. In his speech, Chief Seattle spoke eloquently of the earth's sacredness and of what we now call ecology. He asked, "What will happen when the buffalo are slaughtered, the wild horses tamed, the secret corners of the forest are heavy with the scent of many men, and the view of the ripe hills is blotted by talking wire? It will be the end of living and the beginning of survival."

DePaola, Tomie. *The Legend of the Bluebonnet*. New York: G. P. Putnam's Sons, 1983. (Grades K–3)
A folktale tells how She-Who-Is-Alone, a child of the Comanche People, sacrifices her doll to end a drought. Her warrior doll was made by her parents who had died of hunger. The people send a shaman to listen to the Great Spirits. The shaman reports that the people have become selfish. They must make a burnt offering of their most valued possessions, scattering the ashes to the farthest point of the Earth. That night She-Who-Is-Alone offers her doll to the Great Spirits. In the morning, the people are astonished to see the land covered with bluebonnets. As the people say their thanks, a warm rain falls.

Mayo, Gretchen Will. *Earth Maker's Tales: North American Indian Stories*. New York: Walker & Co., 1989. (Grades 3–4)
This book collects stories from seven different Native American nations that explain earthquakes, floods, daylight, mountains, tornadoes, rainstorms, thunder and lightning, and rainbows. Each chapter is preceded by short summaries of other legends about the earth and the sky. The book explains how stories were passed from generation to generation, shared among nations, and told to European settlers.

Munsch, Robert and Michael Kusugak. *A Promise Is a Promise*. Willowdale, Ont., Canada: Firefly Books, Ltd., 1988. (Grades K–4)

> As the authors explain, "The Inuit traditionally spend a lot of time on the sea ice, so the Qallupilluit were invented to help keep small children away from dangerous crevices." In the story, Allashua disobeys her mother by fishing on the sea ice. Suddenly, the Qallupilluit drag her under the ice. She escapes by promising to bring them her brothers and sisters. After her parents thaw her out, Allashua tells them what she has done. They reply, "a promise is a promise," deciding the only way to rescue their children is to trick the Qallupilluit. As her parents dance to distract the Qallupilluit, they send their children to the sea ice to keep the promise. But because the Qallupilluit are watching the dance, the children are released from the promise and are saved.

Ortiz, Simon. *The People Shall Continue*. Revised ed. San Francisco: Children's Book Press, 1988. (Grades 1–4)

> An overview of Native American history for children written by an American Indian and poet, this book extends in time from creation to the present day. Written in the rhythms of traditional oral narrative, the story encompasses the experiences of Native peoples living in all parts of the United States. As the afterword explains, "In the last part of the story, the concept of 'the People' is enlarged to encompass all peoples living on this land who have been the victims of inhumanity. We must take great care with each other. We must ensure that life continues."

Sewall, Marcia. *People of the Breaking Day*. New York: Atheneum, 1990. (Grades 1–4)

> The Wampanoag people, the "People of the Breaking Day," live in southeastern Massachusetts. They were the Native Americans who greeted the Pilgrims. This book tells of the customs, traditions, spirituality, and way of life of the Wampanoag before the meeting of two very different cultures.

Steptoe, John. *The Story of Jumping Mouse*. New York: Lothrop, Lee & Shepard Books, 1984. (Grades K–4)

> Based on a legend of Northern Plains Native peoples, this story tells of a humble mouse who yearns to know the mysteries that lie beyond the familiarities of home. The first evening of his perilous journey Magic Frog befriends him, imbuing the mouse's legs with extra strength. Magic Frog tells Jumping Mouse he will reach the Far Off Land if he keeps hope alive within him. Along the way, Jumping Mouse meets a bison who has lost his sight and a wolf who has lost his sense of smell. Jumping Mouse uses his magic to restore their senses, but he loses his own ability to see and smell. In despair, he wonders how he will survive. Magic Frog reappears, praising Jumping Mouse's compassion and spirit. He tells Jumping Mouse to jump high into the sky. As he does, Jumping Mouse turns into an eagle, who can live in the Far Off Land forever.

CHAPTER 3
Creating Community

Real community is based on memory, on shared experience over time, continually revivified by comment, by reference, by telling the story over and over again.
—Margaret Mead

INTRODUCTION

On the night of October 1, 1943, German police began arresting Danish Jews. News of the arrests were leaked by several German sources to the Danes, whose response was immediate. Danes took Jews into hiding until they could be transported to the shore. From there, with the help of Danish fishermen, they escaped to Sweden, where the government had arranged refuge.

The rescue operation took three weeks, during which 7,200 Jews and about seven hundred non-Jewish relatives were taken to safety. All segments of the Danish community worked together on the rescue. King Christian X and dozens of economic and social organizations protested the arrests. Danish resistance members helped organize the escape. Danish pastors protested, urging their congregations to assist the Jews. Universities closed down for a week, so students could participate in the rescue.

Even with maximum effort, the rescue was not completely successful. Approximately five hundred Jews were captured and sent to the Theresienstadt concentration camp, but the Danes did not give up. They managed to rescue most of these Jews also, arranging for their transfer before Theresienstadt was closed and its prisoners sent to Auschwitz. By the end of the war, only seventy-seven Danish Jews, out of an estimated pre-war population of eight thousand, had been murdered in the Holocaust.

This action was unparalleled in occupied Europe. Throughout Europe, however, the number of Jews killed varied from country to country. For example, in Germany, Austria, Poland, and the Baltic States, nearly ninety percent of the Jews were murdered, almost three and one-half million people. In Italy, about twenty percent of the Jews were killed, most after German occupation of the country.

There are many reasons why Jews were almost annihilated in some countries but not in others, such as length of occupation, the level of anti-Semitism, the concentration of Jews in ghettos, and the continued existence of a national government. Certainly, however, each country's acceptance or rejection of Jews as community members was an important factor.

The Danes' heroic rescue raises important questions about community. What forces create community? How does a community protect and nurture all its members, including those who may be perceived as different? In times of stress, what motivates people to defend the well-being of all community members? Why do some communities do this, but not others? What values do communities impart to children?

Some of the children's books in this chapter are fanciful, some are serious. They all challenge children to explore the meaning of community, to define their communities, and to think about how community members accept and help each other.

Meaning of Community

The *American Heritage Dictionary* first defines community in its most usual sense, as "a group of people living in the same locality and under the same government." The last definition, truest to the Latin root word for community—"*communis*," meaning common—conveys a deeper meaning of community as connectedness. This entry defines community as "common participation or possession."

Community is more than a place, more than a government, and more than one relationship. John McKnight, a community organizer and professor at Northwestern University, says, "Community exists in the world of associations. Associations are people who come together in groups to work and celebrate, on a face-to-face basis, under their own control. True community occurs when associations come together."

Community is strongest when its members have a multitude of relationships. The more connections, the more shared memory, the more passing of shared experience to new community members, the more communities are able to protect the well-being of all their members.

For adults in a typical community, associated life might look like this.

Children also have personal and associational relationships. Even young children can recognize their communities, learn how they are created, and discover how all people benefit by working cooperatively.

Communities perform important functions. Communities are places where physical, emotional, and relationship needs are best met. They also supply a continuity of human relationships where children, through participation in community life, learn the values and interpersonal skills they need to contribute to their society.

Making Communities Competent

One of the truths demonstrated by the Holocaust is that communities contain the potential for both acceptance and rejection of their members. The Holocaust experience is vivid and stark: a few communities hid or helped Jews to escape, many were passive, others turned in their Jewish neighbors to the Nazis.

This experience, of course, is not limited to the Holocaust. Today, some communities reach out to support and integrate refugees, homeless people, people with disabilities, and members of other groups who can be perceived as different or dangerous. Others enclose themselves, attempting through discrimination, animosity, and sometimes violence to keep people perceived as different out of their neighborhoods and associations.

A community becomes competent in accepting and protecting all its members when people make the effort, through personal and associational relationships, to really learn about each other. Schools need to be competent communities. The books in this chapter teach about community, but children learn the most by observing and emulating adult behavior. When all adult members of the school community—teachers, coaches, counselors, principals, administrators, school board members—put these principles into action, schools transmit the values of competent, caring communities to the next generation.

A competent community:
• appreciates and celebrates diversity among its members;
• makes all people feel welcome and accepted;
• makes an extra effort and takes the time to be courteous, helpful, and responsible—perhaps even to be heroic to one another.[1]

HUMAN RIGHTS AS EXPRESSIONS OF COMMUNITY VALUES

History of Human Rights

The modern legal concept of universal human rights is a recent development. It is, however, rooted in ancient traditions from around the world.

In the West, the Romans placed great emphasis on the concept of *jus gentium*, which were laws Romans found common to the legal systems of their different subject peoples. These commonalities commanded respect as reflections of universal values. The Roman concept of *jus naturale*, natural justice, was derived from the universal values expressed in *jus gentium*. During the middle ages, theologians rediscovered this principle. Thomas Aquinas called it "natural law," the philosophical term still used today.

The theological development of natural law begun in the Middle Ages was affirmed and radically altered by the eighteenth-century American and French revolutions. These revolutions established the foundation of the state in a constitution rather than in a monarchy or theocracy. For the first time, the American Bill of Rights and the French Declaration of Rights of Man and Citizen formally enumerated and defined the rights and freedoms of individuals.

Thus began the development of national human rights law, demanded by the people and encoded in constitutions, legislation, and court decisions. Relying upon these new forms of law, the process of creating national human rights, also called civil rights, spread rapidly through much of Europe and the Americas. By World War II, many countries had adopted their own versions of human rights, making them the law of their land.

The advent of absolute dictatorship in Germany and Russia showed the fallacy of relying upon national human rights for individual protection. The world went to war for political and economic reasons certainly, but also because national human rights laws failed to protect people from governments that assumed absolute authority over their citizens and subject peoples. Because of the doctrine of national sovereignty and the collapse of the League of Nations, there was no method, short of war, for other countries to intervene in the affairs of despotic governments.

The Holocaust and the destruction of World War II shocked and revolted people around the world. Even before the war ended, the Allies began plans for the United Nations. They realized a new forum for international cooperation and the development of common values were essential to protect human life and to forestall the tremendous risk and cost of stopping aggression through warfare.

The Nature of Human Rights

In law, the term "right" is ambiguous. For our purposes, "law" is rules of conduct treated within a community as binding on all its members. "Rights" are claims made by those members upon the community.

One position, called legal positivism, views rights as those claims which are defined and enforced

---

[1] John O'Brien. *Learning about Citizen Advocacy.* Atlanta, GA: Georgia Advocacy Office, 1987, section 5, p. 13.

by law. If a claim is made that cannot be enforced, it is simply not a right. For legal positivists, enforcement is possible when the right is *written* and when there are courts and police to apply and *enforce* the written law. In the United States, for example, citizens have the positive right to freedom of speech because it is written in the Bill of Rights, made applicable to the states by Supreme Court decisions, and enforceable by a judicial system backed by the police power of the state.

A second viewpoint on rights is that conceived by moral philosophy. In this conception, rights are not limited to those that are enforceable. Rights are moral. They are contained in the values necessary for justice. The word *"justice"* comes from a Latin root word meaning righteousness. The human need for justice exists regardless of whether rights are written and enforceable.

So, the crucial question is posed. Are human rights positive rights or moral rights? Are they rights we actually have or rights we ought to have?

This distinction is critical. If students are taught that human rights are those we ought to have but which do not yet exist as positive law, they may fail to grasp that human rights express universal moral values, offering guidance when faced with difficult moral choices. If students are not taught that human rights not only exist but actually protect all people from want and the vagaries of national governments, they may fail to grasp the importance of their future role, as individual citizens and community members, in ensuring human rights for all.

The answer to the question whether human rights are positive legal rights or moral rights is that they are moral rights which many countries have adopted and some actually enforce. In those countries, they are also positive rights. Within the scope of the international community, they are principally moral rights which are perhaps in the process of becoming positive law. The task before us is to find methods for enforcing human rights internationally, so that all people can freely exercise and enjoy them. That this is not the case in much of the world, however, does not vitiate the importance of human rights as statements of moral values.

In *What Are Human Rights?*, Maurice Cranston argues that the assertion that there is only one genuine kind of law, positive law, lacks subtlety and causes mischief. At best, it is frustrating to be told one has a human right but it is not enforceable. Nevertheless, before individuals can protest that a wrong has been done, a correlative right must be stated and recognized. Human rights serve this purpose. People must have the words to claim their rights before rights can be written and enforced.

Second, vesting all legal authority, positive and moral, in government can lead to governments' enacting and enforcing laws that profoundly harm their citizens. Again, the Holocaust provides a chilling example. Before implementing the "final solution," the Nazi party proposed, the Reichstag passed, and the German courts enforced laws stripping Jews of their possessions, access to jobs and schools, and their citizenship. This permitted the majority of the German people to believe these laws were lawful and therefore to be obeyed. There was no alternative body of rights with which to judge the validity of these laws. Human rights documents offer that higher authority.

Conceptually, human rights have the following characteristics:
- Human rights are *inherent;* they attach to each person simply by nature of each person's humanness.
- Human rights are *universal;* they apply to each person regardless of the government under which he or she lives.
- Human rights are *inalienable;* they cannot be separated from the individual or transferred to another person.
- Human rights imply *equality* of all people in terms of dignity, respect, and rights.

Law changes constantly, as people insist that it reflect their values. The status of universal human rights today is essentially the same as the status of moral rights before their embodiment in national human rights law. For example, the rights in our Bill of Rights were moral rights insisted upon by the people of a new nation, and only gradually were incorporated into positive law. Today, our global community is attempting to create and enforce universal human rights under the auspices of the United Nations.

The United Nations and Human Rights

The United Nations was chartered in 1945. One of its first efforts, headed by Eleanor Roosevelt, was adoption in 1948 of the United Nations Universal Declaration of Human Rights. The Declaration is not binding law; it is the first internationally accepted list of those rights that should apply to all people. As such, it is a morally compelling document.

Summary of the United Nations Declaration of Human Rights

1. Right to freedom and equality of rights for all people.
2. Entitlement to all the rights and freedoms in the Declaration, without distinction or discrimination.
3. Right to life, liberty and personal security.
4. Prohibition of slavery and the slave trade.
5. Freedom from torture or cruel punishment.
6. Right to recognition as a person before the law.
7. Right to equal protection of the law.
8. Right to effective national remedies for violation of fundamental rights.
9. Freedom from arbitrary arrest, detention or exile.
10. Right to fair and public hearings.
11. Right to presumption of innocence until proven guilty.
12. Freedom from arbitrary interference with privacy, family, home, correspondence, honor, or reputation.
13. Freedom of movement within a State, and the right to leave a State.
14. Right to seek asylum from persecution.
15. Right to a nationality.
16. Right to marry and have a family; to marry only with full consent; to protection of family.
17. Right to own property.
18. Right to freedom of thought, conscience, and religion.
19. Right to freedom of opinion and expression.
20. Right to freedom of peaceful assembly and association.
21. Right to participate in government and to genuinely universal elections.
22. Right to social security and to economic, social and cultural rights indispensable to dignity.
23. Right to work, to equal pay for equal work, and to unionize.
24. Right to rest, leisure, and to periodic holidays with pay.
25. Right to an adequate standard of living (mothers and children are entitled to special care).
26. Right to education.
27. Right to participate in a community's cultural life.
28. Right to social and international order in which the Declaration's rights can be fully realized.
29. Right to exercise one's duties to the community.
30. Nothing in the Declaration may be interpreted as implying a right to destroy the Declaration's rights and freedoms.

After adopting the Declaration, it took the United Nations another twenty years to agree on international human rights treaties. These treaties are the United Nations Covenant on Civil and Political Rights and the United Nations Covenant on Economic and Cultural Rights.

More than eighty-five countries have accepted these treaties, thereby obligating themselves to bring their national law into compliance with the human rights listed in the treaties. Unfortunately, the United States is not a signatory to either treaty, presumably because it would obligate us to change our national law in unpopular ways. For example, the treaties prohibit the execution of minors, which our Supreme Court has ruled to be constitutional.

Enforcement at the international level remains a significant problem. The United Nations has several complaint processes for violations of human rights, but the United Nations openly acknowledges that it lacks an effective enforcement mechanism. It relies upon investigation, education, and persuasion to implement universal human rights.

So, there is much work to be done to promote and protect human rights. Obviously, the international community has to find a way, either by giving the United Nations a court and armed enforcement capabilities or through some other mechanism, to enforce universal human rights. It would be a powerful lesson for children to understand they have a future role in this process.

In addition, existing documents are not necessarily the final statement on human rights. They can and should be changed as people's values change or expand. One student activity suggested in this chapter is for children to create their own human rights statement for their classroom. Learning that rights are fluid, capable of creation and change, is also a powerful lesson.

Community, Human Rights, and Citizenship

Typically, citizenship is viewed as the right to protection by a government, to vote, and to enjoy other privileges granted by the state. Indeed, this is the definition of citizenship in the *American Heritage Dictionary*.

Only in a legalistic sense, however, is citizenship granted by government. More accurately, citizenship exists when individuals come together in community, demanding their rights from government. John McKnight says citizenship is exercised not solely by voting but rather in an associated life where individuals have a voice and a place to act.

The way people choose to act as citizens in community is a function of their values. For example, if community members see Jews as unworthy of human rights and community acceptance, it is a short step to remaining silent, or even worse, assisting when discrimination and violence take place.

If community members see Jews as people with human rights just like other valued members of the community, it is an easier step to act to protect their neighbors from harm. The Danish experience tells us that when citizens speak up and act on their values as a community, they have tremendous power.

Today, citizens acting in community also have that power. Citizens can reject refugees, or welcome them into their community. Citizens can discriminate on the basis of ethnicity, or work to understand and change racist attitudes. Citizens can monitor, protest against, and stop human rights violations.

Since the Holocaust, we have many examples where citizens have accomplished just this. There were few human rights organizations before 1945; now, over a thousand groups worldwide monitor human rights violations in their communities.

In an introduction to an anthology on human rights, the director of Amnesty International said, "The failures, shortcomings, and immense obstacles experienced in the generation since the signing of the Universal Declaration of Human Rights should never be underestimated. Censorship, illiteracy, government attacks on human rights monitors, cynicism, and deal-making in the councils of power will not be surmounted by the committed few. The movement for human rights must become truly global, carried forward by the millions rather than by the thousands of people if such barriers are to be surmounted."

"But the experience of achievement in adversity and astonishing growth since 1948 provide legitimate reason for hope that the aspirations of the human rights constituency—such goals as making torture 'as unthinkable as slavery'—may be within reach." By teaching children about community, teachers will help prepare today's young students to become part of those millions needed to protect the human rights of their neighbors.

Sources

Cranston, Maurice. *What Are Human Rights?* New York: Taplinger, 1973.Davidowicz, Lucy S. *The War Against the Jews 1933–1945.* New York: Holt, Rinehart and Winston, 1975.

Gilbert, Martin. *Atlas of the Holocaust.* New York: William Morrow, 1993.

Gutman, Israel. *The Encyclopedia of the Holocaust.* New York: Macmillan, 1990.

Machan, Tibor R. "Are Human Rights Real?" *The Humanist* 49 (1989): pp. 28–30.

McKnight, John. "Community." Association for Retarded Citizens/U.S. Converence, Omaha, NE, 1986.

United Nations. *Human Rights: Questions and Answers.* New York: United Nations Department of Public Information, 1987.

LESSON PLAN FOR:

The Mitten, by Alvin Tresselt. Illustrations by Yaroslava. New York: Mulberry Books, 1964. Grades K-4

Story Summary

On the coldest day of winter, the young narrator's grandfather, himself a young boy at the time of the story, loses his mitten. A mouse spies the mitten, popping in to get warm. A frog happens by, and the mouse invites her in before she freezes. Other animals—an owl, a rabbit, a fox, a wolf, a wild boar, and even a big bear—squeeze in. The animals are crowded, but very warm. Finally, an old cricket is invited inside. As she puts one foot in, the mitten splits in half. Just as the mitten splits, the boy discovers he has lost his mitten. He looks for it, but all he can find are some of the ripped pieces and a little mouse scurrying away with a bit of the lining. He is sure his grandmother has finished his new mittens, so he goes home. To this day, the grandfather says he never really knew what happened to his lost mitten.

Concepts Summary

Though a fanciful tale from the Ukraine, *The Mitten* presents issues at the core of community. It asks children to consider what constitutes a community, how and why communities are created, and the effects of acceptance or rejection upon potential community members.

Objectives

The student should be able to:
- define community;
- recognize different forms of community;
- describe how communities are created;
- recognize and describe purposes served by communities;
- understand the importance of individual sharing for communal well-being.

Materials

Books: *The Mitten*, by Alvin Tresselt
   The Mitten, adapted and illustrated by Jan Brett
   The Rabbi's Wisdom, by Erica Gordon
   Christmas on Exeter Street, by Diana Hendry
Art Supplies: Paper and markers, magazines for a collage
Equipment: Building blocks, flannel and yarn, puppets, different types of cloth used to make mittens, pictures of animals in the story

CONCEPT: *DEFINITION OF COMMUNITY*

Discussion Questions

- Where did the animals who crowded into the mitten usually live? Do you think they usually lived with other animals like themselves, or do you think they lived all together?
- Were groups of animals living together in the forest a community? Why or why not?
- Were the animals in the mitten a community? Why or why not?
- Were the people in the story a community? Why or why not?
- How many communities can you find in the story?
- What are some common characteristics of these communities? What are some differences?
- What is your community? What is it like?
- Can people have more than one community? Is your class a community? Your school? Your town?

Activities

Art

- Using blocks or other materials, have children build a model of their community. Each child can describe to the class the physical characteristics of his or her community, also explaining the intangible qualities which make the whole a community rather than simply disparate, unconnected parts.

Drama

- Cut out a large mitten, using yarn to lace it together. Make stick puppets of the animals in the story. Have the class act out the story, placing the puppets inside the mitten as the teacher narrates. The play could be varied by using animals indigenous to your state or by changing the story's location.

Language Arts

- Have children list the different groups they are part of and analyze which are communities and which are not. Have children identify their communities, using their analysis to discuss what turns groups into a community. Help children write their own definition of community.
- This is a "retold" story, based on a folktale. Introduce children to the idea of oral versus written transmission, the moral content of folktales, and storytelling as a method of communicating values. Have children speculate about how storytelling reinforces and transmits community from generation to generation.

Math

- Older children can work on problems related to proportion and ratio. For example, have them calculate the amount of space within a mitten. Compare proportionate pictures of animals for size, calculating the relative space each animal would need.

Science

- Have children compare the tensile qualities of different materials, identifying the materials having the kind of give necessary for expansion. Use this experiment to discuss why people might want to make mittens out of materials that expand.

CONCEPT: *CREATING COMMUNITY*

Discussion Questions

- If the mitten "was just the right size for a tiny mouse," how did all the other animals fit inside?
- Do you think being inside the mitten was comfortable as more animals crowded inside? Why do you think the animals already inside the mitten invited others to join them?
- What does it mean "to set a good example?"
- Are some of the animals who shared the mitten usually enemies? Why do you think they got along inside the mitten?
- If the mitten and the animals inside were a community, how did they create their community?
- What judgments did the animals sharing the mitten make to create their community?
- Do human beings always behave like the animals in the mitten? Why or why not? Can you think of examples in your school or neighborhood where people created a community?

Activities

Art

- Have children draw a picture of their own mittens and the various functions they could provide.

Language Arts

- Have children make up their own mythical community, telling or writing a story of how the community was created and how the creatures who live there get along.
- Older children can be introduced to the concept of "implicit" and "explicit" by discussing how the author implies that each of the animals is left with a piece of the mitten after it explodes. Have children list the facts given in the story, and the inferences that can be made from the facts. Discuss whether they enjoy being told everything or whether they like to add some facts of their own.

Science

- Use examples from the animal kingdom to demonstrate how animals create and live in communities. For example, children can study bees, dolphins, or wolves, analyzing what makes a hive, pod, or pack a community.

CONCEPT: *COMMUNAL WELL-BEING*

Discussion Questions
- What did the mitten do for the animals in the story? Why was this important?
- Why wasn't the boy in the story afraid his hand would be cold all winter after he lost his mitten? Whom did he know would take care of him?
- How do you think the animals stayed warm after the mitten exploded?
- Does this story have a happy or a sad ending?
- What examples in your community compare to the behavior of the animals in the mitten?

Activities

Language Arts

- Have children tell or write a story about how the animals survived the cold winter after the mitten split apart.
- Read and discuss how similar stories can exist in different countries and cultures. For example, *The Rabbi's Wisdom* is a Jewish folktale about a man who learns his home can accommodate all those who need shelter. *Christmas on Exeter Street*, a story from the United States in which a house nearly bursts at the seams, also echoes *The Mitten*'s themes.

Social Studies

- Have children choose a community, such as their classroom, and analyze what it needs to function. Specifically, have children explore the contributions of different community members, ways in which the community obtains important knowledge or resources, and what would happen if community members stopped working together.
- Older children can envision and create a model community, designing buildings, services, community activities, and methods for sharing the community's culture with new members.
- Discuss how people in another culture live together in a community. Older children can examine the ways they live in a community compared to the other culture, analyzing benefits of each.

Science

- Choose an ecological consequence of communal failure to safeguard the environment, such as how improperly disposed waste products contaminate the earth or how overuse of the land contributes to desertification. Explain the science involved in the example. Have children analyze how a community acting together can reverse the process.

Community Resources
People who have service animals, such as someone with a disability or someone who uses a dog sled team, can visit the class to discuss how humans and animals work together.

Children can visit a recycling plant to learn about recycling, new technologies, new materials created from waste products, and how community cooperation makes recycling possible.

Other Recommended Children's Books
Sharing:
The Invisible Hunters, by Harriet Rohmer

Meaning of community:
Let the Celebrations Begin! by Margaret Wild
Swimmy, by Leo Lionni
The Empty Lot, by Dale H. Fife
Angel Child, Dragon Child, by Michele Maria Surat

Ecology:
Brother Eagle, Sister Sky, by Chief Seattle
The People Who Hugged the Trees, by Deborah Lee Rose
Tigress, by Helen Cowcher
A River Ran Wild, by Lynne Cherry

Resources for the Classroom
Caduto, Michael J. and Joseph Bruchac. *Keepers of the Earth: Native American Stories and Environmental Activities for Children*. Golden, CO: Fulcrum Publishing, 1989.
_____. *Keepers of the Animals: Native American Stories and Wildlife Activities for Children*. Golden, CO: Fulcrum Publishing, 1991.
Meagher, Laura. *Teaching Children about Global Awareness*. New York: The Crossroad Publishing Co., Inc., 1991.

Supplemental Children's Books
Pringle, Laurence. *Living Treasure: Saving Earth's Threatened Biodiversity*. New York: Morrow Junior Books, 1991.

LESSSON PLAN FOR:
Sam Johnson and the Blue Ribbon Quilt, by Lisa Campbell Ernst. New York: Lothrop, Lee & Shepard Books, 1983. Grades K-4.

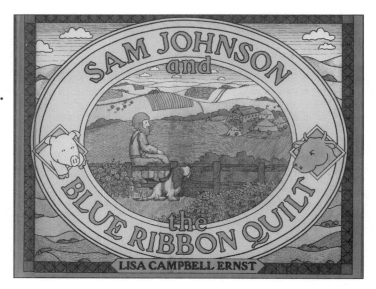

Story Summary

Sam Johnson discovers he has a flair for quilting, but when he attempts to join his wife's quilting club, he is laughed from the room. Believing his rights have been compromised, Sam organizes a men's quilting club. Both clubs decide to enter a quilt competition. On the way there, an accident occurs that damages the quilts. The women and men combine their efforts, making a new quilt fashioned from pieces of the separate quilts.

Concepts Summary

This story presents two major issues. The first, gender diversity, concerns differences between men and women, gender role expectations, stereotypical thinking, and equality. The second issue, working on a project, raises interesting questions about community. Why do people choose to compete or cooperate? Why do people work cooperatively to meet their needs, and in this process, produce useful and beautiful artifacts? How does a crisis affect a community? How do written or unwritten rules affect community cohesiveness?

Objectives

The student should be able to:
• understand the concepts of gender, stereotype, equality, competition, cooperation, and community;
• recognize ways women and men are different and similar;
• learn that talent is not gender-specific;
• analyze how society historically assigns interests and work based on gender, how this is changing, and how this change can affect a community;
• analyze how working on a project creates community, recognizing that this process exists in many cultures.

Materials

Books: *Sam Johnson and the Blue Ribbon Quilt*, by Lisa Campbell Ernst
Documents: Declaration of Independence, U.S. Constitution, Emancipation Proclamation
Art Supplies: Cloth scraps for making quilts, rulers, and tracing paper

CONCEPTS: *GENDER DIVERSITY, EQUALITY*

Discussion Questions

• Why did Sam's wife chuckle nervously when he showed her his handiwork?

- What was Mrs. Johnson's attitude toward Sam's new interest? Why?
- In the story, who decided only women made quilts? Was this fair?
- Why is making a quilt usually thought of as women's work?
- Can you think of other examples of women's work? Men's work? Where do you think these ideas come from?
- Why would men want to make a quilt? Does quilt-making fit with your examples of men's work?
- How are the women and men in the story the same? Different? How are the girls and boys in your class the same? Different?
- How do you think Sam would feel if he were not allowed to make a quilt?
- Can you think of occasions when you were not allowed to do something just because you were a boy or girl? How did you feel? Would it make a difference if you had decided this for yourself?
- If boys and girls are different in some ways, can they still be equal? What does "equal" mean to you?

Activities

Language Arts

- Have children use answers from the discussion questions to give examples of the following terms: different, same, gender, gender role, stereotype, and equality.
- Have children tell or write a story, using these concepts, where traditional gender roles are reversed. Ask children to consider what obstacles they might encounter because of stereotypes and how they would overcome them.

Social Studies

- Show a copy of the Declaration of Independence and read, or ask children to find, the part that meant the most to Sam and the other men. Other documents, such as the Constitution or the Emancipation Proclamation, can be introduced.
- Have children analyze why people write down which rights are important to them and why this is useful.
- Have children define gender equality in their own words and develop a list of rights based on this for their classroom. The definition and list can be made into a poster, displayed, and used to resolve questions and disputes in the classroom community.

Math

- Have children write a story problem using gender-neutral language, for example a doctor sees five patients and a nurse sees seven. The answer should consider not only the number of patients treated during the day but assumptions about the gender of the nurse and doctor.

CONCEPT: *COMMUNITY COOPERATION*

Discussion Questions

- How did the people in the story make quilts? What would you need to know to make a quilt? How could you learn these skills?
- Why do people make quilts?

- What is the crisis in this story? How was the crisis solved? Can you think of examples of a crisis in your life? What did you do?
- Why did the men and women stop competing and start cooperating?
- What good things happened when they worked together? What do you think Sam, his wife, and the other people learned from working together?
- How are competition and cooperation opposites?
- When can competition be good? Bad? When can cooperation be good? Bad?
- Besides making quilts, what other cooperative activities do people do to take care of themselves and survive?
- How can working cooperatively help a community to care for its members?

Activities

Art

- Look at different quilts and discuss various designs. Discuss whether the quilts tell anything about who made them.
- Children can design or make small quilts from scraps that tell their personal story. Or children can draw a quilt. Each of the border designs in the book comprises a traditional quilt pattern, such as "hole in the barn door." Using different geometric designs, children can create their own patterns and assign them fanciful names.

Language Arts

- Have children imagine telling a story by using a quilt form. Each square could consist of some vivid description expressed in a few words, with each frame adding another detail to the narrative.

Social Studies

- Discuss the history of quilting. Compare it with other crafts that are both beautiful and practical. For older children, this could be a research project, with each child assigned to discover a craft made by a particular culture, learning how it is made and used.
- Have children conduct an experiment in cooperative activities and gender roles. One example would be to plan a winter camping trip or picnic. Have children decide what they would need to stay warm, to eat, and to survive a snowstorm. Watch for gender assumptions, such as boys assigned to collect wood or girls assigned to cook. After the activity is planned, discuss what they learned about their assumptions and about working together as a community.

Math

- Children can learn how math skills are essential to quilt-making. Have children draw a quilt made of geometric shapes and then use a measuring stick to reproduce the components for a life-size quilt. (Tracing skills can also be practiced.) Children can actually make the large quilt out of construction paper.

Science

- Explore different ways of keeping warm, for example an oil furnace, an electric space heater, wood fires, warm clothes and blankets, another person's body heat. Compare ways people from different cultures in cold climates use the resources around them to keep warm. Consider different ways community members work together to create warmth during winter.

Community Resources

Children can bring quilts from home. Quilters can come to the classroom to discuss their craft. Women and men who have nontraditional occupations can discuss their work and experiences. People with winter camping experience can explain the equipment and cooperation needed to live outdoors during the winter. Several people could be invited, so that different methods can be compared, e.g., traditional Native American methods compared with high-tech equipment.

Other Recommended Children's Books

Gender:

The Paper Bag Princess, by Robert Munsch
Bea and Mr. Jones, by Amy Schwartz

Community cooperation:

Angel Child, Dragon Child, by Michele Maria Surat
My Grandmother's Journey, by John Cech
Somebody Loves You, Mr. Hatch, by Eileen Spinelli
The Lily Cupboard, by Shulamith Levy Oppenheim
Mrs. Katz and Tush, by Patricia Polacco

Quilts:

The Rag Coat, by Lauren Mills
Tar Beach, by Faith Ringgold

For the Classroom

Anti-Defamation League. *The Wonderful World of Difference: A Human Relations Program for Grades K-8*. New York: Anti-Defamation League, 1986.
Caduto, Michael J. and Joseph Bruchac. *Keepers of the Earth: Native American Stories and Environmental Activities for Children*. Golden, CO: Fulcrum Publishing, 1989.

Supplemental Children's Books

Scholes, Katherine. *Peace Begins With You*. Boston: Little, Brown and Co., 1994.

LESSON PLAN FOR:

***Blueberries for Sal*, by Robert McCloskey. New York: Puffin Books, 1948, 1976. Grades K-2.**

Story Summary

Little Sal and her mother go to Blueberry Hill to pick blueberries for the winter. Meanwhile, on the other side of the hill, Little Bear and his mother are eating blueberries, storing food for their winter's hibernation. Little Sal loses sight of her mother. She thinks she finds her, happily following along, but it is really the mother bear. Little Bear, who has also lost his mother, goes off to search, finding Little Sal's mother instead. When Little Bear's mother hears the sound of blueberries hitting the bottom of a pail, she looks behind her and discovers Little Sal. Little Bear's mother, who is old enough to be shy of people, rushes off to search for her own child. Little Sal's mother, when she feels someone taking tremendous amounts of blueberries from her pail, looks behind her and sees Little Bear. Little Sal's mother, who is old enough to be shy of bears, rushes off to find her daughter. The people and bears unscramble, and each gather enough blueberries to last for the long winter.

Concepts Summary

In this whimsical story, humans and animals live cooperatively, sharing resources necessary to meet their needs. Their tale offers another perspective on community: community as an environment used by many creatures.

Objectives

The student should be able to:
- Understand the nature of the community shared by people and bears;
- Learn that people and animals occupy the same world and depend on the same resources;
- Recognize the similarities and differences between the two sets of mothers and children;
- Analyze the plot to understand what happens in the story.

Materials

Book: *Blueberries for Sal*, by Robert McCloskey
Art Supplies: Paper, markers, magazines for collages
Equipment: Pails, blueberries, dried peas dyed blue, or marbles, United States or world map

CONCEPT: *SHARING RESOURCES*

Discussion Questions
- Why are blueberries important to people? Why are they important to bears?
- What do Little Sal and Little Bear have in common? What do their mothers have in common?

- What might happen to bears if people decided to keep them away from Blueberry Hill?
- What might happen to people if there were so many bears on Blueberry Hill that they were afraid to pick blueberries?
- Why do you think Little Bear's mother didn't chase Little Sal and her mother off Blueberry Hill?
- Why do you think Little Sal's mother didn't chase Little Bear and his mother off Blueberry Hill?
- What makes this story have a happy ending?
- How could this story have an unhappy ending?

Activities

Art

- Ask children to find their favorite picture in the story, and to describe why they like it.
- Have children draw Blueberry Hill, showing some of its other natural resources and animals which might use them.

Language Arts

- Have children identify each step in the story's plot. Discuss how each step is necessary for the next to occur. Change an element of the plot, asking children to tell or write a new ending based on possible consequences caused by the change.
- Many words come from the way something sounds, such as "kerplunk." Have children identify other words that come from sounds, and create new words that imitate sounds.

Geography

- Identify locations in the U.S. where blueberries grow, including where they are grown and harvested for sale. Discuss the geographic features that make certain parts of some states ideal for blueberry production.

Math

- Divide children into teams of different sizes, scatter the blueberries, dried peas, or marbles, and hold a contest to see which team can fill the pail the fastest. Have each child count the number of objects he or she contributed. Use the contest to demonstrate the relationship between the number of people doing a job and the length of time necessary to complete the job.

Science

- Discuss how blueberries grow and what they provide by way of nourishment. As a project, children can create an appropriate environment in their class and grow blueberries, or other nourishing plants.

CONCEPT: *COMMUNAL ENVIRONMENT*

Discussion Questions

- Is Little Sal's mother kind to Little Bear? Why?
- Is Little Bear's mother kind to Little Sal? Why?
- What is Little Sal's community? What is Little Bear's community? What parts of their communities do they have in common?
- Why do you think the mothers are shy about bears and people?
- What are some of the ideas this story teaches about bears, other animals, and people?
- Can you think of any other animals who might live on or use Blueberry Hill as their community?
- Do you think people and animals might share places other than a hill like Blueberry Hill? What other places might they share?
- Do you think it is important for people and animals to share their communities? When is this a good idea? When can this be a bad idea?
- What do you think your community might be like if there were no animals?

Activities

Art

- Have children draw pictures or make a collage of animals that live in their state. Make a wall display with the pictures.

Language Arts

- Have children create their own definition of community to include the animals which share their ecosystem.
- Have children list the different animals they have seen, including domestic and wild animals. Using the answers to the discussion questions, have children tell or write a story about what their community would be like if all these animals disappeared.

Social Studies

- Choose a different geographical region of the United States or a different country, and describe the people and animals who live there. Have children draw parallels between this community and their ecosystems in their state.

Science

- Using the animals on the wall display, prepare lessons on the different animals. Describe each animal's habitat, and what the animal contributes to its larger ecosystem.

Community Resources
Invite people who rely on blueberries for their livelihood or who study blueberries to teach a class about blueberries.

Other Recommended Children's Books
Interactions between animals and humans:
My Buddy, by Audrey Osofsky
Hawk, I'm Your Brother, by Byrd Baylor
Why Mosquitoes Buzz in People's Ears, by Verna Aardema

Ecology:
Tigress, by Helen Cowcher
The Empty Lot, by Dale H. Fife
The Great Kapok Tree, by Lynne Cherry
The People Who Hugged the Trees, by Deborah Lee Rose
A River Ran Wild, by Lynne Cherry

Resources For the Classroom
Baker, Michael O. *What Would You Do? Developing and/or Applying Ethical Standards*. Pacific Grove, CA: Midwest Publications, 1989.
Caduto, Michael J. and Joseph Bruchac. *Keepers of the Animals: Native American Stories and Wildlife Activities for Children*. Golden, CO: Fulcrum Publishing, 1991.
Martinez, Jimmie and Arlene Watters. *US: A Cultural Mosaic*. San Diego, CA: San Diego Public Schools, 1979.

Supplemental Children's Books
Durrell, Ann and Marily Sachs, eds. *The Big Book for Peace*. New York: Dutton Children's Books, 1990.
Foster, Joanna. *Cartons, Cans, and Orange Peels. Where Does Your Garbage Go?* New York: Clarion Books, 1991.
Lepthion, Emilie U. and Joan Kalbacken. *Recycling*. Chicago: Children's Press, 1991.
Pringle, Laurence. *Living Treasure: Saving Earth's Threatened Biodiversity*. New York: Morrow Junior Books, 1991.

LESSON PLAN FOR:

Uncle Willie and the Soup Kitchen,
**by DyAnne DiSalvo-Ryan. New
York: Morrow Junior Books,
1991. Grades 1-4.**

Story Summary

The narrator, a young boy, is watched over
after school by his Uncle Willie. Uncle
Willie works in a soup kitchen because
"sometimes people need help." When the
boy sees homeless people, the Can Man
rummaging through garbage, and an old
woman sleeping on a park bench—he feels
sad and a little scared. His mother suggests
he spend a day at the soup kitchen to learn
more about people who need help. At first he is nervous, but then he pitches in, helping to make soup
and fruit salad, setting the tables, serving and cleaning up. He sees Frank the Can Man, and thinks he
sees the old woman too. By the end of the day, he feels at ease, proud of his contribution.

Concepts Summary

Reading and talking about an urban soup kitchen can give children an opportunity to explore fear of
people who seem different, the condition of people who are less well-off, how a community responds
to need, and the good feelings that come from helping others. Beyond the issues apparent on the
story's surface, this book raises other abstract concepts. The book lends itself to an exploration of the
consequences of rejection from community, how people can make community inclusive, and the
importance of human rights for protection of all a community members.

Objectives

The student should be able to:
- define community;
- learn some of the consequences when a community does not protect all its members;
- understand that those with homes differ from those without homes in some ways, but perhaps not
  in all ways;
- identify ways individuals contribute to communal well-being, and the benefits of such work;
- define and apply the concepts of citizenship and human rights to situations in his or her community.

Materials

Book: *Uncle Willie and the Soup Kitchen*, by DyAnne DiSalvo-Ryan
Documents: U.S. Constitution and Bill of Rights; United Nations Declaration of Universal Human
Rights
Art Supplies: Paper, poster board, markers, cloth, yarn, clay
Music: Sheet music or recording of "This Land Is Your Land"
Drama: Costumes for merchants, soup kitchen workers, and homeless people
Cooking: Soup pot, vegetables, seasoning, protein sources

CONCEPT: *CITIZENSHIP*

Discussion Questions

- What is the community in the story? How many community members can you list?
- How many different people can you identify in your community? Is the police officer a community member? How about the librarian, doctor, grocer, your mother and father?
- Why does Uncle Willie call people at the soup kitchen "citizens"?
- Are you a citizen of your community? What makes you a citizen?
- What is a homeless person? Are homeless people always treated like citizens? Why or why not?
- What manners does Uncle Willie observe while assisting people who come to the soup kitchen?

Activities

Art

- Children can draw or make collages of the different citizens who make up their community.

Music

- Teach children to sing (or play a recording) of "This Land Is Your Land." Lead a discussion on what the song says about belonging and citizenship.
- Older children can research the history of "This Land Is Your Land"; for example, who wrote it and the historical conditions in the United States when the song was written.

Language Arts

- Using answers to the discussion questions, have children analyze what makes a person a citizen. Have children tell or write a story about what citizenship means to them personally.

Geography

- If "This Land Is Your Land" was taught, have children identify the geographical areas mentioned in the song on a map of the United States.

Social Studies

- Lead a discussion on what makes a person a citizen of the United States. Older children can research how immigrants to the United States become citizens.
- List some of the rights of citizenship in the United States, such as the right to go to school or the right to vote. Have children analyze the responsibilities created by citizenship. Older children can be introduced to the Constitution and Bill of Rights in terms of the benefits and responsibilities of citizenship.

CONCEPT: *CONSEQUENCES OF EXCLUSION*

Discussion Questions

- What did Uncle Willie mean when he said that "If it wasn't for George we'd all be in hot water?"
- How did "Underfoot" get his name? What did Uncle Willie mean when he said that "Underfoot works the night shift down in the basement?"
- Who contributes to the soup kitchen and what do they receive in return?
- What do homeless people have in common? Do you think all homeless people are alike? Why or why not?
- From the information in the story, what are some of the ways people's lives change if they are homeless?
- How do you think a person might become homeless? Do you think homeless people are part of their communities? Why or why not?
- Even if you didn't have a home, do you think you would still be the same person inside? Why or why not?
- Can you think of other people who might be excluded from full participation in community life? How about people who speak a language other than English? How about people who have a disability? How about very old people?
- Why might these people be left out of community life? What do you think the consequences might be for them?

Activities

Art

- Have children make a "survival bag" out of cloth and yarn. Brainstorm what they would most need in their bags. Have children make some of these things with art supplies.

Language Arts

- Have children tell or write an imaginative story about the life of Frank, the Can Man, or the old woman who slept on the bench.
- For older children, define "inclusion" and "exclusion," drawing parallels between these concepts and belonging to a community. Children can analyze how the homeless people in the story were both excluded and included in community life. Children also can write a story about a time they were excluded from a family or community activity, and how they felt about it.

Social Studies

- Ask children what they can tell about homeless people from the pictures in the story. Analyze what the pictures say about how homeless people are different from and the same as people who have homes. Discuss what the similarities and differences tell about homeless people.

Science

- For older children, introduce a lesson on malnutrition: what causes it, what its effects are, and how it can be cured. Have children brainstorm about methods for identifying and helping people in their community who might be malnourished.

CONCEPTS: *COMMUNITY WELL-BEING AND HUMAN RIGHTS*

Discussion Questions

- Why does the town in the story have a soup kitchen? Does the soup kitchen provide other things besides meals? What?
- What are some important rules in a soup kitchen for those who serve and for those who are served?
- What food did Mr. Anthony give to the soup kitchen? Why do you think he did this?
- Who else made the soup kitchen work? What did each of them provide?
- At the beginning of the story, what is the attitude of the boy towards the Can Man? What happens at the end of the story that tells you his attitude has changed?
- Do you think the boy liked working in the soup kitchen? Why? What do you think he learned?

Activities

Art

- Have children draw the vegetables that went into the pot of soup in the story.

Language Arts

- Discuss what makes the town in the story a community. List the different people who contribute to the soup kitchen, discussing what they give to the soup kitchen and what they receive in return.
- Have children brainstorm about what they could contribute to a soup kitchen, and write a story about their ideas.

Drama

- Using their ideas about what they could contribute, have the students write and act a play about starting and operating a soup kitchen in their community.

Social Studies

- Use the concept of citizenship to discuss and analyze human and legal rights. For example, all people have a human right to have enough to eat. Some poor people may have a legal right to food stamps, but others may not.
- Have children list the human rights of the people at the soup kitchen, and then discuss what their community can do to assure these human rights.
- Children also can list the human rights they would like to have, such as the right to food and shelter, to live in a family, to go to school, to have a job when they grow up. Older children can compare their list to that in the United Nations Declaration of Universal Human Rights, analyzing why human rights are universally important.
- Using the rights identified in these activities, children can decide on those human rights they want for their community, classroom, or school. Children can make a wall poster, using these rights to govern their community.

Math

- Have children identify how many people ate at the soup kitchen on the day this story takes place. Different story problems can be derived. For example, if all 121 people had seconds on soup, how many bowls of soup would have been served? How many if half the people had seconds? If everyone has half a piece of chicken in his or her soup, how many pieces of chicken will they need to serve 121 people?

Science

- Have children create a delicious soup, with each child contributing an ingredient that provides an essential nutrient. If possible, make the soup and serve it for lunch.

Community Resources

The explanatory note, "About Soup Kitchens," located at the beginning of the book can be used to introduce children to the soup kitchen or shelter for homeless people in their community. Children can contribute food to a soup kitchen or food bank.

Other Recommended Children's Books
Citizenship:
How My Family Lives in America, by Susan Kuklin
Molly's Pilgrim, by Barbara Cohen
POWWOW, by George Ancona

Exclusion:
The Woman Who Outshone the Sun, by Alesandro Cruz Martinez
The Rag Coat, by Lauren Mills
The Children We Remember, by Chana Byers Abells

Community well-being:
Riches, by Esther Hautzig
Stevie, by John Steptoe
A New Coat for Anna, by Harriet Ziefert
A Chair for My Mother, by Vera B. Williams
Miss Rumphius, by Barbara Cooney

Resources for Teachers

Resources For the Classroom
United Nations. *Human Rights: Questions and Answers*. New York: United Nations Department of Public Information, 1987.

Additional Recommended Children's Books on Community

Understanding community:
Ancona, George. *POWWOW*. San Diego: Harcourt Brace & Company, 1993.

> In this beautifully photographed account of the annual Powwow at the Crow Fair in Montana, Ancona describes the activities and values of the many Native Americans who gather at this, the largest of the Powwows held in the United States and Canada. The book explains the different roles of men, women, and children at a Powwow; the role Powwows play in keeping traditions and friendships alive and vibrant; and how Native Americans have incorporated some elements of modern technology into their dances and rituals without changing their essential heritage.

Cherry, Lynne. *The Great Kapok Tree*. San Diego: Gulliver Books, 1990. (Grades K–2)

> In the dense Amazon rain forest, a man is chopping down a great Kapok tree. The animals who live among its branches watch him silently. Hot and weary, the man lies down to rest. One by one, the forest creatures emerge to whisper in his ear. Among others, the snake, the bee, the monkey, the toucan, the jaguar, and finally a small child from the Yanomamo tribe beg him not to destroy their home. They tell him how important every tree is in the rain forest. Suddenly, the man wakes up. He and the creatures stare silently at each other. The man picks up his axe and walks out of the rain forest.

Cooney, Barbara. *Miss Rumphius*. New York: Puffin Books, 1982. (Grades K–4)

> The narrator tells the story of her great aunt, Alice Rumphius, the Lupine Lady. As a girl, Alice lived in a city by the sea, where her grandfather told her stories of faraway places. Alice decided that she too would travel and live beside the sea. Her grandfather said there was a third thing she must do. Alice must do something to make the world more beautiful. When she grew up, she did visit faraway places and did buy a house by the sea. She did not know how to make the world more beautiful, however, until she discovered that the lupine flowers in her yard had spread to a neighboring field. Miss Rumphius decided to scatter baskets of lupine seeds throughout her community. Every year when they bloomed, her community was indeed more beautiful.

Fife, Dale H. *The Empty Lot*. San Francisco: Sierra Club Books, 1991. (Grades K–4)

> Harry Hale owns a vacant lot he has not visited for years. He decides to sell it, quickly receiving three offers. When he visits the lot to decide on a price, he is surprised to discover that the town

has grown all around his empty lot. He is even more surprised to discover that his lot is home to thousands, maybe millions, of insects, birds, small animals, and even children. Harry decides not to sell after all. His empty lot is occupied, every square inch.

Hautzig, Esther. *Riches*. New York: Harper Collins, 1992. (Grades 3–4)
Samuel and Chaya-Rivka live in a small town on the river Vilia. They had worked hard in their small store and had become wealthy. As they grow older, they think about no longer working, but work seems the best way to please God. Samuel consults a wise rabbi for advice. The rabbi tells Samuel that for three months he should drive a horse and cart, and that Chaya-Rivka should read and think about the holy books. Although puzzled, they follow the advice. At the end of the three months, they realize they had found wisdom and performed work pleasing to God. Samuel had discovered the beauty of nature, and had helped people by giving them rides while asking for nothing in return. Chaya-Rivka had new knowledge, including the knowledge to appreciate Samuel's charity in the context of the Holy books.

Levitin, Sonia. *The Man Who Kept His Heart in a Bucket*. New York: Dial Books for Young Readers, 1995. (Grades K–4)
Jack's heart has been broken, so now he keeps it in a bucket. He is alone, without the ability to feel pleasure, joy, or love. When he goes to get fresh water for his heart, a golden carp, who turns into a beautiful maiden, steals his heart and gives him a riddle he must solve. As Jack solves the riddle, which he can do only by reaching out to members of his community, he learns about feelings and love.

Lionni, Leo. *The Biggest House in the World*. New York: Alfred A. Knopf, 1968. (Grades K–3)
When a small snail wishes he had the biggest house in the world, his father tells him the story of another snail who made his shell grow into a huge house. The house is admired, but when the cabbage leaves are gone, this snail cannot leave with the others to find new food. He and his shell shrivel away. The young snail realizes that his small house, like those of the other snails comprising his community, is best.

Polacco, Patricia. *Mrs. Katz and Tush*. New York: Bantam Books, 1992. (Grades K–4)
Mrs. Katz, an elderly Jewish widow, and Larnel, an African American boy, live in the same building. Larnel knows Mrs. Katz is lonely, so he brings her a kitten. She names the kitten Tush, asking Larnel to help take care of Tush. Larnel loves visiting Tush, but he also loves Mrs. Katz's stories of her childhood in Poland. Over time, Larnel discovers that African Americans and Jews share a common history of triumph and suffering. Mrs. Katz, Tush, and Larnel become family, and through the years share the joy of graduations, weddings, and new babies.

Pushker, Gloria Teles. *Toby Belfer Never Had a Christmas Tree*. Gretna, LA: Pelican, 1991. (Grades K–4)
Toby Belfer is a Jewish girl living in a small, all-Christian town. Toby invites her friends to join in the celebration of Hanukkah, just as Toby has joined in their celebrations by trimming Christmas trees and singing carols. Toby introduces her friends to potato latkes and the game of dreidl. Best of all, she tells the story of Hanukkah, a story of the Jews' quest for religious freedom, and of the miracle celebrated by the Festival of Lights.

Russo, Marisabina. *A Visit to Oma*. New York: Greenwillow Books, 1991. (Grades K–4)
Celeste spends Sunday afternoons with her great grandmother, Oma, an immigrant who does not speak English. While Oma talks, Celeste imagines the story she thinks Oma is telling. This week, the story is about Oma's arranged marriage to a man she does not love, her courage in leaving, and her happiness when she finds Leo, her true love. The gentleness and creativity in their relationship allows them to overcome the language barrier.

Steptoe, John. *Stevie*. New York: Harper Trophy, 1986. (Grades K–2)
Robert lives with his mother and father. Life is good, until Stevie moves in. Stevie's mother works all week and cannot take care of him. Robert does not like Stevie at all. He is a crybaby, always wanting his own way. He breaks Robert's toys, and gets Robert in trouble with his father. It is only when Stevie's parents move away, taking Stevie with them, that Robert misses Stevie. He remembers the fun they had playing together, realizing Stevie was like a little brother.

Community cooperation:

Cech, John. *My Grandmother's Journey*. New York: Bradbury Press, 1991. (Grades 1–4)
Based on true events, the book begins when Korie asks her grandmother for a story. Grandmother lived in Russia with her family. A gypsy woman told Grandmother that the day would come when she prayed for a crust of bread or to endure for one more hour. The Russian Revolution came, and the family lost everything. They traveled the countryside, taking whatever work was available. Then came World War II, and again their world was destroyed. Grandmother had a baby daughter by the banks of a river. They survived only because strangers helped them when they saw the young baby. They were captured by Nazis and sent to Germany as slave laborers, but they survived even this. When peace came, they emigrated to the United States, where at last they had a house, a place where Grandmother can rest her feet.

Cherry, Lynne. *A River Ran Wild*. San Diego: Harcourt Brace & Company, 1992.
Cherry tells the true story of the clean-up of the Nashua River in Massachusetts. Native peoples who originally settled by the river named it Nash-a-way, or "River with a Pebbled Bottom." The Nash-a-way supported a thriving Native culture until the land was occupied by colonists. White people cut down the trees, dammed the river, and eventually polluted it with waste from industrial factories. As a result, the river could no longer support wildlife and fish. In modern times, Oweana, a descendant of the original Native people, had a vivid dream telling him the river should be cleansed. He went to his friend Marion, an environmental activist. Together they organized a successful campaign to return the Nashua to its original state. Today, the Nashua is clean, full of wildlife, and a river where the pebbled bottom can be seen by all who use it.

Cowcher, Helen. *Tigress*. New York: Farrar, Straus & Giroux, Inc., 1991. (Grades K–4)
A tigress climbs with her cubs to the edge of the sanctuary. Beyond, a herdsman watches his goats and oxen graze. Suddenly, monkeys shriek their warning that danger is near, and the tigress strikes. A young bullock is killed, and later a camel. The herdsman cannot afford this loss, and neither can his friends. With the sanctuary ranger, they wait that night by the camel carcass. When the tigress and her cubs approach, they set off bright lights and firecrackers. The tigress and cubs flee in fear, but to the safety of the sanctuary. The tigress and her family are saved, as are the herdsmen's valuable animals.

Hendry, Diana. *Christmas on Exeter Street*. New York: Alfred A. Knopf, Inc., 1989. (Grades K–4)
Two days before Christmas, the Mistletoes' house on Exeter Street begins to welcome Christmas guests. First Grandma Ginny and Grandpa George, then the other grandparents, family, and friends arrive, filling the house. Some guests are expected, others are welcomed because they have nowhere else to go. Mrs. Mistletoe manages to find space for everyone to sleep, even the baby, who sleeps in the sink, and three very thin aunts, who are tucked into cupboard shelves. Because each guest has something special to share, Christmas dinner is wonderful.

Levinson, Riki. *Watch the Stars Come Out*. New York: E. P. Dutton, 1985, paperback, 1995. (Grades 1–4)
This story-within-a-story describes the immigrant experience of millions of children who came to the United States around the turn of the century. A young brother and sister travel in steerage

aboard a ship for twenty-two days. The journey is difficult, but others help them. They watch the passengers struggle with the conditions on the ship, learning about survival. The brother and sister arrive at Ellis Island. They meet their mother, father, and big sister who have preceded them, and they begin a new life in a tenement.

Lionni, Leo. *Swimmy*. New York: Pantheon Books, 1968. (Grades K–2)
Swimmy's school of fish is eaten by a big fish. Swimmy escapes, swimming away to see the wonders of the ocean. When he discovers another school of fish like him, he teaches them to swim in the shape of a big fish, so that they can chase the actual big fish away.

Mills, Lauren. *The Rag Coat*. Boston: Little, Brown & Co., 1991. (Grades 1–4)
Nina's family is poor. Her father works in the coal mines and her mother makes quilts with other mothers for additional money. Nina cannot go to school; she has to stay home to help her mother, and besides, she does not have a coat to wear. When her father dies from black lung disease, it seems she will never go to school. The quilting mothers, though, offer to make her a coat from scraps. Nina carefully chooses the scraps that have the best stories. When Nina wears her coat to school, the other children laugh at her for having a "rag" coat. She runs away, until she remembers her father saying, "People only need people, and nothing else." Nina returns to school, where she tells the story of each piece of her coat.

Phillips, Mildred. *The Sign in Mendel's Window*. New York: Macmillan Publishing, 1996. (Grades 1 –4)
Mendel and his wife, who live in the tiny town of Kosnov, decide to rent half their store for extra money. Tinker, an out-of-towner who says his job is to think, offers to rent. He seems to be the perfect tenant, until he brings police to Kosnov and accuses Mendel of stealing. The police are about to take Mendel to jail when Mendel's wife and neighbors come to Mendel's rescue, proving that Tinker, not Mendel, is the real thief.

Spinelli, Eileen. *Somebody Loves You, Mr. Hatch*. New York: Bradbury Press, 1991. (Grades K–2)
Mr. Hatch is all alone. He goes to work alone, eats alone, and spends his evenings alone. He eats the same food and does the same things every day. Then one day, the postman delivers a large box of candy, with the note, "Somebody Loves You." Buoyed by this message, Mr. Hatch begins to laugh, help his neighbors, and enjoy himself. When he learns that the candy was delivered to the wrong address, he believes that nobody loves him after all, and he goes back to his old habits. But all his new friends miss him. He learns that everybody loves Mr. Hatch.

Williams, Vera B. *A Chair for My Mother*. New York: Mulberry Books, 1982. (Grades K–2)
The young narrator's mother waitresses in a diner. It is hard work. In addition, all their possessions had been destroyed in a fire. Family and neighbors welcome them to their new apartment, donating what furniture and household goods they could. Meanwhile, the mother and daughter save every bit of money for a comfortable chair by putting all of the mother's tips in a big jar. Sometimes, Grandma, aunts and uncles add money, too. Finally, the big jar is full. The family shops and shops until they find just the right chair.

Ziefert, Harriet. *A New Coat for Anna*. New York: Alfred A. Knopf, Inc., 1986. (Grades K–4)
Anna needs a new coat. Because of the war, there are none to buy. Her mother promises her a coat when the war is over, but even after it ends, the stores are empty. No one has any money. Anna's mother, though, finds the solution. She trades with the farmer for wool, with an old woman to spin the wool into yarn, and with the tailor to make the coat. Anna and her mother gather lingonberries to dye the yarn a beautiful deep red. When the coat is finished, Anna invites all the people who helped make her coat for Christmas dinner. They agree it is the best Christmas in a long time.

CHAPTER 4

Confronting Prejudice

The world is too dangerous to live in—not because of the people who do evil, but because of the people who stand by and let them.
—Albert Einstein

INTRODUCTION

The Holocaust is an example of the ultimate consequences of prejudice and hatred, one of the worst examples in world history. The Holocaust, however, was not inevitable. Although the Holocaust was caused by a confluence of historical and contemporary events, including virulent hatred of the Jews, the perpetrators could have been stopped. Why they were not, until it was too late for millions of people, is the subject of this chapter.

The children's books introduced here offer examples of different forms of prejudice that children are likely to encounter. The stories help children to understand prejudice, its consequences, and methods available to children for confronting prejudice. The books are thematically rich, offering many opportunities for class discussion and activities. They also are multicultural, helping children to understand the extent of prejudice in our world.

Just as in life, several of the books do not offer a happy resolution. These may be the most powerful stories. By examining the characters' behavior in these books, children are challenged to examine and develop moral values. These books also provide context for older children to begin Holocaust study.

Examining prejudices of others is easier than confronting our own. If teachers are to lead children in an understanding of prejudice, it is imperative that they examine their own attitudes and behavior. Several books recommended in the Teacher Resource Bibliography, such as *Creating a Bias-Free Classroom*, are useful resources for this work.

KEY CONCEPTS

"Prejudice" often is used as a catchall phrase for a larger group of concepts. Careful presentation of distinctions between these concepts will help children to correctly analyze prejudice.

Predilection is a simple preference for one individual, group, language, culture, etc., as opposed to another. It is an inevitable and natural consequence of humanness. We all have predilections. Not only are these value-neutral, they also are internal guides to the types of activities, hobbies, or jobs we are most likely to enjoy. Predilections, however, can be the first step to prejudiced beliefs if they are accompanied by stereotypes.

Stereotype is the belief that all people in a certain group have common characteristics and behaviors. Stereotypes are used to form prejudgments about members of the group. Stereotypes are endemic in our culture. Examples of common stereotypes are: Franco-Americans are dumb, African Americans are lazy, Italians are criminals, Irish are drunks, Jews are greedy, and Native Americans are shiftless.

Prejudice is a negative, irrational attitude toward a group of people. Prejudice is characterized by a cognitive component (stereotypes about a group) and an affective component (dislike for a group). Prejudice is irrational because it is based on inaccurate "pictures in our mind" which have negative connotations. It is negative judgment without basis.

Discrimination is characterized by a behavioral component that denies individuals or groups equality of treatment. It restricts the life choices and chances of an outgroup—generally but not always a minority group—in comparison to the dominant group. Discriminatory behavior results in the exclusion of an outgroup based on group membership rather than on individual knowledge or abilities. Discrimination aimed at various groups is often described by "isms," such as racism, sexism, ageism, classism, anti-Semitism, or handicapism.

Oppression is very severe discrimination. The *Oxford English Dictionary* defines it as "to affect with a feeling of pressure, constraint, or distress; to trample down or keep under by wrongful exercise of authority of superior power or strength." The archaic definition is simply "to crush." Oppression occurs when a dominant group defines a norm for humanness and uses it to judge other groups. These judgments are then backed by the economic power of the dominant group and threats or acts of individual and institutional violence. The genocide of Native Americans, the enslavement of African Americans, and the mass murder of Jews in the Holocaust are examples of oppression.

Scapegoating is the transfer of shame, fear, and suffering from one group to another. Scapegoating is based on stereotypical beliefs about a group, usually one with limited power, and the acting out of aggression on that group. Scapegoating increases during times of stress, such as depression, famine, or revolution. For example, the Nazis scapegoated Jews for Germany's loss in World War I.

In summary, prejudice is an irrational, negative *attitude* based on stereotypical thinking, and discrimination is exclusionary *action* based on prejudice. Not all discrimination is oppression. Discrimination becomes oppression when its goal is to subjugate an entire group through economic sanctions and violence.

As prejudice develops, it scapegoats the victims for the consequences of the discriminators' behavior. Over time, prejudice and discrimination become part of the structures of belief shaping the culture of a people. These belief structures:
• are learned involuntarily from a previous generation;
• are shared broadly within the culture;
• may persist even after the conditions that originally caused them are gone.
As a result, prejudice and discrimination are extremely resistant to change.

DEFINITIONS FOR CHILDREN

The Anti-Defamation League of B'nai B'rith, in *The Wonderful World of Difference*, offers the following definitions for children:
Stereotype: the belief that all people of a certain group will be the same and behave in the same way;
Prejudice: judging people without really knowing them;
Discrimination: keeping someone out of activities or groups just because of who they are and what groups they belong to.

CHALLENGING PREJUDICE IN THE SCHOOLS

James Lynch, in *Prejudice Reduction and the Schools*, calls upon teachers to be "transformative intellectuals," seeing prejudice reduction not as an Utopian ideal but rather as a necessary and natural evolution of society. But if prejudice is an attitude learned from many sources and is extremely resistant to change, what can schools reasonably be expected to do? First, schools must be models of acceptance of diversity and of intolerance of prejudice. Second, schools must teach children how to think critically.

Being able to think is the key. In *Reducing Adolescent Prejudice*, Nina Grabelko and John Michaelis conclude that development of skills leading to cognitive sophistication have the greatest, long-lasting impact on prejudice reduction. By defining concepts, teaching thinking processes, and developing moral values, teachers help children gain the abilities they need to identify and confront prejudice appropriately and effectively.

Because studies show that typical teaching methods tend not to change attitudes, teaching critical thinking skills is imperative. The effects of exhortation—telling children to be above prejudice—pass quickly. This approach leads children to see the teacher as the one with the "correct" answer. It does not assist children to analyze and take steps when confronted with prejudice.

Similarly, the presentation of multicultural information by itself does not change attitudes. Knowing that certain African Americans are talented jazz musicians does not lead to an intuitive understanding that African Americans are stereotyped and discriminated against in the United States. Presenting accurate, interesting information about different cultures is important, but not enough.

The development of cognitive sophistication requires the teaching of concepts, thinking processes, and valuing processes. To confront prejudice, children first need to understand and differentiate among such concepts as stereotype, prejudice, discrimination, bias, sexism, and racism.

Second, children need critical thinking skills, such as the ability to compare, classify, and generalize; to analyze and synthesize; to infer, hypothesize, and predict; and to understand perceptions other than one's own.

Finally, children need values to reason morally and to take appropriate action. The importance of values cannot be overemphasized. Many of the men who planned and implemented Hitler's "final solution" were the products of one of the most respected educational systems in the world. Without concomitant teaching of moral values that protect diverse people, education can lead to intellectual bigots who perpetuate rather than challenge prejudice.

Because values are frequently associated with religion, the teaching of values can be a difficult issue for schools. Our country, however, was founded on values. One approach would be to introduce children to the values underpinning our national human rights law, as expressed in the Declaration of Independence, Bill of Rights, Gettysburg Address, Emancipation Proclamation, and civil rights laws. By teaching these documents as expressions of universally held beliefs important to all peoples of the United States rather than simply as historical documents, teachers can transmit democratic values and help children apply these to contemporary examples of prejudice.

A second approach would be to use international human rights values as expressed in the United Nations Declaration and Covenants on human rights. (These documents are summarized in Chapter 3, "Creating Community.") Children can analyze which rights are violated by prejudice and discrimination, why these rights are important, and what children can do about it. Children also can develop a rights statement for conduct in their classroom, exploring the underlying values of each right. Even very young children can think through the impact of fighting, teasing, and bullying on themselves and their classmates.

USING CHILDREN'S BOOKS TO CONFRONT PREJUDICE

Because books in this chapter present stories that are typical of children's experiences, they help children to think through and confront the meaning and impact of prejudice. The stories also demonstrate a variety of ways those who experience prejudice overcome it, as well as how those who see prejudice act on their values. In other words, the stories lead children to apply concepts, to think critically, and to use moral values in contexts relevant to their young lives. They encourage active learning and participation rather than passive reception of revealed knowledge.

Another book that can be used to teach about prejudice is *Terrible Things*, which can be found in Chapter 5, "Beginning Holocaust Studies." This book, subtitled "An Allegory of the Holocaust," presents one of the central challenges of *The Spirit That Moves Us*. What can individuals do when confronted with violence and power greater than the capacity of a single individual to resist? What happens when individuals refuse to recognize the danger? What are the consequences of confronting that power or failing to confront it? What can individuals acting as a community do?

Terrible Things allows children to respond to these questions in the context of a fictional animal story. The story is a bridge, both to study of the Holocaust and to an understanding that as adults, they may have to face real "terrible things."

What do the children in your classroom need to understand about prejudice? To develop the critical thinking, skills, and values to confront prejudice? When students have the analytical skills and moral values to recognize and stand up to prejudice, they can be important actors in the fight to supplant hatred with peace. They can change the world. The books in the chapter give teachers a place to begin the lessons that can indeed transform society.

Sources

Allport, Gordon W. *ABC's of Scapegoating*. 9th ed. New York: Anti-Defamation League, 1983.
_____. *The Nature of Prejudice*. 2nd ed. Reading, MA: Addison-Wesley, 1979.
Anti-Defamation League. *The Wonderful World of Difference: A Human Relations Program for Grades K-8*. New York: Anti-Defamation League, 1986.
Grabelko, Nina Hersch and John U. Michaelis. *Reducing Adolescent Prejudice*. New York: Teachers College Press, 1981.
Levin, Jack and William Levin. *The Functions of Discrimination and Prejudice*. 2nd ed. New York: Harper & Row, 1982.
Lynch, James. *Prejudice Reduction and the Schools*. East Brunswick, NJ: Nichols Publishing Co., 1987.
Matiella, Ana Consuelo. *Positively Different: Creating a Bias-Free Environment for Young Children*. Santa Cruz, CA: ETR Associates, 1991.
Pharr, Suzanne. *Homophobia, A Weapon of Sexism*. Inverness, CA: Chardon Press, 1988.

LESSON PLAN FOR:
Amazing Grace, **by Mary Hoffman. Illustrations by Caroline Binch. New York: Dial Books, 1991. Grades K-4.**

Story Summary

Grace loves stories, whether she hears them, reads them, or makes them up. Possessed with a marvelous imagination as well as a strong flair for the dramatic, she acts the stories out, always giving herself the most exciting parts. Thus, it is natural when her teacher announces a classroom production of Peter Pan, that Grace wants to play the lead. One classmate says she can't because she's black. When a saddened Grace relates the day's events to her mother and grandmother, they tell her she can be anything she wants to, if she puts her mind to it. Inspired by her family's support, her own indomitable spirit, and an excursion to a weekend ballet starring a lovely Trinidadian dancer, Grace shines during her audition, leaving no doubt in anyone's mind as to who will play Peter Pan.

Concepts Summary

Using the realistic story of children "putting down" a classmate who is in some way different, *Amazing Grace* introduces the concepts of stereotype, prejudice, and discrimination. The book leads to an exploration of differences in physical appearance, talent, and personality. When a difference becomes a stereotype, consequently leading to prejudice and discrimination, children see some of the hurtful and damaging consequences of prejudicial beliefs. By examining what Natalie and Raj say, children can analyze various responses to being excluded from an activity because of prejudice.

Objectives

The student should be able to:
- distinguish types of human difference;
- define stereotype, recognizing that stereotypes come from false perceptions of difference;
- define and distinguish prejudice and discrimination, relating the story's action to the concepts;
- recognize the consequences of prejudice and discrimination in the story and find real life examples;
- analyze various responses to prejudice and discrimination, including both non-violent and violent responses.

Materials

Book: *Amazing Grace*, by Mary Hoffman
Video: *"Behind the Mask"*
Art Supplies: Pictures from magazines for a collage

CONCEPT: *DIFFERENCE*

Discussion Questions
- How do the children in the book's pictures look the same? Look different?
- How is Grace different from the other children? How is she the same?
- Which of Grace's differences are because of how she looks? Which because of what she is good at? Which because of how she gets along with the other children?
- What are some of the ways Grace, Natalie, and Raj are different? Whose friend would you want to be? Why?

Activities

Art

- Children can draw pictures, or make a collage out of magazine pictures, of ways people are physically different.

Language Arts

- Children can list words that describe difference. Have children list three things they like about themselves (or each other). One characteristic should be physical, one a talent, and one a personality trait. Make a big poster of all the positive ways the children in the class are different. Older children can write a story about how their differences make them special.

Social Studies

- Using the list of ways that children in the class are physically different, discuss how physical differences are caused. Watch the video, "Behind the Mask," and discuss social meanings of difference.
- Have children distinguish between physical differences and differences in talent and personality. Children can brainstorm on the causes of disparate talents and personalities.

CONCEPT: *STEREOTYPE*

Discussion Questions

- What are some of the things Grace's classmates thought she could do because of who she was?
- Do you think their ideas were positive or negative? What would make them positive? What would make them negative?
- Do you think their ideas were true? Why or why not? Can you tell whether someone will be good at something by how they look? How?
- What are some of the differences between how Grace was treated at the beginning of the story and how she was treated at the end?
- Do you think characters in a story should always be recreated in drawings or on the stage in the same way? Examples to think about: Martin Luther King and Peter Pan (a real person and a fictional story character).

Activities

Language Arts

- Have children look at the list of physical differences among their classmates and decide whether any of the differences can lead to stereotypes. Discuss what the stereotypes are and where they might come from. Have children develop a definition of stereotype.
- For older children, choose a group that has traditionally been stereotyped. Have children list the stereotypes they might have heard about this group of people. Locate an old children's book perpetuating the stereotypes and read it to the class. Help children identify stereotypical words, images, and beliefs. Read a second book presenting truthful, positive attributes of the same group. Have children analyze the differences, discussing what they would learn if exposed to only one of the books.

History

- Extend the concept of stereotyping by presenting a history lesson on the chosen group. (Older children can do a research project.) Help children analyze historical events to discover how stereotypes created long ago continue to exist.

Concept: *Prejudice and Discrimination*

Discussion Questions
- Why did Raj and Natalie think Grace shouldn't try out for Peter Pan? What other reasons might have made them say those things?
- How did Grace feel when she thought she shouldn't try out? How would you have felt?
- Who helped Grace overcome her sadness? How did they help?
- Did Natalie's feelings about Grace change after the auditions? Why?
- What is prejudice? (A simple definition is to pre-judge.)
- What does "Don't judge a book by its cover" mean? How does it relate to this story? Do you know any other sayings that mean the same thing?

Activities

Language Arts

- Have children identify how they could tell Natalie was prejudiced and how this resulted in discriminatory comments against Grace. Have children develop their own definition of discrimination.
- Have children tell or write a story about a time their feelings were hurt because they were teased or excluded from an activity. In their story, ask them to distinguish between prejudiced attitudes and discriminatory action.

Social Studies

- List some groups in the United States who historically have experienced and continue to experience prejudice and discrimination. Have students identify the characteristics of these groups that others use as an excuse for prejudice, such as religion, race, being physically or mentally challenged, speaking a language other than English, or place of birth. Have children analyze whether these characteristics suggest that people in these groups would be good friends.
- Using the example of an historically prejudged group discussed in previous activities, have children consider what actions could be taken by them and their community to rectify the injustice of prejudiced actions toward them.
- Older children can write to an organization representing the group, asking what the group wants from society in terms of justice. Children can brainstorm in small groups or as a class to decide what they can do in their school to teach other students about prejudice, and to assure that members of this group are accepted.

Community Resources
Ask a member of a group commonly discriminated against to visit the class and discuss the nature of prejudice and discrimination against this group. Children can discuss with the visitor ways to change prejudice in their school and community.

Other Recommended Children's Books
Difference:
Why Am I Different? by Norma Simon
People, by Peter Spier
Black Is Brown Is Tan, by Arnold Adoff

Prejudice
The Adventures of Connie and Diego, by Maria Garcia
Tillie and the Wall, by Leo Lionni
Who Belongs Here? by Margy Burns Knight
The Rag Coat, by Lauren Mills
Why Do You Call Me Chocolate Boy? by Carol Parker
White Socks Only, by Evelyn Coleman
The Story of Ruby Bridges, by Robert Coles

Justice
Follow the Drinking Gourd, by Jeanette Winter
Amazing Grace: The Story Behind the Song, by Jim Haskins
How Many Days to America? by Eve Bunting

Resources for Teachers
Allport, Gordon W. *The Nature of Prejudice.* 2nd ed. Reading, MA: Addison-Wesley, 1985.
Langone, John. *Spreading Poison: A Book About Racism and Prejudice.* Boston: Little, Brown and Co., 1993.

Resources For the Classroom
Anti-Defamation League. *The Wonderful World of Difference: A Human Relations Program for Grades K–8.* New York: Anti-Defamation League, 1986.
Cummings, Marlene A., et al., eds. *Individual Differences: An Experience in Human Relations for Children.* Madison, WI: Madison Public Schools, 1976.
Matiella, Ana Consuelo. *Positively Different: Creating a Bias-Free Environment for Young Children.* Santa Cruz, CA: ETR Associates, 1991.
Sonnenschein, Francis M. and Jay S. West. *Our Umbrella of Friendship: An Activity Book for Young Children (K–3) to Celebrate Diversity and Fight Prejudice.* New York: Anti-Defamation League, 1989.
Teaching Tolerance Project. *Starting Small: Teaching Tolerance in Preschool and the Early Grades. Alabama: Southern Poverty Law Center, 1997.*

Supplemental Children's Books
Stewart, Gail B. *The Facts about Discrimination.* New York: Crestwood House, 1989.
Wilt, Joy. *Checking 'Em Out and Sizing 'Em Up: A Children's Book about Opinions and Prejudice.* Waco, TX: Word, Inc., 1980.

LESSON PLAN FOR:
Tar Beach, by Faith Ringgold. New York:
Crown, 1991. Grades 2-4.

Story Summary

This beautifully illustrated book combines fiction, autobiography, and African American history. Cassie, the eight-year-old narrator, has a dream: to be free to go wherever she wants for the rest of her life. One night, on the "tar beach"—the rooftop of her family's Harlem apartment building—her dream comes true. She flies over the city. She sees the George Washington Bridge, her most prized possession, which her father helped to build; and the union building, which her father was not allowed to join because of his skin color. Cassie learns that, "Anyone can fly. All you need is somewhere to go that you can't get to any other way."

Concepts Summary

The experience of Cassie's father demonstrates consequences of prejudice against African Americans.
Cassie's story offers an opportunity to explore ways oppressed people find the strength to confront and overcome prejudice. In this instance, Cassie uses the richness of her African American culture and her ability to dream of a better future to imagine the actions she can take to overcome prejudice.

Objectives

The student should be able to:
- recognize aspects of discrimination confronting African Americans and other minority groups;
- recognize aspects of African American culture, understanding how pride in cultural heritage can combat prejudice;
- understand the concept of imagination, using it to envision a dream for a society free of prejudice;
- learn that several books on the same theme, when read together, can lead to greater understanding of similarities among diverse peoples.

Materials

Books: *Tar Beach*, by Faith Ringgold
       Galimoto, by Karen Lynn Williams
       Cherry Tree, by Ruskin Bond
       Ben's Trumpet, by Rachel Isadora
       The Rag Coat, by Lauren Mills
       Sam Johnson and the Blue Ribbon Quilt, by Lisa Campbell Ernst
       The Day of Ahmed's Secret, by Florence Heide and Judith Gilliland
       Hawk, I'm Your Brother, by Byrd Baylor
       Everybody Cooks Rice, by Norah Dooley
       How My Parents Learned to Eat, by Ina R. Friedman

African American art:
Children of Promise: African-American Literature and Art for Young People, by Charles Sullivan

African American folktales:
The People Could Fly, by Virginia Hamilton
The Knee-High Man and Other Tales, by Julius Lester

African American music:
Teaching Music with a Multicultural Approach, by William M. Anderson

Art supplies: Scraps of material and paste, construction paper, crayons/markers, paper air planes, and kites

CONCEPT: *DISCRIMINATION*

Discussion Questions
- Why wasn't Cassie's father allowed to join the union? Do you think this was fair? Why or why not?
- How do you think being unable to join the union affected Cassie's father? Cassie's family?
- What does Cassie want to do to change the discrimination experienced by her family? Can you think of some ways she might make this happen? Can you think of some ways you might help?
- Has anyone you know experienced discrimination? What was it? How did it make them feel?

Activities

Language Arts

- Have children identify discriminatory acts in the story. Help them analyze why these acts are discriminatory. Have children develop their own definition of discrimination.
- Have children imagine their school has a union which provides benefits to students, such as special field trips or help with homework. Have children tell or write a story about what they would miss and how they would feel if they were excluded because of the color of their hair.

History

- Prepare a lesson on discrimination experienced by African Americans. To extend the lesson, these experiences can be compared to those of another group historically discriminated against in the United States, such as Native Americans or Japanese Americans.
- The author's note gives information on the historical exclusion of minorities from trade unions. Older children can learn about different types of unions, the purpose of unions, why minorities were kept from joining unions, the impact of this discrimination, and what minority groups have done to change the pattern of discrimination in unions.

CONCEPT: *CULTURAL HERITAGE*

Discussion Questions
- From the clues in the story, can you tell where Cassie lives? What other information would you need?
- Why do you think the family calls their roof a beach? What do you think they imagine their "tar beach" to be? Can you think of any times when you imagined that the place you were playing was really something else?

- Why does Cassie's family like to picnic with friends? What do you think this gives them?
- Does your family spend time with other families? What kinds of things do you do together? Does this make you feel like you belong to a big family? Why?

Activities

Art

- Each page of the book is bordered with quilt designs from the author's original story quilt. Children can draw their own story quilt about their cultural heritage. (See the author's note for more information about story quilting.) Have children tell their quilt's story to the class.
- Look at the pictures and discuss what the quilt tells about Cassie's cultural heritage. Children can compare these designs to the quilts in *The Rag Coat* and *Sam Johnson and the Blue Ribbon Quilt*, noting differences and similarities. Other examples of quilting as a cultural heritage can be introduced.
- Show children other examples of African American art. Choose several examples, discuss their relationship to African American history, and discuss how they interpret African American culture. Have children create an art work related to an aspect of African American culture.

Language Arts

- Demonstrate how pictures can tell stories. Show pictures from a storybook without the text, or pictures from other sources, such as paintings. Have children discuss what the pictures tell them, or write a story to accompany the pictures.
- African American folktales, especially those originating during slavery, were often allegories of the struggle against oppression. Read several folktales. Younger children can enjoy them as examples of African American culture. Older children can analyze them for what they say about slavery.

Music

- Play examples of gospel music. Help children analyze how the messages in gospel music gave and continue to give African Americans, and others, strength to overcome oppression and to hope for a better future.

Social Studies

- *The Day of Ahmed's Secret, Galimoto,* and *Cherry Tree* are contemporary stories about children who live in other countries who also use their imagination and determination to carry out a project. Read these stories, asking children to draw parallels about the similarities of wants, desires, and the drive to succeed among children from diverse cultures.
- *Tar Beach's* themes and images are rich with connections to other books in *The Spirit That Moves Us.* Some possible connections are quilts (*The Rag Coat* and *Sam Johnson and the Blue Ribbon Quilt*); dreams for the future (*Ben's Trumpet, Hawk, I'm Your Brother,* and any of the books about immigrant families); and the kinds of foods families like to eat (*Everybody Cooks Rice* and *How My Parents Learned to Eat*). Using these books, children can identify common themes, discussing how people are influenced by their culture.

CONCEPT: *IMAGINATION*

Discussion Questions

- How does Cassie fly? What does flying mean to her?
- Do you think Cassie can really fly? What are some of the ways you might "fly" without leaving the ground?
- What is Cassie's dream for herself and her family? How does flying help Cassie imagine her dream?
- What do you dream for yourself and your family's future?

Activities

Art

- Children can illustrate a story about what they see when they fly in their imagination.

Language Arts

- Imagination is an important part of the story. Children can imagine they fly to a place they have always wanted to visit, and tell or write a story about what they see.
- Children can imagine a dream for the future and write a story about their dream. Part of the story could be to write about what they can do to turn their dream into reality. *Ben's Trumpet* (lesson plan in Chapter 1) can be read with *Tar Beach* as another example of dreams for the future.

Science

- Discuss the ancient human desire to be able to fly, using examples such as the myth of Icarus or the story in *Hawk, I'm Your Brother*. Children can experiment with paper airplanes, kites, or other devices to understand flight.

Community Resources

Invite a representative of the National Association for the Advancement of Colored People (NAACP) to discuss African-American history as it relates to prejudice, discrimination, and the civil rights movement. Ask the representative to brainstorm with the children on ways to recognize stereotypes and prejudice, and methods they can use in their school to confront prejudice.

Other Recommended Children's Books

Prejudice:

Follow the Drinking Gourd, by Jeanette Winter
Amazing Grace: The Story Behind the Song, by Jim Haskins
Why Do You Call Me Chocolate Boy? by Carol Parker
Ceremony—In the Circle of Life, by White Deer of Autumn

Imagination:
The Red Balloon, by A. Lamorisse

Resources for Teachers

Langone, John. *Spreading Poison: A Book About Racism and Prejudice.* Boston: Little, Brown and Company, Inc., 1993.
Perlmutter, Philip. *Divided We Fall.* Ames, IA: Iowa State University Press, 1992.

Resources for the Classroom

Blackaby, Susan. *One World: Multicultural Projects and Activities.* Mahwah, NJ: Troll Associates, 1992.
Derman-Sparks, Louise. *Anti-Bias Curriculum.* Washington, D.C.: National Association for the Education of Young Children, 1997.
Hayden, Carla D., ed. *Venture into Cultures.* Chicago: American Library Association, 1992.

Supplemental Children's Books

Stewart, Gail B. *The Facts about Discrimination.* New York: Crestwood House, 1989.

LESSON PLAN FOR:
***Angel Child, Dragon Child,* by Michele Maria Surat. New York: Scholastic, 1983. Grades 1–4.**

Story Summary

With most of her family, Ut has emigrated from Vietnam to the United States. Because there was not enough money to bring everyone, her mother stayed behind. Ut does not like her new American school, or Raymond, the boy who picks on her every day. After they fight, the principal instructs Ut to tell Raymond about herself. Raymond's task is to listen and to write it down. As Ut tells Raymond about her life and he turns it into a story, they become friends. After the principal reads Ut's story to the entire school, Raymond suggests the school hold a fair to raise money to bring Ut's mother to America. The fair is a success. On the last day of school, Ut's mother rejoins her family.

Concepts Summary

Ut's story portrays Vietnamese culture as well as the prejudice frequently experienced by immigrant children in their new schools. The principal's solution, having Raymond listen to Ut's story, is one effective method for confronting prejudice. Raymond's change in attitude and his idea to hold a fair demonstrate how people can work together to redress prejudice and to welcome new members to the community.

Objectives

The student should be able to:
- learn basic facts about Vietnamese culture, history, and relations with the United States;
- recognize ways people from different cultures can be perceived as "different";
- learn about prejudice and discrimination against immigrants;
- learn to confront prejudice by understanding people from different cultures;
- understand how to redress prejudice by working together as a community.

Materials

Books: *Angel Child, Dragon Child*, by Michele Maria Surat
          Uncle Willy and the Soup Kitchen, by DyAnne DiSalvo-Ryan
Video: *"Prejudice: Answering Children's Questions"*
Equipment: World map or globe

CONCEPT: *CULTURAL DIFFERENCES*

Discussion Questions

- For Ut, how was America different from Vietnam?
- What made Ut seem different from the other children in her class?
- Can you think of ways Ut was the same as the other children in her class?
- What was Ut's full name? Why was she called Ut?
- What are some of the nicknames used in your family?
- What are some of the things the people at the fair learned about Vietnam?

Activities

Language Arts

- Several Vietnamese words are used in the story. The children can list the words and decipher their English translation. (The story also has phonetic pronunciations for each word.)
- The information in the Afterword explains Ut's family name, her first name, and her nickname. Compare this to how children are named in Western countries.
- Read *The Little Weaver of Thai Yen Village*. Compare the experiences of the two protagonists. Children can identify what they learned about Vietnamese culture from the two books. Have children explore how different books on the same subject lead to greater knowledge and understanding of a group of people.

Geography

- Locate Vietnam and China on a map or globe. Have children speculate why one is called Little Dragon and the other Big Dragon. Have children draw a map of Vietnam.

Social Studies

- Older children can research and write a report about different aspects of Vietnam; for example, its geography, national foods, or holidays.

History

- For older children, a lesson on the modern history of Vietnam, including the United States' involvement in the Vietnam War, can be introduced to explain the Vietnamese boat people, the refugee camps, and why Ut's family emigrated to the United States.

Math

- Using the distance key on the map, have children compute the distance Ut traveled from Vietnam to the West Coast of the United States. Additional computations can be made by varying the route and location of Ut's home.

CONCEPT: *PREJUDICE AGAINST IMMIGRANTS*

Discussion Questions

- When was Ut an Angel Child? A Dragon Child?
- How did Ut act in her new school?
- How do you think Ut felt in her new school? Why?
- Why do you think Ut didn't like Raymond?
- Were Ut's attitude and behavior examples of prejudice or discrimination? Why or why not?
- Why do you think Raymond didn't like Ut? What changed his mind?
- Were Raymond's attitude and behavior examples of prejudice or discrimination? Why or why not?

Activities

Language Arts

- Have children apply the concepts of prejudice and discrimination to Ut's and Raymond's attitudes and behavior before they became friends.

Social Studies

- Choose another group of immigrants to the United States. Introduce a lesson on how this group has been perceived as "different," how it has assimilated, and how it has maintained its cultural identity. An immigrant group from Europe—such as the French, Irish, or Italians—might be useful to explore how people who appear physically similar to the majority still can be seen as different.
- Introduce a lesson explaining why people from different parts of the world have different physical traits, e.g., height, skin color, eyelid shape. (A portion of the video, "Prejudice: Answering Children's Questions," offers a good lesson on this topic.) Have children explore how different traits demonstrate environmental adaptability.

CONCEPT: *CONFRONTING PREJUDICE*

Discussion Questions

- What changed Raymond's mind about Ut? What important lesson did Raymond learn by writing Ut's story?
- How did Raymond act once he knew Ut's story?
- What changed Ut's mind about Raymond? How did Ut act once Raymond wrote Ut's story?
- Why do you think learning about and helping Ut's family changed Raymond?
- Can you think of any times you became friends with someone you didn't like at first? What changed your mind?
- Why do you think the principal read Raymond's story about Ut to the whole school? What do you think the children and teachers learned by hearing Ut's story? What did you learn?
- Who helped put on the fair? Do you think Ut and Raymond could have put on the fair by themselves? Why not?
- Do you think Ut's and Raymond's school and community changed from planning and attending the fair? How might they have changed?
- If you were Raymond, how would you have felt when Ut came home and saw her mother?
- How do you think Raymond will feel about and act toward Vietnamese people when he grows up?

Activities

Art

- Have children illustrate the story they wrote about a classmate for the following Language Arts activity.

Language Arts

- Divide children into pairs. Have one child tell a story about his or her life and the other child write the story, and then reverse roles. Children can discuss what they learned by writing a classmate's story.
- Have children prepare an appropriate list of questions and write letters to people of Asian descent living in your state asking about their experiences. When they receive the replies, children can analyze the stories for examples of inclusion and exclusion, prejudice and acceptance. Children can brainstorm on how they might respond as individuals and as a community to the letters. For example, with

permission from the authors, the letters can be reproduced in a booklet, and distributed to other students in their school.

Social Studies

- Children can choose a nationality represented by people in their school or community and plan a fair, researching the appropriate decorations, foods, and activities.
- *Uncle Willy and the Soup Kitchen* (lesson plan in Chapter 3) also demonstrates how people working together can accomplish what an individual cannot. Children can identify a problem in their community, then design and carry out a project to alleviate the problem. (Note: If this involves people in need or with disabilities, they should be asked first *if* they wish to be helped and what would be most helpful for them.) Some ideas might be activities to make children with disabilities welcome in their schools, adopting a family through one of the international relief agencies, or collecting food for the local soup kitchen or food bank.

Community Resources

Ask an immigrant from a minority group new to your state and a member of an ethnic group with a long history in your area to visit the class. Have them talk about methods for retaining their cultural heritage and whether they have experienced prejudice.

Other Recommended Children's Books

Vietnam:
Lee Ann, by Tricia Brown
Talking Walls, by Margy Burns Knight

Immigration:
Molly's Pilgrim, by Barbara Cohen
How Many Days to America? by Eve Bunting
My Grandmother's Journey, by John Cech
Talking Walls: The Stories Continue, by Margy Burns Knight
Watch the Stars Come Out, by Riki Levinson

Prejudice:
Tillie and the Wall, by Leo Lionni
Who Belongs Here? by Margy Burns Knight
Why Do You Call Me Chocolate Boy? by Carol Parker

Community response:
The Rag Coat, by Lauren Mills
The Sign in Mendel's Window, by Mildred Phillips
A New Coat for Anna, by Harriet Ziefert
A River Ran Wild, by Lynne Cherry

Resources for Teachers

Beilke, Patricia F. and Frank J. Sciara. *Selecting Materials for and about Hispanic and East Asian Children and Young People.* Hamden, CT: Library Professional Publications, 1986.
Knoll, Tricia. *Becoming Americans.* Portland, OR: Coast to Coast Books, 1982.

Resources For the Classroom

Blackaby, Susan. *One World: Multicultural Projects and Activities.* Mahwah, NJ: Troll, 1992.

Kan, Betty Sing Luke. *The Asian American Experience.* Arlington, VA: The REACH Center for Multicultural and Global Education, 1987.

Knight, Margy Burns and Thomas V. Chan. *Talking Walls Teacher's Guide* and the *Talking Walls: The Stories Continue Teacher's Guide.* Gardiner, ME: Tilbury House, 1992.

Li, Marjorie H. and Peter Li, eds. *Understanding Asian Americans: A Curriculum Resource Guide.* New York: Neal-Schuman Publishers, Inc., 1990.

Supplemental Children's Books

Lucas, Eileen. *Peace on the Playground: Nonviolent Ways of Problem-Solving.* New York: Franklin Watts, Inc., 1991.

LESSON PLAN FOR:

The Hundred Dresses, by Eleanor Estes and Louis Slobodkin. New York: Harcourt Brace Jovanovich, 1944, 1971. Grades 3-4.

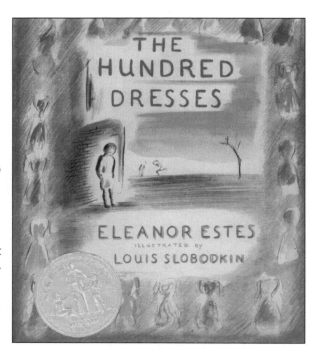

Story Summary

Wanda Petronski lives in the wrong part of town, has a funny name, and wears the same faded blue dress to school every day. She does not talk much, except when she blurts out, "I have a hundred dresses at home." Peggy, the most popular girl in class, starts the game by teasing Wanda about her "dresses." The other girls soon join in. Maddie, poor like Wanda but Peggy's best friend, stays silent. When Wanda's drawings for the drawing contest are shown, her classmates discover Wanda does have the dresses. She had drawn one hundred of them, each one beautiful. The day the teacher announces Wanda has won the contest, her father sends a note to the class. His family is moving to the big city, where they will not be made fun of for their strange name and ways. Maddie and Peggy feel terrible, recognizing too late they have hurt Wanda. Maddie decides she will never again be silent when someone is bullied.

Concepts Summary

The Hundred Dresses was originally published toward the end of World War II. By replicating in a classroom a flagrant example of prejudice, the book leads children to insight into consequences of prejudice. The story continues to be relevant to the experiences of recent immigrant groups to the United States. It challenges children to examine their moral values when confronted with prejudice, asking them to consider what they would do in similar situations.

Objectives

The student should be able to:

- apply the concepts of stereotype, prejudice, and discrimination to events in the story and find experiences in their own lives;
- recognize the consequences, for individual members of the community and for the community as a whole, of discriminating against those perceived as "different";
- identify moral values children could apply to this and similar situations;
- learn ways to stand up for one's values.

Materials

Book: *The Hundred Dresses*, by Eleanor Estes
Art supplies: Poster board, drawing materials
Equipment: World map

CONCEPTS: *STEREOTYPE, PREJUDICE, AND DISCRIMINATION*

Discussion Questions

- Why wasn't Wanda popular with her classmates?
- What made Wanda's name funny?
- Why didn't the children in the story like Boggins Heights? Are there any parts of your town that you are afraid of? Why?
- How was Wanda seen as different? Were there reasons other than her name and clothes?
- How was Wanda similar to and different from the other children in her class? Why do you think the children focused on Wanda's differences rather than her similarities?
- Why do you think Peggy invented the dresses game?
- How do you think Wanda felt about the game?
- How do you think Maddie felt about the game?
- Why do you think Maddie let the dresses game continue?
- What is a "Polack"? Do you think that this is a hurtful word? Why?

Activities

Language Arts

- Have children apply the concepts of prejudice and discrimination to examples in the story. Discuss how Wanda was stereotyped, the prejudiced beliefs held by other children, and how these prejudiced beliefs were translated into discriminatory action.
- Children can identify other words that stereotype groups of people, discuss why these words are hurtful, and list respectful words to identify groups of people.
- Have children write a story about a time they were teased and how they felt.

Geography

- Have children locate Poland on the map. Identify past and recent immigrant groups to the United States. Children can locate the countries from which these groups emigrated.
- Identify the Native American groups living in New England and the Maritime Provinces, and locate their Nations on the map. The original migration of Native Americans from Asia across the Bering Straits also can be introduced.

Social Studies

• Using the map to show the origin of groups who are now Americans, lead a discussion on the extent to which the United States consists of people originally from other places. Given this, have children analyze why many groups continue to experience prejudice and discrimination.

CONCEPT: *CONSEQUENCES OF PREJUDICE*

Discussion Questions

• Do you think Wanda wanted to be friends with her classmates? Why?
• Why did Wanda tell her classmates she had so many dresses and pairs of shoes?
• What was Wanda's community in the story? Did she have more than one?
• What were her classmates' communities? Did they have more than one?
• Is your classroom a community? Why or why not? What other communities do you belong to?
• For the contest, why did the girls design dresses and the boys design motorboats? Do you think that boys would like to design dresses, or that girls would like to design motorboats? What are some things that both girls and boys might like to design?
• Why did Wanda and her family move away? How do you think they felt? How would you feel if your family had to leave your home because you were discriminated against?
• What did the class lose when Wanda moved away? What could Wanda's classmates have done differently to keep this from happening?

Activities

Art

• Children can have a drawing contest, acting as a community by deciding together what to draw and how to judge the contest.

Language Arts

• Use answers to the discussion questions to define the children's classroom community. Have children randomly pick a classmate's name, identifying what their classroom community would lose if he or she moved away.

Social Studies

• Have children imagine they have moved to a country in another part of the world. The class can do a research project on this country's people: their appearance, dress, customs, schools, etc. Have children analyze how they might be seen as different in this country and explore how they would like to be treated by their new peers.

History

- *The Hundred Dresses* was published in 1944. A brief history lesson on World War II can be tied to the lessons in the story. Children can be introduced to the idea that historical events influence literature, and that literature often interprets and gives meaning to history.

Math

- Have children analyze why the author chose a "hundred" dresses for the story. The importance of the number "hundred" can be discussed; for example, a hundred years is a century; hundred is a key number in the metric system; many products, such as reams of paper, come in hundreds or multiples of hundreds.

CONCEPT: *MORAL VALUES*

Discussion Questions

- What did Maddie and Peggy do to try to make up for teasing Wanda?
- What did Maddie decide to do if she were ever in a similar situation? Why did she decide this? How did her values change?
- What would you have done if you were Maddie? Why?

Activities

Art

- Children can make illustrated posters of the values identified in the following Language Arts activity.

Language Arts

- Have children identify the moral values that led to Maddie's feelings and actions after Wanda moved away. Have children list and define the values important in their classroom, such as playing fairly, listening to each other, being friendly.

Social Studies

- After the class reads *Terrible Things* (Chapter 5), have them make connections between the community of animals in the forest and the community of students portrayed in *The Hundred Dresses* classroom. For example, the animals peacefully coexisted, but did not stand up for other animals when the Terrible Things appeared, with catastrophic consequences. Some of the children in *The Hundred Dresses* actively discriminated, while others were silent, also with serious consequences for Wanda and the community. Children can discuss the similarities and differences when the threat to the community is from *outside* aggressors as compared to prejudice and discrimination from *inside* the community.

History

- Extend the lesson by making connections between the discrimination in the story and an example of real discrimination in the United States. For example, children can learn about the African American civil rights movement, identifying the victims of discrimination, their response, their supporters among white and minority peoples, the bystanders, and the changes in the United States as a result.

Community Resources

Adults who are members of ethnic groups with a history of discrimination can be asked to visit the classroom to discuss their experience in school and how they would have liked their classmates to have responded.

Other Recommended Children's Books

Prejudice:
Terrible Things, by Eve Bunting
Who Belongs Here? by Margy Burns Knight

Community:
Mrs. Katz and Tush, by Patricia Polacco

Immigration:
Buba Leah and Her Paper Children, by Lillian Hammer Ross
How My Family Lives in America, by Susan Kuklin

Moral Values:
The Ring and the Window Seat, by Amy Hest
Follow the Drinking Gourd, by Jeanette Winter
Brother Eagle, Sister Sky, by Chief Seattle
The Invisible Hunters, by Harriet Rohmer, Octavio Chow, and Morris Vidaure
The Lily Cupboard, by Shulamith Levey Oppenheim

Resources for Teachers

Perlmutter, Philip. *Divided We Fall*. Ames, IA: Iowa State University Press, 1992.

Resources for the Classroom

Anti-Defamation League. *The Wonderful World of Difference: A Human Relations Program for Grades K–8*. New York: Anti-Defamation League, 1986.
Baker, Michael O. *What Would You Do? Developing and/or Applying Ethical Standards*. Pacific Grove, CA: Midwest Publications, 1989.
Knight, Margy Burns and Thomas V. Chan, *Who Belongs Here? Teacher's Guide*. Gardiner, ME: Tilbury House, Publishers, 1993.

Supplemental Children's Books

Stewart, Gail B. *The Facts About Discrimination*. New York: Crestwood House, 1989.

LESSON PLAN FOR:
White Wash, by Ntozake Shange.
New York: Walker & Co., 1997.
Grades 2-4.

Story Summary

A young African-American girl, Helene-Angel, is traumatized when a gang attacks her and her brother on their way home from school and spray paints her face white. Mauricio, her brother who was beaten in the attack, carries her home where their grandmother tends to them both. Helene-Angel retreats to her room for a week as news media and neighbors talk about the incident. After praising her and trying to cajole her out of her room, Grandma insists that she be strong and come out. Still feeling very embarrassed, she opens the door to her classmates who have come to support her and to accompany her back to school. Helene-Angel then is able to encourage her disheartened brother with the words, "You know, we've got a right to be here, too."

Concepts Summary

Based on a series of true incidents, this powerful story tells of a terrible racial incident that becomes a lesson in group support and triumph. It is particularly good to help explore the emotion of fear, the feelings that accompany it, and the grief following the trauma. It highlights the need to recognize, identify, and share with others the immobilizing emotional results of prejudice.

Objectives

The student should be able to:
- recognize the concepts of prejudice and discrimination in the events of the story;
- identify and describe the feelings of fear, anger, and embarrassment and understand how these feelings can have a physical as well as emotional affect on people;
- recognize the need to understand, encourage, and support people experiencing those fears;
- identify the grief that follows such a traumatic event and examine ways of coping with fear.

Materials

Books: *White Wash*, by Ntozake Shange
 The Story of Ruby Bridges, by Robert Coles
Art supplies: 12 x 18 drawing paper, crayons, markers, colored pencils
Video: *Rapsody in Orange*, available through the Anti-Defamation League.

CONCEPTS: *PREJUDICE AND DISCRIMINATION*

Discussion Questions
- Where do you think Helene-Angel lives?
- Why did she have to wait for her brother to walk her home from school? How did she feel about

this? How did Mauricio feel about it?
- Why did she walk behind Mauricio?
- Who were the Hawks? Why did they call Helene-Angel and her brother "mud people"?
- Why do you think the Hawks painted her face? What happened to Mauricio?

Activities

Language Arts

- Have the children write a paragraph describing the setting of the story. (Older students can write more.) Then have them add another paragraph giving details from the story or the illustrations that support their descriptions.

Math

- Using the school building shown on the first page of the story, have the children estimate how many classrooms might be in it and give the reasoning behind their estimate.

Music

- Show a video about living in the city and have children describe the sounds heard.

Social Studies

- Have older children look up information or news articles about gangs and discuss why they exist, what problems they create and what alternative activities there are for young people. Students may want to share their own experiences with gangs.

CONCEPTS: *RECOGNIZING FEELINGS AND DEVELOPING COPING SKILLS*

Discussion Questions
- What did Helene-Angel do in class at school that made her feel embarrassed? Can you describe an experience when you felt that way?
- What were Helene-Angel's feelings after the attack? How did that fear affect her senses?
- How did Mauricio feel? Grandma? What details give you clues to their feelings?
- How did Helene-Angel cope with her feelings after the incident? How did Grandma try to help? Why did Grandma call her a hero?

- Why did Helene-Angel feel embarrassed after the attack?
- Who helped Helene-Angel feel good about herself again? How?
- What do you know about the members of Helene-Angel's family?
- Helene-Angel thought Mauricio looked "like a dog with his tail between his legs." What does that mean? Who helped him with his feelings?
- Helene-Angel said, "We've got a right to be here, too." What did she mean?

Activities

Language Arts

- Helene-Angel retreated to be alone right after the attack. Have students break up into small groups of two or three and brainstorm additional appropriate ways to cope with fear and prejudice. Share those ideas with the whole class. Discuss also inappropriate ways to cope with fear.
- Read *The Story of Ruby Bridges* by Robert Coles. Compare the settings, characters and methods of coping with those in *White Wash*.

Science

- Research the human body's nervous system and discover how the body, especially the senses, reacts to different emotions.

Art

- Use 12 x 18-inch drawing paper and draw a line down the middle. On one side have children draw a situation showing fear. On the other side have them draw one appropriate way to cope with that fear.

Guidance

- Have the guidance counselor use role-playing or other activities with the students to highlight coping strategies for situations involving fear, anger, and embarrassment.

Other Recommended Children's Books

Fat, Fat, Rose Marie, by Lisa Passen
Angel Child, Dragon Child, by Michele Maria Surat
The Hundred Dresses, by Eleanor Estes
The Black Snowman, by Phil Mendez
White Socks Only, by Evelyn Coleman

Molly's Pilgrim and *Make a Wish*, by Barbara Cohen
The Christmas Revolution, by Barbara Cohen
Remember My Name, by Sara H. Banks

Community Resources

If there are no available guidance personnel in the school system, invite a trained community person
to do the same type of guidance activities with the students.

Resources for Teachers

The following free resources are available from Teaching Tolerance:
P O Box 548, Montgomery, AL 36101-0548
Order Fax: 334-264-7310
Editorial fax: 334-264-3121
Phone: 334-264-0286
Teaching Tolerance, a semiannual magazine
Starting Small: Teaching Tolerance in Preschool and the Early Grades, a video and text
The Shadow of Hate: A History of Intolerance in America, video and text

Additional Recommended Children's Books on Prejudice

Understanding basic concepts:

Browne, Anthony. *Willy and Hugh.* New York: Alfred A. Knopf, Inc., 1991. (Grades K–2)
Willy is lonely. He is smaller than the other gorillas, and without friends. One day, Willy runs
into Hugh in the park. Compared to Willy, Hugh is a huge gorilla. Rather than blame Willy for
the collision, though, Hugh apologizes. While they are watching the other runners, Buster Nose,
a mean gorilla, tries to pick on Willy. Hugh sticks up for him, so Buster Nose backs down. Willy
and Hugh visit the zoo, where people are in cages, and the library, where Willy reads to Hugh.
As they leave, Hugh is frightened by a spider. This time, Willy helps Hugh by carefully moving
the spider away.

Garcia, Maria. *The Adventures of Connie and Diego.* Rev. ed. San Francisco: Children's Book Press,
1987. (Grades K–4)
Connie and Diego's adventures, told in Spanish and English, begins in the Land of Plenty.
Unlike their sisters and brothers, the twins are born with bodies of many colors. All their brothers and sisters laugh at them. Connie and Diego get tired of this, so they run away. They search
the forest, the ocean, the sky, and the jungle for a place where they can belong. Because they
cannot survive in these places, none of the animals they meet can help them. Finally, the jungle
tiger tells them to look at themselves. They are human, their many colors do not matter. Connie
and Diego go home. After searching the world, they know they belong with their brothers and
sisters.

Lamorisse, A. *The Red Balloon.* New York: Doubleday, 1956. (Grades 1–3)
Pascal, a young Parisian boy, sees a red balloon atop a lamppost and catches it. While becoming
friends, he discovers the balloon has magic powers. Like any devoted friend, the balloon stays
with Pascal, hovering outside his window and following him to school. Pascal, in turn, takes
special care of the balloon. A group of bullies tries to steal the balloon, but Pascal and the balloon
protect each other as best they can. When the bullies burst the balloon, all of the captive balloons
in Paris come to Pascal's rescue.

Lionni, Leo. *Tillie and the Wall.* New York: Alfred A. Knopf, Inc., 1989. (Grades K–2)
"The wall had been there ever since the mice could remember." The mice love to talk about it,

but never try to see the other side. Tillie, the youngest and most curious mouse, lies awake at night, imagining a strange and fantastic world beyond the wall. Unlike the older mice, she does not let her fear conquer her curiosity. Tillie tries to climb the wall, to drill a hole through it, and to walk to its end. Every attempt fails, until an earthworm shows Tilly how to dig under the wall. When Tillie arrives at the other side, she discovers—not the strange and fantastic world she had imagined—but regular mice, just like herself. The mice on both sides celebrate in honor of Tillie, who first showed them the way under the wall.

Taking action against prejudice:

Cohen, Barbara. *Molly's Pilgrim.* New York: Bantam Skylark, 1990. (Grades 2–4)
Molly and her family have moved from Russia to the United States, where third grade is difficult for Molly. She is the only Jewish child in class. Her clothes and accent set her apart. As Thanksgiving approaches, the teacher tells each student to make a small doll, Indians for boys and Pilgrims for girls. Molly's mother makes a beautiful doll; unfortunately, it looks just like Molly's mother, not like the Pilgrims in Molly's school books. Molly is ashamed, but her teacher understands the doll's true meaning. Molly's family has emigrated to the United States to find religious freedom, just like the first Pilgrims. The teacher explains that the Pilgrims got the idea for Thanksgiving from the Jewish Harvest Holiday, Sukkot. Molly's doll is given a place of honor on the teacher's desk to remind the class that Pilgrims still come to America.

Haskins, Jim. *Amazing Grace: The Story Behind the Song.* Brookfield, CT: The Milbrook Press, Inc., 1992. (Grades 3–4)
Through the story of John Newton, an Englishman who worked in the slave trade for many years, the author tells how Africans were captured and transported on slave ships for sale in the United States. Later in life, Newton, who becomes a minister, writes "Amazing Grace." As he grows older, he realizes his greatest sin has been taking part in slavery. He spends the rest of his life working to outlaw the slave trade. For two hundred years, "Amazing Grace" has been sung in churches and in concerts to celebrate freedom.

Knight, Margy Burns. *Who Belongs Here?* Gardiner, ME: Tilbury House, 1993. (Grades 1–4)
Nary was born in Cambodia. His parents are killed by the Khmer Rouge, but he and his grandmother escape to a Thai refugee camp. After several years in the camp, they are sponsored for immigration to the United States by an American family. Nary enjoys his new freedom, but he is sometimes treated badly. Other students call him "chink" and "gook," telling him to go home. His teacher helps the class understand what it means to be a refugee and an immigrant. Nary continues to work hard to make the United States his new home and to retain his Khmer heritage. His wish is for people in his new country to learn to get along.

Parker, Carol. *Why Do You Call Me Chocolate Boy?* Boothbay Harbor, ME: Gull Crest, 1993. (Grades K–4)
Brian is nine, African American, and a new student in his all-white class. Some of his classmates call him "chocolate boy," refusing to let him play with them during recess. After several incidents, Brian punches one of the boys. He does not want to go back to school because he hates himself for being different. Brian's mother calls his teacher, telling her the whole story. Brian's teacher asks the school guidance counselor to meet with her class. The counselor explains racism, frankly confronting the attitudes that had hurt Brian. She asks the students to give presentations on their family backgrounds. Brian tells the class about slavery and his family's rise from their slave origins. Brian's classmates understand what they have done by discriminating against him, finally welcoming him to their school.

Winter, Jeanette. *Follow the Drinking Gourd.* New York: Alfred A. Knopf, Inc., 1988. (Grades K–4)
Long before the Civil War, African Americans enslaved in the South traveled the underground
railroad to freedom. This story, based on true events, tells how information about the railroad
was passed to the slaves. Peg Leg Joe, one of the railroad conductors, travels from plantation to
plantation teaching a simple song. The song, "Follow the Drinking Gourd," is actually a map to
freedom, for hidden in its lyrics are directions for the underground railroad. When James is
about to be sold to another master, he, his wife Molly, their son Isaiah, old Hattie and her grand-
son George, decide to escape. They follow the drinking gourd—the Big Dipper—along the
perilous journey. After receiving help from many on the way, they escape to freedom in Canada.

CHAPTER 5

Beginning Holocaust Studies

Anyone who does not actively, constantly engage in remembering and making others remember is an accomplice of the enemy. Conversely, whoever opposes the enemy must take the side of his victims and communicate their tales, tales of solitude and despair, tales of silence and defiance.
—Elie Wiesel

INTRODUCTION

The Holocaust is a horrifying part of our collective history. Adults have difficulty comprehending the Holocaust's events and consequences. Even more difficult is finding the words to explain the Holocaust to children.

Educators should consider carefully the maturity level of their students when deciding when to teach this material. The featured literature is suitable for third and fourth grades. The core concepts in *The Spirit That Moves Us* can be taught without it. If teachers decide to use this chapter's literature, however, they will impart a compelling, powerful lesson on consequences of prejudice. They also will set the stage for future Holocaust studies by their students.

DEFINITIONS

Holocaust Holocaust, from a Greek word, means "a sacrifice totally burned by fire." It is the most common term applied to the Nazi genocide of Jews and murder of other victims between 1933 and 1945.

Shoah Shoah is a Hebrew word meaning annihilation, and is also used to describe the genocide of Europe's Jews.

Victims Victims are people who are injured, destroyed or sacrificed; people who are subject to oppression, or mistreatment. Jews and Roma (Gypsies) were the two groups targeted for complete annihilation in the Holocaust. Approximately six million were murdered. Approximately five million other people—political prisoners, communists, people with disabilities, gay men, Russian prisoners of war, Jehovah's witnesses, resistance and underground members—also were murdered.

Bystanders Bystanders are those who know about a victim's oppression but choose to do nothing.

Perpetrators Perpetrators are people who bring about or carry out a crime. Holocaust perpetrators included Nazi government and party officials; special police and security forces; many soldiers in the regular German army; bureaucrats in Germany and the occupied countries involved in implementation of the Holocaust; and police and civilians who assisted in the rounding up, deportation, and murder of victims.

Ghetto A ghetto is an area where the Nazis confined Jews. Some ghettos, such as that in Warsaw, were walled and cut off from the city. Tens of thousands of Jews who moved into ghettos died of starvation and disease. Concentration of Jews in central areas also made possible quick deportation to the death camps.

Camps The camps were established by the Nazis to imprison victims, create slave labor, and carry out the Holocaust. They built approximately three thousand labor, transit, prisoner of war, concentration, and death camps.

Concentration Camps Concentration camps were prisons for victims. They also supplied slave laborers. One of the first camps, Dachau, was built about ten miles outside of Munich. Other examples of concentration camps were Buchenwald, Bergen-Belsen, and Ravensbruck. Hundreds of thousands of prisoners died in the camps due to starvation, disease, and murder.

Death, or Extermination, Camps These camps were built for the purpose of mass murder. The camps, all in Poland, were Chelmo, Belzec, Treblinka, Sobibor, Majdanek, and Auschwitz. Parts of Majdaneck and Auschwitz were also concentration camps. Millions of victims were gassed to death in these camps.

Resistance Resistance is an act that combats the dehumanization and death of victims. Victims resisted in many ways. Spiritual resistance included conducting schools and worship services in the ghettos and camps. Slave laborers frequently sabotaged materials in the factories. Armed resistance included fighting by Jewish partisan groups, the Warsaw ghetto uprising, and prisoner rebellions in Auschwitz, Sobibor, and Treblinka.

Righteous Gentiles Righteous Gentiles, also known as the "Righteous among Nations," are non-Jews who risked their lives to rescue Jews during the Holocaust.

Nazi A Nazi was a member of or sympathizer with the National Socialist German Workers (Nazi) party. Adolf Hitler led the Nazi political movement, and after 1933 was also Chancellor and military leader, combining political, government, and military institutions under one rule.

Persecution Persecution is the act of oppressing or harassing someone.

War War is a period of armed conflict.

Immigrants Immigrants are people who come to a country to take up permanent residence.

Refugees. Refugees are people who flee, especially those who flee to another country to escape danger or persecution.

TOPICS AND LESSONS

However teachers design their curriculum, Holocaust study should include the following topics. This chapter's lesson plans explore these topics. Materials annotated in the Teacher Resource Bibliography offer most of the necessary background information.

- **Jewish Culture and Religion** It is imperative that children understand Jews as ordinary people, who, like all peoples, have some unique religious and cultural customs that are part of their way of life. Several books annotated in this Guide, such as *Toby Belfer Never Had a Christmas Tree*, introduce Judaism without reference to the Holocaust. Stereotypes and anti-Semitism should be confronted openly, so that children know Jews did nothing to cause or deserve the Holocaust.

- **Prewar European Jewish Life** Children will better understand how the Holocaust altered Jewish life if they have a concept of life before the Holocaust. The lesson plan books offer a view of Jewish life in Eastern and Western Europe.

- **Historical Context.** The Holocaust occurred in a context of anti-Semitism, oppression, economic depression, and war. A brief introduction to these topics will help children understand how the Holocaust happened. We caution teachers, however, not to oversimplify "causes." The Holocaust is a complex event with numerous interactive causes. Teaching context is more accurate than teaching causes.

- **Holocaust History** The Holocaust is not synonymous with World War II, so it should be taught within the context of but separate from the war. The first phase of the Holocaust occurred from 1933–1939, between the Nazi rise to power and the beginning of World War II. During this period, the Nazis stripped German Jews of all their rights as citizens, and established concentration camps. The second phase, from 1939–1945, marked the ghettoization of Jews, construction of the death camps, and genocide. The number of people murdered was made possible by Germany's military conquests, but this phase existed apart from its war effort.

- **Holocaust Victims** Jews and Roma (Gypsies) were the only groups targeted for complete annihilation, but millions of others also died. As appropriate, this chapter's books tell individual stories of Jews caught in the Holocaust without describing the extent of the horror they faced. A fuller explo-

ration of the victims' fate should be left until children are older.
- **Resistance, Survival, and Healing** Jews did resist. Some survived and were able to go on with their lives. Righteous Gentiles, and in some instances governments, rescued Jews. Several of this chapter's books emphasize ways victims survived, healed, and were helped by others.

TEACHER PREPARATION

Preparation is an essential step in Holocaust education. Teachers must know enough to place the Holocaust in context, to be scrupulously accurate about events, to know what is and is not appropriate for third and fourth grade children, and to know how to answer unexpected questions.

The Holocaust poses questions universal in their applicability to situations where those in power grossly abuse human rights. What does it mean to be human and inhuman? Why do innocent people suffer? Why do victims not stop the violence? How do survivors bear the pain of being alive when all friends and family have perished? Why is it important to remember and bear witness? Teachers should be ready to help students explore answers to these very difficult questions.

The Spirit That Moves Us references a variety of materials about the Holocaust. The United States Holocaust Memorial Museum has published a pamphlet called "Guidelines for Teaching about the Holocaust." It is essential reading, and is reproduced in Appendix A. Two short summaries, also from the Holocaust Museum, are a good place to begin learning Holocaust history. These articles are also reproduced in Appendix A.

For teachers who want a thorough historical grounding, any of the adult histories annotated in Appendix B will accomplish the task. For teachers who want a simpler introduction, any of the histories written for middle and secondary students, also annotated in Appendix B, provide sufficient background. Several of these histories offer the additional advantages of numerous first person accounts, photographs, chronologies, and maps.

Videos, while not supplanting books, also offer historical background. *The Longest Hatred*, a history of anti-Semitism, and *Genocide*, covering the major historical events of the Holocaust, are particularly recommended for teachers. [Note: *Genocide* includes graphic footage of the murder of Jews. The film is disturbing, and intensely moving. It is not appropriate for students.]

It is important for teachers to review as many of the children's books in this chapter as possible. While all are excellent, they vary greatly in their emotional impact. Depending on children's maturity, an appropriate book for one class may be completely inappropriate for another.

While a rabbinical student, Rabbi Lewis Keurass offered this prayer for dedication of a Torah that survived the Holocaust.

> *For the times we saw another's anguish,*
> *But we could not bear the burden;*
> *For the times when we gazed upon loneliness and fear,*
> *And we withdrew our hands;*
> *For the times when all we offered was the*
> *callousness of indifference,*
> *We ask your forgiveness.*
> *And with this hope of forgiveness, we dare to hope*
> *for strength in the days ahead—*
> *that indifference may turn to caring,*
> *and caring bring forth deed.*

STUDENT PREPARATION

Children need a social and cultural context before reading Holocaust books. It is best to introduce the Holocaust only after books on diversity and prejudice have been taught. *Terrible Things* provides a bridge between a fictional example of prejudice and historical reality.

Students may have intense emotional reactions to the books, but also may have difficulty with emotional expression. Teachers should encourage emotional response, assuring children that almost everyone who learns about the Holocaust feels sadness, anger, fear, and confusion. Having children keep a journal of their thoughts and feelings is a good way to monitor emotional reaction.

A special difficulty in Holocaust education is walking the fine line between honesty about the Holocaust's destruction and causing so much despair that children cannot comprehend the literature. The reality is that nothing good came out of the Holocaust. Most of the children's books, however, include examples of survival, healing, and growth by those who lived through the Holocaust. Others recount stories of resistance and rescue. As long as children are not left with the impression that genocide is useful because people respond with courage and growth, emphasizing this material can help children confront the Holocaust.

In order to address parental concerns, teachers should inform parents that they intend to read Holocaust books in the classroom. Teachers who have used these books report that parents typically do not object to them.

TEACHING THE BOOKS

The books recommended here are stories simply told, without graphic pictures of violence or the camps. They are divided between fictional and factual stories.

Each book approaches the Holocaust in a different way, which is valuable because the Holocaust is not one but many different stories. Although there are commonalities, each Holocaust victim had a unique experience.

So that children understand this, we encourage teachers to read several of the books at least. The lesson plans suggest complementary books annotated in this and other chapters.

After the books are read, teachers may wish to lead a discussion of what students learned that is relevant to their lives.

Among lessons the children recount, the authors encourage teachers to make clear the following ideas. One point is the importance of awareness of prejudice. Unless people see and hear, they cannot respond. The Holocaust offers too many examples of bystanders who did nothing because they closed their hearts and minds to the suffering of others.

A second point is the importance of taking a stand, acting in whatever ways available when people are at risk of harm. The Holocaust offers examples of heroic response, and sometimes terrible consequences. By discussing different ways they can take a stand, children can learn about the risks and rewards of speaking out against injustice.

A third point is the importance of witnessing by listening to those who were harmed and telling others their stories. Several of the books teach that witnessing brings knowledge to the listener, healing to the story teller, and victory over the abuser. From their studies, children can learn that witnessing is an action of great power and healing.

A fourth point concerns prevention of future genocides. There is no one answer, but if as a result of Holocaust studies children begin walking a life-path of seeing and responding to injustice, teachers will have met the central goal of *The Spirit That Moves Us*.

All of the lessons taught by the books in *The Spirit That Moves Us*—why diversity is a gift, how different cultures enrich us, the goodness and power inherent in true community, ways to confront and change prejudice—come together in these books.

Sources

Berenbaum, Michael. *The World Must Know: The History of the Holocaust as Told in the United States Holocaust Museum.* Boston: Little, Brown and Company, Inc., 1993.

Gutman, Israel. *The Encyclopedia of the Holocaust.* New York: Macmillan, 1990.

Merriam-Webster's Collegiate Dictionary. 10th ed. Springfield, MA: Merriam-Webster, 1993.

> *First they came for the communists,*
> *and I did not speak out—because I was not a communist.*
> *Then they came for the socialists,*
> *and I did not speak out—because I was not a socialist.*
> *Then they came for the labor leaders,*
> *and I did not speak out—because I was not a labor leader.*
> *Then they came for the Jews,*
> *and I did not speak out—because I was not a Jew.*
> *They came for me—*
> *and there was no one left to speak out for me.*
> —Reverend Martin Niemoeller

THEMES IN HOLOCAUST CHILDREN'S LITERATURE

Prewar European Jewish life:
Memories of My Life in a Polish Village
When Hitler Stole Pink Rabbit
Buba Leah and her Paper Children

Historical overview:
Promise of a New Spring

Escape:
When Hitler Stole Pink Rabbit
Memories of My Life in a Polish Village

Hidden children:
The Lily Cupboard
A Picture Book of Anne Frank

Ghettos and camps:
The Number on My Grandfather's Arm
The Yanov Torah
Let the Celebrations Begin!
A Picture Book of Anne Frank

Righteous Gentiles:
Memories of My Life in a Polish Village
The Lily Cupboard
Let the Celebrations Begin!

Survival and healing:
The Number on My Grandfather's Arm
Memories of My Life in a Polish Village
The Yanov Torah
Promise of a New Spring

German experience:
Rose Blanche

Allegory:
Terrible Things

LESSON PLAN FOR:
Terrible Things, by Eve Bunting. Philadelphia: The Jewish Publication Society, 1989. Grades K-4.

Story Summary

This book, an allegory of the Holocaust written for young children, has meaning for children of every age. The animals in the clearing are content. They share the trees, the shade, and the cool brown water of the forest pond. Without warning, Terrible Things come for every creature with feathers, catching all of the birds in their fearsome nets. Little Rabbit wonders what is wrong with feathers, but Big Rabbit silences him. The clearing returns to normal, until the Terrible Things come back, this time for all creatures with bushy tails. The Terrible Things return again and again, until only the rabbits are left. The rabbits scream for help, but no one is left to hear. All the rabbits are carried away except Little Rabbit, who hides behind a pile of rocks. Sadly, he leaves the clearing to warn other forest creatures about the Terrible Things.

Concepts Summary

Terrible Things challenges children to grapple with the consequences of violence against an entire community. It uses the device of unknown bullies, who have no apparent reason for prejudice against the peaceful animals, to illustrate the nature of bullies and bystanders. It demonstrates the consequences of failure to act as a community when faced with danger. Because the story does not resolve these problems, it offers the opportunity for children to explore their values and develop their own solutions.

Objectives

The student should be able to:
- identify the story's different communities and how each reacted to prejudice and violence;
- recognize connections within and between communities, learning that what happens to others can affect everyone;
- define peace and violence, recognizing the difference between them;
- recognize bullying behavior and its consequences;
- recognize bystander behavior and its consequences;
- identify and analyze individual and community responses to bullies and violence.

Materials

Books: *Terrible Things*, by Eve Bunting
 The Mitten, by Alvin Tresselt
Art supplies: Magazines for collage pictures, paste, white tape for school building outline, drawing supplies, large piece of paper for history time line
Drama: Animal puppets or costumes
Equipment: United States map, newspapers for current events stories

CONCEPTS: *COMMUNITY AND PEACE*

Discussion Questions

- What is the forest like before the Terrible Things come?
- Do the different animals have their own community? What makes each group a community?
- Are all the animals in the forest clearing a community? What makes them a community?
- Before the Terrible Things came, did the animals get along with each other? Do you think this is an example of peace? What are some examples of living together peacefully in your community?
- Where does Little Rabbit go at the end of the story?
- Do you think there might be an even bigger community of animals? What could that community be?

Activities

Art

- Using pictures from magazines, children can make a collage of the different communities within their school. The class can assemble these into a big picture of their school community. These can be displayed on the wall within an outline of their school building.

Language Arts

- Read *The Mitten*. Have children compare how the animals in both stories lived together peacefully.

Social Studies

- Have children identify and list the different communities within their school community; e.g., their classrooms, all third graders, teachers. Children can identify the characteristics that make each group a community, and compare these to the different communities in the story.
- Have children give examples of how their communities live together peacefully and identify some different components of peace, e.g. listening to each other, playing together, including everyone in a party, talking about problems rather than fighting.

CONCEPTS: *BULLIES AND VIOLENCE*

Discussion Questions

- What are the Terrible Things?
- How do the Terrible Things make the animals afraid? If the Terrible Things use violence to make the animals afraid, does this make them bullies?
- Can you think of examples where bullies made you feel afraid? What did you do?
- Do you think the Terrible Things are powerful? What makes them powerful?
- How did the other animals in the forest feel when the Terrible Things came for the birds, the squirrels, the fish, and the porcupines?

Activities

Art

- Have children imagine and draw pictures of their conceptions of the Terrible Things. Show the pictures to the class and identify characteristics, such as the Terrible Things are big, have weapons, look scary. Relate these characteristics to the pictures in the story and to real life bullies.

Language Arts

- Younger children can tell a story about a time when bullies scared them and how they wanted to respond. Older children can read a book with the same theme and write an essay about the similarities and differences of the bullies in the two stories. Help children develop their own definitions for peace and violence.
- Compare the Terrible Things with other "evil" beings in children's fairy tales, such as the witch in *Hansel and Gretel* or the wolf in *Little Red Riding Hood*. Have children analyze how these archetypes are different than the Terrible Things; for example, these beings want something specific from the victims. Discuss how the intended victims in the fairy tales responded to the threat to their lives, and compare this with the way the animals responded.

History

- This story is a good place to introduce real examples of oppression through violence. For older children, examples from United States history can be used to extend the story's lessons, such as the slavery of African Americans or the internment of Japanese Americans during World War II.
- Using the history lesson taught above and the lessons from *Terrible Things*, have children analyze how the historical example might have been different if the bystanders had changed their behavior.

Social Studies

- Bring a newspaper or magazine account of a contemporary example of bullies and violence. Discuss what the children could do if confronted with this situation.

CONCEPT: *PREJUDICE*

Discussion Questions

- Do you think the Terrible Things are prejudiced against the animals? Why or why not?
- Do you think the Terrible Things have reasons to hate the animals? If not, why are they violent?
- Can this be true for people too? Can one group of people hate another without really knowing anything about it?
- Why do you think the Terrible Things wanted to capture the animals and take them away? What would the Terrible Things have to gain from doing this?

Activities

Language Arts

- Using answers from the discussion questions, have children analyze what prejudice and discrimination mean in the absence of explicit reasons for the Terrible Things' violence.
- Have children tell or write a story about prejudice from their own experience. As part of the story, ask children to consider what they might do to help those discriminated against and to confront those who are prejudiced.

Social Studies

- Discuss reasons people use to justify hurting others. Explore whether hurting others can be justified.
- For older children, use newspapers to find current local and national examples of prejudice. Using the concepts introduced in *Terrible Things*, have children analyze these examples. For example, children can identify the group discriminated against, what the prejudice is, and why it might exist; the group with the prejudicial attitudes, how it is discriminating, and what members have to gain from discrimination; and the consequences of prejudice and discrimination for both groups.
- Teach a lesson on various forms of human behavior related to the lessons in the story. Explain why and how people become prejudiced, develop into bullies, and use violence to get their way. Children can brainstorm about ways to help people change. For example, a bully might be afraid and lonely, and thus be helped by being brought into a group and encouraged to change his or her behavior. A prejudiced person might fear someone different because of lack of knowledge, and thus be helped by being given accurate information.

CONCEPT: *BYSTANDERS*

Discussion Questions

- What do the other animals do when the Terrible Things come for all the animals with feathers? What questions does Little Rabbit ask Big Rabbit?
- What does Big Rabbit tell Little Rabbit to do? Does this make Big Rabbit a bystander to violence?
- Can you think of examples in your community when people acted like bystanders?
- Why does each group in the forest feel safe until the Terrible Things come for them?
- What excuses do members of each group of animals make for not helping each other? What are the consequences of this?
- Why do the other animals make excuses? What might have happened if the animals had tried to protect each other?

- At the end of the story, what does Little Rabbit do? Is he still a bystander or something else? Does Little Rabbit show courage when he goes to warn animals in other clearings?

Activities

Language Arts

- Children can write a play (younger children can role play with puppets) where Little Rabbit finds another forest clearing with animals who do not know about the Terrible Things. Different children can play the parts of Little Rabbit, Terrible Things, bystanders, and animals who want to take action. Children can imagine what might happen if some of the animals listened to Little Rabbit, convinced the bystanders to take action, and as a community confronted the Terrible Things.

Social Studies

- Contrast the concepts of prejudice, bystanding, and empathy. Using these concepts, discuss what makes people empathize with some groups but not with others. List the reasons. Have children analyze how people might respond when a group they feel empathy for is hurt or in danger, and how people might respond when a group they feel prejudiced against is hurt or in danger.
- Have children suggest what they could do if they or their friends were bullied. Explore the power people have to stop a bully; for example, speaking out rather than staying silent, asking others for help, forming groups to protect themselves, or escaping when bullies have too much power for an immediate confrontation.
- Extend the lesson for older children by choosing a current event that includes all of the elements in *Terrible Things*. Children can identify the bullies and victims in these real stories, describing how the bullies use violence. Children can identify bystanders and those who take action, exploring their feelings about these events. Finally, children can identify actions they can take individually (sending a donation to a relief organization) or collectively (as a class, writing their congressional representatives).

Community Resources

Ask victims of prejudice from different communities to visit the classroom and talk about their experiences, specifically how they would have liked others to have responded to prevent the prejudice or discrimination from occurring.

Other Recommended Children's Books

Community:
Swimmy, by Leo Lionni
The Mitten, by Alvin Tresselt

Bullies:
Willy and Hugh, by Anthony Browne
Who Belongs Here? by Margy Burns Knight
The Red Balloon, by A. Lamorisse

Prejudice:
The Adventures of Connie and Diego, by Maria Garcia
The Little Weaver of Thai-Yen Village, by Tran-Khanh-Tuyet

Bystanders:
Follow the Drinking Gourd, by Jeanette Winter
The Ring and the Window Seat, by Amy Hest
The Hundred Dresses, by Eleanor Estes

Resources for Teachers

For background information, see any of the Holocaust histories and personal accounts in the Teacher Resource Bibliography.

Allport, Gordon W. *ABC's of Scapegoating.* 9th ed. New York: Anti-Defamation League, 1983.

Kushner, Harold S. *To Life! A Celebration of Jewish Being and Thinking.* Boston: Little, Brown and Company, Inc., 1993.

Trepp, Leo. *The Complete Guide of Jewish Observance.* New York: Behrman House, Inc./Summit Books, 1980.

Yinger, Milton. *Anti-Semitism: A Case Study in Prejudice and Discrimination.* New York: Anti-Defamation League, 1964.

Resources for the Classroom

Ben-Asher, Naomi and Hayim Leaf, eds. *The Junior Jewish Encyclopedia.* 11th ed. New York: Sheingold, 1991.

Chaikin, Miriam. *Menorahs, Mezuzas, and Other Jewish Symbols.* New York: Clarion Books, 1990.

Supplemental Children's Books

Edwards, Michelle. *Blessed Are You: Traditional Everyday Hebrew Prayers.* New York: Lothrop, Lee & Shepard Books, 1993.

Gross, Judith. *Celebrate: A Book of Jewish Holidays.* New York: Platt & Munk, 1992.

Patterson, Jose. *Stories of the Jewish People.* New York: Peter Bedrick Books, Inc., 1991.

Stewart, Gail B. *The Facts about Discrimination.* New York: Crestwood House, 1989.

LESSON PLAN FOR:
Best Friends, by Elisabeth Reuter. Germany: Yellow Brick Road/ Pitsopany Presses, 1993. Grade 4.

Story Summary

Judith and Lisa were best friends who lived in Germany. They played together all the time. Judith was Jewish, Lisa was not. In school they began to hear about Adolph Hitler and to be taught that "good German people had blond hair and blue eyes" and that bad Jewish people had "hooked noses, dark hair and a cunning look in their eyes." They learned to salute "*Heil,* Hitler" and wave flags with swastikas on them. They were also told that the Jews were responsible for all the problems—no jobs, no money, and small apartments. When Judith was taunted by other students at recess, Lisa came to her defense. Lisa could not understand why everyone was treating Judith so badly just because she was Jewish and why her parents did not want her to play with Judith. The girls had to invent hand signals in order to arrange play time when Lisa's parents were not home. The repeated lies about the Jews finally sank in and one day when they were playing together Lisa made an anti-Semitic remark and Judith ran home. After a few days Lisa was sorry, but she couldn't apologize because Judith no longer came to school. Soon after this incident came the "night of broken glass" which became known as *Kristallnacht*. The next morning Lisa was terrified at the broken windows in Judith's house and her disappearance. She wanted to make friends again with Judith, but though she looked at every little girl wearing a yellow star she never found Judith again.

Concepts Summary

This is a story about normal, healthy friendship and the repeated lies of prejudice that attempt to destroy it. It is also about the power of fear—what happens when people allow themselves to believe lies and to be led astray, and what happens when people do not stand firm against evil and falsehood. Within the story *Kristallnacht* is simply described. Elisabeth Reuter presents very clearly, in story form based on fact, how children as well as adults were manipulated to believe that it was because of the Jews that life was so difficult in Germany. It is a warning of what can happen if we allow ourselves to feel superior to others.

Objectives

The student should be able to:
• recognize the positive aspects of friendship;
• recognize the normal difficulties of friendship;
• understand what happens when people feel more important than others;
• recognize the fear of adults under pressure;
• identify the swastika and its meaning;
• describe the events of *Kristallnacht*;
• explore how to prevent prejudice.

Materials

Books: *Best Friends*, by Elisabeth Reuter
            Promise of a New Spring, by Gerta Weissmann
            I Never Saw Another Butterfly, by Hana Volavkova
Art supplies: Drawing paper

CONCEPTS: FRIENDSHIP

Discussion Questions
• What was the relationship between Judith and Lisa? Where did they live? How did they feel about each other?
• Did they always get along perfectly? What happened when they quarreled?
• Is it normal to argue when you are friends? Why do friends become angry with each other? Has that ever happened to you? What are some ways you can restore a relationship?
• How did Lisa show that her friendship for Judith was very strong? Did Lisa take any risks for her friend?

- What questions did Lisa ask her parents? What were their answers?
- How did they make it difficult for Lisa to be friends with Judith? Why didn't they want the girls to be friends anymore?
- What happened between Lisa and Judith that destroyed their friendship? How could that have happened when they were such good friends?
- How did Lisa feel as soon as Judith left? Why do you think she was angry and embarrassed?
- When Judith didn't come to school anymore, how did Lisa feel? How do you know she wanted to be friends with Judith again?
- How do you know Lisa was sorry about what she had done? Do you think what happened changed how Lisa felt and behaved when she grew up?

Activities

Guidance

- Have children make a list of the qualities they would wish to have in a friend. Students can work in groups of twos and threes and combine the lists afterward or each student can develop his/her own list.
- Discuss the difficulties that occur in friendships. Make a list of ways to restore a friendship that has been broken.
- Have students share the feelings they experience when a friend does not treat them well in a particular situation.

Language Arts

- Have students write a story about a situation that has broken or hurt a friendship. Let students who wish read their stories to the class. Have the class discuss ways to repair friendships.

Art

- Have children examine the illustrations to see what they can tell about Germany in the 1930s and 1940s—school, clothing, architecture, toys, media.

CONCEPTS: *LIES, FEAR AND PREJUDICE*

Discussion Questions

- How did school change for the girls after Hitler became the leader of Germany?
- What was taught in school that made Judith feel uncomfortable? Why did she feel self-conscious?
- How was school changing for Judith? Do you think school changed for Lisa?
- What clues were given that tell you life was difficult in Germany?
- What did the teacher ask the children to do when they went to their homes? Why?
- What were students taught about Jewish people? Do you think these things were true?
- How were Germans discriminating against Jews? What is prejudice? What events in this story are examples of prejudice?

- What happened the night of *Kristallnacht*? Why is it known as the "Night of Broken Glass"?
- What did the yellow star mean? Where was it seen?
- Who was afraid in the story? Why were they afraid? How did the fears of Lisa's parents hurt Lisa and Judith? What do you think makes people afraid?
- After Judith's family disappeared, why did Lisa's mother want her to "just forget everything"?

Activities

Social Studies

- Have children make a list of all the lies that were told in this story. Discuss why they think each one is a lie. What experiences or knowledge do they have that make them feel this way? Discuss how people can be convinced that such lies are true.
- Encourage students to talk with friends, relatives or community members about German customs, architecture, clothing, school, toys, and media of the World War II era. Try to find out what the cone-shaped items are at the beginning of the book.
- Have students look up the word "propaganda" in the dictionary. Guide a discussion of other places where they see propaganda in our society. Look particularly at media and advertising.

History

- Research the origin and meaning of the swastika.
- Research the yellow star. Discover if there were other symbols used by the Nazis to mark Jews or other targeted groups.

Language Arts

- Read *The Promise of a New Spring* or *Remember Not to Forget* to the students. Define the terms war, genocide and Holocaust. Describe the origin of the word "Holocaust." The lesson can be extended by demonstrating other words that have been created or used to name a particular event.
- Discuss how genocide is a general concept that can apply to many historical events, and how the Holocaust describes a specific genocide. Use this to explain why "genocide" is not capitalized while "Holocaust" is always capitalized. Have children identify other pairs of words that demonstrate that concept.
- Read some of the poems in *I Never Saw Another Butterfly*. Have children write a poem based on what they felt after hearing the poems.

Art

- Children all over the country created tiles with symbols of the Holocaust on them that are displayed on a wall in the U. S. Holocaust Memorial Museum in Washington, D.C. Have children create their own paper "tile" with symbols or pictures on them that signify the meaning of this event and why we should never forget what happened.

LESSON PLAN FOR:

The Lily Cupboard: A Story of the Holocaust, by Shulamith Levey Oppenheim. New York: Harcourt Brace Jovanovich, 1992. Grade 4.

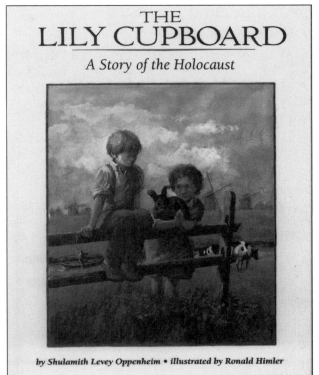

THE
LILY CUPBOARD
A Story of the Holocaust

by Shulamith Levey Oppenheim • illustrated by Ronald Himler

Story Summary

It is 1940 in Holland. Miriam's parents take her to a farm family who have agreed to hide her and keep her safe from the soldiers. Miriam is Jewish; the farm family is not. They give Miriam a rabbit, whom she names after her father. She keeps her rabbit safely hidden in the secret lily cupboard, just as her parents sent her to the farm family to be safely hidden in the countryside.

Concepts Summary

Many Jewish families, recognizing the Nazi threat, sent their children to Gentiles (non-Jews) willing to hide them. This story highlights both the feelings of Miriam and her parents as well as the understanding and care given by the Gentile family. It demonstrates Miriam's significant need to always have the rabbit to cling to for comfort. The risk for the farm family is also evident.

Objectives

The student should be able to:
• recognize the need the Jewish people had to hide;
• understand the risk taken by Gentiles as well as the care and sensitivity shown by them;
• begin to comprehend the many different and difficult feelings involved for the Jewish child, her parents, and the Gentile family;
• recognize the child's need for something tangible to hold on to during the separation from her parents;
• understand the indefiniteness of the child's stay.

Materials

Books: *The Lily Cupboard,* by Shulamith Levey Oppenheim
In My Pocket, by Dorrith M. Sim
Waiting for Anya, by Michael Morpurgo
Number the Stars, by Lois Lowry
A Picture Book of Anne Frank, David A. Adler

Equipment and supplies: Encyclopedia, Internet access, books on art history and the Netherlands (including art and artists), map of Europe

CONCEPTS: *HIDING*

Discussion Questions

- Why did Miriam need to hide? Who decided she should hide?
- Where did she go? Who was in the family where she stayed?
- How long might Miriam have had to stay there?
- Did Miriam have to stay in hiding all the time, day and night?
- How would she know when the soldiers were coming? How would she know when to come out?
- Did you ever play hide and seek? Do you remember enjoying it? What is different about Miriam's hiding?

Activities

Language Arts

- Read *In My Pocket* to the students. Compare Miriam's experience with that of Dorrith Sims.
- Read the chapter book *Waiting for Anya*. Have the children write a journal entry after each chapter or two. Compare the hiding experience and setting of the twelve children to that of Miriam.

History

- Read the chapter book *Number the Stars* to the students. Include the epilogue that addresses its historical accuracy. Discuss what the Danish people did to keep their Jewish citizens from being taken away by the Nazis. Also research the Dutch response. Compare the responses of the two countries and discuss what the risks were and how they were the same or different and why.

Social Studies

- Research the geography and history of the Netherlands. Discuss where in the Netherlands Miriam might have been.

CONCEPT: *FEELINGS*

Discussion Questions

- About how old do you think Miriam is?
- What does Miriam have to do to get ready to hide? Who helps her? How does Miriam feel about doing this? How does her mother feel?
- What does she decide to take? Why does she leave her dolls?
- Miriam says her heart feels like a little stone lantern without a candle. What does that mean? What words would you use for the same kind of situation?
- How does Miriam describe the family she will be staying with? What does the countryside look like?
- What is her first day and night like? What does the family do to make her feel better?

- Who understands her feelings best? Why do you think so?
- Why won't Miriam hide without Hendrik? Why are Nello and his father so worried?
- Why didn't Nello's father just grab Miriam and put her in the cupboard without Hendrik?
- How do you think all of them are feeling when the soldiers come?
- What is the most important thing Miriam has to do while she's in the cupboard?
- Do you think Miriam only had to hide once while she was there? What other information would help you to be able to answer that question?

Activities

Math

- Have the students check the clock, close their eyes and be absolutely quiet for five full minutes without looking at the clock to see how much time has passed. Each student can raise their hand when they think five minutes has gone by. As each student raises his/her hand have them look at the clock to check and write down how many minutes has elapsed. Then have them imagine what it would be like to have to do that for at least thirty minutes or more.

Language Arts

- Have the children write a story about what they think happens after this story ends.
- The students can write a paragraph about a time when they went away from their parents for a period of time. Included should be what they took with them and what their feelings were. It may help to ask them to remember what it was like for them to do this for the very first time.

Guidance

- Guidance personnel in the school may have other activities that could be used to explore feelings around being separated from parents.
- Read *A Picture Book of Anne Frank*. Compare Anne's situation with that of Miriam. Talk about setting, people involved, feelings, and ways of coping with being in hiding.

Social Studies

- Read a book about Harriet Tubman and/or about the Underground Railroad experiences in this country. Compare the hiding situations including houses used. Investigate the part of the country near your school to see if it is connected in any way with the Underground Railroad and find out if there are any houses in the area that may have been used.

Art

- Have children draw a picture of one thing they could take with them into hiding (or if they moved, or went to camp) that would help them feel more secure.
- Research famous artists of the Netherlands. Using clues from the book find copies of famous Dutch paintings of places resembling where Miriam was in hiding.

Other Recommended Children's Books
Chapter Books:
Twenty and Ten, by Claire Huchet Bishop
Jacob's Rescue: A Holocaust Story, by Malka Drucker
Hiding From the Nazis, by David A. Adler
Hide and Seek and *Anna Is Still Here*, by Ida Vos
Anne Frank: A Life of Hiding, by Johanna Hurwitz
A Knock at the Door, by Eric Sonderling

LESSON PLAN FOR:
***The Number on My Grandfather's Arm*, by David A. Adler. Philadelphia: The Jewish Publication Society, 1989. Grade 4.**

Story Summary
A loving relationship between a young girl and her Grandfather is portrayed in text and black-and-white photographs. When the girl notices a number tattooed on her Grandfather's arm, her Grandfather tells her of the atrocities committed by the Nazis against Jews, even describing Auschwitz, the camp he was in. "We were no longer people to them. We were numbers." Moved, the young girl comforts her Grandfather.

DAVID A. ADLER

The Number on My Grandfather's Arm

Photographs by Rose Eichenbaum

Concepts Summary
The photographic illustrations in this book help a child understand the reality of the Holocaust for real people living ordinary lives. It recounts simply the basic outline of Nazi plans and events including concentration camps. Students begin to understand the terrible loss of families and extreme difficulty survivors have when describing what happened to them, including their feelings of shame.

Objectives

The student should be able to:

- begin to understand, in a simple form, Nazi history and beliefs;
- recognize what a concentration camp was;
- understand that the Holocaust happened to real people who had been living normal lives;
- recognize and empathize with Holocaust victims about the difficulty and pain they have in sharing their stories;
- begin to understand the survivor's terrible loss of family members.

Materials

Books: *The Number on My Grandfather's Arm*, by David A. Adler

Rose Blanche, by Roberto Innocenti

Let the Celebrations Begin! by Margaret Wild

The Big Lie: A True Story, by Isabella Leitner

I Never Saw Another Butterfly, by Hana Volavkova

One Grain of Rice, by Demi

Art supplies: Drawing paper, markers, crayons, colored pencils, water colors, fabric scraps, glue, scissors, etc.

Supplies: Large map of Europe

Music: Tape of Klezmer music

CONCEPTS: *NAZI HISTORY*

Discussion Questions

- Who was the ruler of Germany during the 1930s and 1940s? What were the people who followed him called?
- What did the Nazis believe? What did they plan to do?
- What kinds of things happened to the Jewish people? What rights did they lose?
- What other countries were involved?
- Why did grandpa begin to talk about what happened?
- Why do you think the Nazis printed numbers on the arms of people who were put in concentration camps?
- What was a concentration camp used for? What was it like there?

Activities

Art

- Show some of the pictures in *I Never Saw Another Butterfly*. Explain who drew these, discussing how children could create art in a concentration camp.
- Have children create an original work of art in the medium of their choice that reflects their feelings about the persecution of the Jews by Nazis.

Language Arts

- Read *The Big Lie: A True Story* by Isabella Leitner to understand more about existence in Auschwitz.
- Read *Rose Blanche*. Discuss why Rose saw the persecution in her country while the adults in the story helped persecute Jews or ignored the persecution. Ask children whether Rose is the sort of person they would like to be. Help children analyze the risks and benefits of responding to persecution.

Social Studies

- Make a list of the ways Jews were persecuted that are described in this book. Guide a discussion of what human rights have been abridged.
- Help children list some of their rights as United States citizens. Lead a discussion on why we have these rights and where they come from. This is a good time to introduce the Bill of Rights. Have children write a story describing how their lives might change if any of these rights were taken away.

CONCEPTS: *SHATTERED AND LOST LIVES*

Discussion Questions

- What was life like for Grandpa when he was young? Where was this?
- What was Grandpa's occupation? Where does he live now?
- Why did Grandpa hide the number on his arm? How do you know it was very difficult for him to talk about what happened during World War II? What do you think was the hardest thing for him to remember?
- How did his granddaughter feel? What did she say to support him?
- In what ways did what he experienced in Europe change his life forever?

Activities

Art

- Talk about Grandpa's memories of his early life. Have children draw pictures of something they remember from their early years, including people. Talk about what it would be like if those people in their picture were not living now.
- Discuss why the illustrations in the book are done in black and white and why photographs are used instead of drawings. Guide the discussion to stress the sadness and realism that these methods emphasize.

Language Arts

- Read *Let the Celebrations Begin!* Discuss how the characters in this book begin to have new life. Talk about the possible problems that might occur as a result of the kinds of experiences that occurred in the concentration camp.

Geography

- On a large map of Europe, locate the countries identified by Grandpa where the Jews were hated. Research the countries that Hitler's Nazis took over and locate all of them on the map.

Math

- To help understand the magnitude of six million, first read *One Grain of Rice*. Then have children pile a hundred books on the floor. Guide them to figure out how many piles they would need to make one million—then six times that.

Music

- Introduce children to Klezmer music, the traditional music of Eastern European Jewry. This music is enjoying a comeback and tapes or CDs are available.

LESSON PLAN FOR:

Child of the Warsaw Ghetto, **by David A. Adler. New York: Holiday House, 1995. Grade 4.**

Story Summary

This is the story of Froim Baum, a Holocaust survivor now living in the United States, who was born to a poor Jewish family in Warsaw in 1926. The boy's personal biography is woven together with the history of Hitler's rise to power, the Nazi invasion of Poland, the raging anti-Semitism, the herding of more than 400,000 Jews into the walled Warsaw Ghetto, and finally the death camps. Froim found shelter in the orphanage of the beloved Janusz Korczak and moved between there and home. Later came escape for Froim and his family to a relative's home in Plonsk, Nazi capture, enslavement in death camps, and survival of two of the brothers.

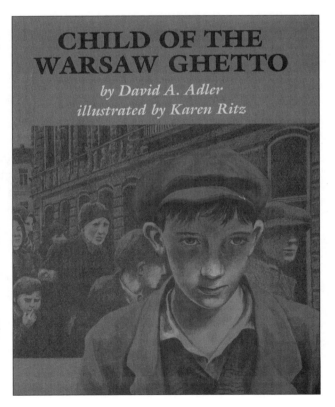

CHILD OF THE WARSAW GHETTO

by David A. Adler
illustrated by Karen Ritz

Concepts Summary

Packed with history but understandable for young readers, this is mainly a story of Polish Jews and the Warsaw Ghetto woven into events of the Holocaust from the beginning to camp liberation. Adler has told the story with restraint in a way that is stark, factual and extremely powerful, but not so over-whelming that a child would be traumatized. The colors in the illustrations convey the feeling of the setting. Both historical chronology and a realization of the severity of ghetto conditions are presented in this book, along with information about Jewish resistance.

Objectives

The student should be able to:
• understand the basic historical facts surrounding the rise of Nazism and its introduction into Poland;
• recognize the conditions and struggles of poverty and oppression;
• understand the horrors and results of prejudice and war;
• understand the concept of loyalty in spite of personal danger;
• discuss the basic history of and living conditions in the Warsaw Ghetto;
• understand and explore forms of Jewish resistance that occurred;
• explain why and how we know about this history;
• explore why and how people survived these nightmarish experiences.

Materials

Books: *Child of the Warsaw Ghetto*, by David A. Adler
            Memories of My Life in a Polish Village, by Toby Knobel Fluek
            Marc Chagall, by Ernest Raboff
            Tar Beach, by Faith Ringgold

Equipment and supplies: Map of Europe, encyclopedia, Internet access (please see Internet information on page 9), long piece of paper for timeline, 12 x 18-inch drawing paper, markers, crayons, paints

CONCEPT: *POLISH JEWS AND NAZISM*

Discussion Questions

• Describe the Baum family's life in the 1920s when Froim was born. What was their financial status?
• What tragedy happened that made life even more difficult for the Baums?
• What was the most serious problem the family had? What did Froim do to help their situation?
• What was happening politically in neighboring Germany? How did that affect Poland?
• What happened in September of 1939 that made everything much worse in Warsaw?
• How was life worse for Polish Jews than for other Polish citizens?
• Where did Froim live during this time? Was there anything about his life that was happy? Who made a difference for Froim?
• What event happened in April of 1940 that changed everything for the Jews in Warsaw?

Activities

Geography

- Make copies of a map of the entire European continent. Have students locate Poland on the map. Label all the countries including Poland and indicate the dates they were invaded by or surrendered to the Nazis.

Social Studies

- Research Poland to discover its culture and societal structure, particularly before the war.

Language Arts

- Read *Memories of My Life in a Polish Village 1930-1949*. Compare Toby's story with that of Froim. This is especially meaningful because they are both accounts of real people.
- Examine the straightforward, factual writing style which this author (and also Toby Knobel Fluek in *Memories)* uses to tell the story and compare it to styles used in fictional stories.

Geography

- Have children look at a map of Europe to find the region where Toby Knobel Fluek lived.

Art

- Compare the style of the illustrator of this book to that of Toby Knobel Fleuk in *Memories* and to that of Marc Chagall in his paintings of Eastern European life found in the book *Marc Chagall*.

Math

- Figure out what year Chaim Baum was born and/or how old Froim was when the war ended in 1945.
- Look up the value of a *zloty*. Research the value of a *zloty* in 1926 and then in 1945 (and other selected years in between) and convert to dollars, if information is available.

CONCEPTS: *WARSAW GHETTO AND SURVIVAL*

Discussion Questions

- Describe the living conditions in the Warsaw Ghetto. Include such topics as housing, schools, culture, work, food, and security.
- How was Froim able to survive? What things helped him do better than many other Jews? What does it mean that Froim didn't look Jewish?
- Why did the Nazis want the Jews to leave the ghetto in July of 1942? How did they get people to volunteer to leave?
- What happened to the Orphans' House? Why wasn't Froim involved? Why didn't Janusz Korczak go free when he was apparently given the chance? Why did Froim want to go with them?
- How did Froim escape the ghetto?
- What events happened in the Warsaw Ghetto after Froim's family left? How do you think things would have been different for Froim if they had stayed?
- How was the second attempt by the Nazis at "resettlement" in January of 1943 different from the first one? What did "resettlement" mean? Why did Jews resist the second time?
- What happened in April of 1943? How was this different both for the Nazis and for the Jews?
- What events happened to Froim and his family after escaping from the ghetto?
- What different ways did Jewish people use to resist the Nazis?
- Why do you think Froim survived? How many different ways did he use to survive throughout this whole time?
- How do we know the facts about the events of this time?

Activities

History

- On a long piece of paper guide students to make a large timeline from 1926 to 1945. Have children place all of the events described in this book in the proper year in which they occurred. Label the Warsaw Ghetto events in a different color from the others. Using a third color add important events in Nazi Germany, such as when Hitler became Chancellor, passage of the Nuremberg laws, and *Kristallnacht*. Discuss how events in Germany influenced events in Poland.
- Use Holocaust history books or the Internet (please see Internet information on page 9) to find a map of the city of Warsaw in 1940. Locate the area of the Warsaw Ghetto.
- Students can research more information and write a brief report on German General Jurgen Stroop or Mordechai Anielewicz.
- Have students research the number and location of the death camps.
- More advanced students could research what was happening in the United States during the time of the Warsaw Ghetto.

Math

- Have children use the map of the Warsaw Ghetto and/or research information to find out how much area was covered in square yards or square meters. Then help children figure out how many people there would have been per square yard or square meter.
- Have children conceptualize the three million Polish Jews murdered and/or the six million total Jewish deaths by collecting a thousand objects (pennies, poker chips, bottle tops, etc). Explain that to have one symbolic object for every Jewish person killed, the class would need to make six thousand of these collections.

Language Arts

- Read *Tar Beach*. Compare the inner city problems with those from Froim's family. Discuss what is the same and what is different.
- Have students write a letter (not to be sent) to Froim reflecting their own thoughts about his experiences and how he coped with the events of his life.
- Have students write three questions they would ask Froim if they were to meet him today.

Social Studies

- Make a list of all the problems faced by Froim and his family. Discuss what they did to try to solve each one. Compare those problems with situations occurring in places around the world that may be somewhat similar.
- Discuss how the Holocaust could have happened. Make a list of the circumstances and decisions that were allowed to happen that ultimately led to death camps. Then list things that could have been done to stop the progression at any point. This activity can be done in teams and then lists combined into one.

Art

- Talk about the illustrations in the book. Discuss how they help convey the story's message, especially the use of color. Have students divide a 12 x 18-inch piece of drawing paper into two sections. Have them draw a picture of a positive situation using appropriately vivid colors on one side and on the other side use dark or muted colors to draw a difficult or negative situation.

Science

- Have children list the kinds of medical difficulties mentioned in the book. Follow up with research on symptoms, causes, and remedies for these conditions or diseases.

Other Recommended Children's Books

Hear O Israel: A Story of the Warsaw Ghetto, by Terry W. Treseder
Winter in the Morning: A Young Girl's Life in the Warsaw Ghetto and Beyond 1939-1945, by Alvin Tresselt
The Warsaw Ghetto Uprising, by Elaine Landau
Warsaw Ghetto, by Conrad Stein
Flowers on the Wall, by Miriam Nerlove

LESSON PLAN FOR:

Passage to Freedom: The Sugihara Story, by Ken Mochizuki. New York: Lee & Low Books, Inc., 1993. Grade 4.

Story Summary

It's July 1940, a year before the German army was ordered into Russia, and young Hiroki Sugihara and his family are living in Lithuania where his father is the Japanese consul. One morning they awake to find their house surrounded by hundreds of desperate men, women, and children—Jews who escaped from Nazi soldiers in their native Poland. If they can get visas to travel through the Soviet Union to Japan, they may be able to go on from there to safety. Moved by their plight, yet afraid for the safety of his own family, Hiroki's father Chiune asks the Japanese government for permission to write the visas. Three times he is refused, at which point he decides to disobey his government because he cannot disobey God. With the agreement of his family, he begins the overwhelming task of handwriting 300 visas a day for more than a month until he is ordered to leave Lithuania. As their train pulls out of the station, he is still throwing permission papers out the window to more waiting people. In an important afterword, the real Hiroki Sugihara recalls the events that occurred from that day to the present time.

Concepts Summary

Hiroki, the five-year-old son of Japanese Consul Chiune Sugihara, narrates this powerful family story of compassion, courage and conscience. It carries an added dimension of heroism and brotherhood above and beyond political pressures and in the face of potential risk for his young family. The story is seen through the eyes of a child who has his own needs and concerns, but clearly understands the belief of his parents that all persons have the same worth. The story, set in its political/historical context, shows that one person can indeed take a stand and make a difference.

Objectives

The student should be able to:
- understand the basic political situation in Lithuania in 1940;
- recognize the courage of Chiune Sugihara and his family;
- recognize that obeying your conscience may mean disobedience to authority;
- understand that personal risk may be necessary in order to stand up for what is right;
- understand that one person can make a difference;
- recognize first-person writing style;
- evaluate the reasons why a particular artistic style is used for the illustrations in the story.

Materials

Books: *Passage to Freedom: The Sugihara Story*, by Ken Mochizuki
        Heroes and *Baseball Saved Us*, by Ken Mochizuki
        Samantha Smith: A Journey for Peace, by Anne Galicich
        Journey to the Soviet Union, by Samantha Smith
        A variety of age-appropriate biographies

Equipment and materials: Map of Europe, encyclopedia, timeline paper, Internet access

CONCEPT: *HISTORICAL SETTING*

Discussion Questions

- What was the occupation of Hiroki Sugihara's father? Where were they living? Where did Mr. Sugihara do his work?
- In what year does the story take place?
- Why were hundreds of people outside the Sugihara house? Where had they come from?
- What did Hiroki notice about these people—dress, physical condition, ages?
- What did these people want Hiroki's father to do? Why were they anxious to get this done soon?
- What was the problem preventing Mr. Sugihara from writing the visas? How did he try to solve this problem?
- Why do you think the Japanese government would not give Hiroki's father permission to write the visas?

Activities

Geography

- Locate the country of Lithuania on a map of Europe and identify the surrounding countries. Identify major geographical features (mountains, rivers, lakes, seas, etc.).

Social Studies

- Research the culture, customs, traditional folk costumes, etc., of Lithuania.
- Have children research the culture, customs, traditional folk costumes, etc. of Latvia and Estonia and compare them with those of Lithuania.

History

- Have children research Lithuanian history between 1918 and 1993. Students can make a timeline and mark the major political events, particularly when Lithuania was its own nation and when it was occupied. Mark the time period of the event in this story on the timeline in a different color.

Language Arts

- Identify the voice that tells the story and discuss with the students the first-person style of writing. Compare that with some stories written in the third person. Have the students write a personal anecdote using first-person writing.
- Help children analyze how historical events can be used to create literature, and how literature can make history personal and real.

CONCEPTS: *COURAGE, CONSCIENCE AND RISK*

Discussion Questions

- What decision did Mr. Sugihara have to make? Whose opinion did he ask before he decided what to do?
- Why was this decision so difficult? What might happen if he decided to help the Jews?
- What were the reasons Hiroki's father finally decided to help the Jewish refugees?
- What does it mean to obey your conscience? What did Mr. Sugihara mean when he said, "I may have to disobey my government, but if I don't, I will be disobeying God"?
- From reading this story, what do you think were important beliefs in the Sugihara family? What events in the story help you answer this question?
- What is courage? Why did it take courage to help Polish Jews?
- What does it mean to take a risk? How is that different from not taking a risk? Can you give an example of when you or someone you know took a risk? What might have happened when they took this risk?
- Are there any times when it is not advisable to take a risk?
- Once Hiroki's father decided to help, what made it so hard to complete the task?
- What things did the other members of the Sugihara family do to help Hiroki's father do as much as possible?
- Did Mr. Sugihara get discouraged at any time? How do you know? What kept him going?
- Why did the family have to stop helping? Do you think they should be concerned about the place they were being sent?
- What future difficulties were there for Mr. Sugihara because of his decision? How did this decision change his life? Do you think he ever regretted what he did?
- How do you know that this person and his family made a difference?

Activities

Language Arts

- Have children brainstorm a list of famous people who have exhibited a great deal of courage and note what they did that was courageous.
- Children can choose any biography from the school or class library to read and then do a report on the person they chose. They should include an analysis of whether the person exhibited courage in any way.
- Read a biography of Samantha Smith and discuss what children think she did to make a difference. Brainstorm a list of other people who alone have made a difference in the world such as Ghandi, Martin Luther King, Jr., Oscar Schindler, etc. Include what they did to make a difference. Try to include other children on the list. Help children understand that they don't have to be adults to make a difference and that one person alone is able to effect change or raise awareness of an issue.

- Write a letter to the author of this book telling him why you appreciate the telling of this story.
- Read another of Ken Mochizuki's books and compare the subjects, illustrations, and methods of telling the stories.

Art

- Study the illustrations in this book. Discuss such things as the focus on the faces and the colors used that create the feeling of old photographs. Discuss also what feelings the colors evoke. Have children experiment with drawings of situations using colors that they feel will convey somber and compassionate feelings.
- Compare the illustrations in this book with those in another book about a similar topic.

Math

- Have children estimate how many visas Mr. Sugihara could possibly have written if he wrote the full three hundred each day from the time he started until he left on the train to Berlin. Discuss what information is missing from this story that would help get the total number more accurately.

History

- Ask children to use research sources including the Internet to learn more about the Sugihara family and this incident. (Please see Internet information on page 9.) Information about "Sugihara survivors" could be particularly interesting.

Science

- Have children find out the names of the muscles in the arm that would be affected by so much writing, and how they work. Discover if there are any ways in addition to massage that would help relieve the pain and stiffness Mr. Sugihara suffered.

Other Recommended Children's Books
Rose Blanche, by Roberto Innocenti
The Lily Cupboard, by Shulamith Levey Oppenheim
The Christmas Menorahs: How a Town Fought Hate, by Janice Cohn

Resources for Teachers
It's Our World Too!: Stories of Young People Who Are Making a Difference, by Phil Hoose
The Kid's Guide to Service Projects: Over 500 Ideas for Young People Who Want to Make a Difference, by Barbara A. Lewis.

Additional Recommended Children's Books on the Holocaust

Adler, David A. *A Picture Book of Anne Frank*. New York: Holiday House, 1993.
  This book is a biography of Anne Frank rather than a condensation of her famous diary. As such, it offers an account of one family's odyssey through the Holocaust: leaving their home, living in hiding, deportation to Auschwitz, Anne's and her sister's deaths in Bergen-Belsen from starvation and disease, and the discovery of her diary in 1947. The author places Anne's story in the larger context of the Holocaust, citing the number of people murdered and referring to other groups of Holocaust victims.

Innocenti, Roberto. *Rose Blanche*. New York: Stewart, Tabori & Chang Publishing, 1985.
  Rose Blanche lives in a small German town during World War II. Although she notices the trucks full of soldiers, life goes on as before, until she sees a boy run from the back of a truck. He is immediately caught by the town mayor. Rose wonders what happened to the boy, so she follows the truck's tracks out of town, where she discovers a concentration camp. She gives the food in her bag to the children on the other side of the barbed wire. As often as she can, she returns with food. At the end of the war, she goes to the camp one last time. It is a foggy day and soldiers are everywhere. The camp is empty; a shot is fired. Rose does not return. Over time, spring arrives at the deserted camp.

Klein, Gerda Weissmann. *Promise of a New Spring*. Chappaqua, NY: Rossel Books, 1981.
  Subtitled "The Holocaust and Renewal," this book describes through text, photographs, and drawings the rise of the Nazis, the war that followed, and the Holocaust. The text explains that the Holocaust was as terrible for human beings as a forest fire is for nature. Each year, animals and plants in the forest live through the cycle of seasons. An evil hand may try to destroy the forest by setting it on fire, but some life survives and spring comes again. Similarly, the few who survived the Holocaust have an important task: to remember what the world was like before so much was destroyed, and to tell their memories to all who will listen, especially children.

Wild, Margaret. *Let the Celebrations Begin!* New York: Orchard Books, 1991.
  Miriam lives in Hut 18, Bed 22, of a concentration camp. As liberation approaches, Miriam and other women in the camp plan a special party for the children. The young children know no other life, but Miriam remembers toys, her own bedroom, and chicken dinners. The women make toys out of scraps of material; they even cut off pieces of their own clothes. When soldiers arrive to liberate the camp, the children receive their toys and the celebration begins.

References for Teachers and Students
Fiction:

Ackerman, Karen. *The Night Crossing*. Random House, Inc., N.Y. 1995.
  Young Clara, older sister Marta, and their parents encounter many dangers as they escape Nazi-occupied Austria to Switzerland.

Adler, David A. *One Yellow Daffodil: A Hanukkah Story*. Gulliver Books, San Diego, 1995.
  During Hanukkah two children help a Holocaust survivor to once again embrace his religious traditions.

Bishop, Claire Huchet. *Twenty and Ten*. Puffin Books, N.Y. 1988.
  Based on the true story of twenty French orphans who helped hide and protect ten Jewish refugee children during the German occupation.

Drucker, Malka. *Jacob's Rescue: A Holocaust Story*. Bantam Skylark, N.Y. 1993.
  In answer to his daughter's questions, a man recalls the terrifying years of his childhood when a

brave Polish couple, Alex and Mela Roslan, hid him and other Jewish children from the Nazis. Based on a true story.

Feder, Paula K. *The Feather-Bed Journey*. Albert Whitman & Co., Morton Grove, IL 1995.
As she tries to repair a torn feather pillow, Grandma tells about her childhood in Poland, about the Nazi persecution of the Jews during World War II, and about the origin of this special pillow.

Ginsburg, Marvell. *The Tattooed Torah*. Union of American Hebrew Congregations, N.Y. 1983.
A Torah confiscated and put into storage by the Nazis in Czechoslovakia during World War II finds a new home in an American congregation after the war.

Hoestlandt, Jo. *Star of Fear, Star of Hope*. Walker and Co., N.Y. 1995.
Nine-year-old Helen is confused by the disappearance of her Jewish friend during the Nazi occupation of Paris.

Innocenti, Roberto. *Rose Blanche*. Creative Education, Inc., Minn. 1995.
Beautifully illustrated work which encourages questions and individual response to the story of a young girl who discovers a concentration camp in the woods near her town and begins to carry food to its inhabitants.

Jules, Jacqueline. *The Grey Striped Shirt, How Grandma and Grandpa Survived the Holocaust*. Alef Design Group, Los Angeles, 1993.
When a nine-year-old Frannie finds a gray striped shirt in the closet, she asks questions which lead her grandparents to tell her about their experiences of the Holocaust.

Kerr, Judith. *When Hitler Stole Pink Rabbit*. Dell, N.Y. 1987.
Tale of German family, including a nine-year-old daughter, who fled from Germany to England in the early 1930s.

Lakin, Patricia. *Don't Forget*. William Morrow & Company, Inc., N.Y. 1994.
Heartwarming story set against the backdrop of a postwar Jewish neighborhood in which Sarah learns the past should never be forgotten.

Lowry, Lois. *Number the Stars*. Houghton Mifflin Co., Boston, 1989.
Newberry Award-winning tale of the efforts of the Danish people to save their Jewish citizens as told by 10-year-old protagonist Annemarie.

Matas, Carol. *Daniel's Story*. Scholastic, N.Y. 1993.
Daniel, whose family suffers as the Nazis rise to power, describes ghetto and concentration camp experiences and his eventual liberation.

McSwigan, Marie. *Snow Treasure*. E. P. Dutton & Company, N.Y. 1942.
Norwegian children elude the German occupation forces and manage to slip a gold shipment past the Nazis. Based on a true story.

Morpurgo, Michael. *Waiting for Anya*. Viking, N.Y. 1991.
Benjamin needs the help of the entire French village to smuggle twelve Jewish children over the border to safety in nearby Spain.

Nerlove, Miriam. *Flowers on the Wall*. Margaret K. McEldry Books, N.Y. 1996.
Rachel, a young Jewish girl living in Nazi-occupied Warsaw, struggles to survive with her family and maintains hope by painting colorful flowers on her dingy apartment walls.

Sachs, Marilyn. *A Pocket Full of Seeds*. (Scholastic Inc., N.Y. 1973) Puffin Books, Penguin Books USA Inc., N.Y. 1994.
A Jewish girl separated from her family struggles to survive her loss.

Sim, Dorrith M. *In My Pocket*. Harcourt, Brace & Company, San Diego, 1996.
     Fear and uncertainty afflict everyone on the boat on the morning in July 1939 when Jewish children sail from Holland to the safety of a new life in Scotland. Honest, autobiographical account of the Kindertransport told in a child's voice.

Treseder, Terry W. *Hear O Israel: A Story of the Warsaw Ghetto*. Atheneum, N.Y. 1990.
     A Jewish boy describes life in the Warsaw Ghetto and his family's ultimate transfer and decimation in the camp of Treblinka.

Vos, Ida. *Anna Is Still Here*. Houghton Mifflin Co., Boston, 1993.
     Thirteen-year-old Anna, who was a hidden child in Nazi-occupied Holland during World War II, gradually learns to deal with the realities of being a survivor.

_____. *Hide and Seek*. Houghton Mifflin Co., Boston, 1991.
     A young Jewish girl living in Holland tells of her experiences during the Nazi occupation, her years in hiding, and the after shock when the war finally ends.

Non-Fiction:

Abells, Chana Byers. *The Children We Remember*. Kar-Ben Copies, Maryland 1983. Greenwillow Books, N.Y. 1986.
     A sensitive photo essay which focuses both on the children who perished and those who survived.

Adler, David A. *A Picture Book of Anne Frank*. Holiday House, N.Y. 1993.
     Biography of famous diary writer geared for younger children.

_____. *We Remember the Holocaust*. Henry Holt & Co., N.Y. 1989.
     Discusses the events of the Holocaust and includes personal accounts from survivors of their experiences of the persecution and the death camps.

Amdur, Richard. *Anne Frank*. Chelsea House Publishers, N.Y. 1993.
     Traces the life of the young Jewish girl whose diary chronicles the years she and her family hid from the Nazis in an Amsterdam attic.

Baldwin, Margaret. *The Boys Who Saved the Children*. J. Messner, N.Y. 1983.
     Illustrated with photographs, this tells how a young man and his friends saved the lives of children in the Lodz Ghetto.

Bauman, Janina. *Winter in the Morning: A Young Girl's Life in the Warsaw Ghetto and Beyond 1939-1945*. The Free Press, N.Y. 1986.
     A memoir depicting a descent from ease and security to hardship and fear in wartime Warsaw.

Brown, Gene. *Anne Frank: Child of the Holocaust*. Blackbirch Press, Inc., Woodbridge, CT 1991.
     Biography of the thirteen-year-old Jewish girl whose diary, published after her death in a Nazi concentration camp, made her famous all over the world.

Cohn, Lilo. *A Shadow Over My Life*. Gefen Publishing House, Ltd., Jerusalem 1994.
     The author's early childhood in Berlin and the impact on her young life of Hitler coming to power.

Friedman, Ina R. *Escape or Die: True Stories of Young People Who Survived the Holocaust*. J. B. Lipincott Co., N.Y. 1985.
     Twelve true stories of young Jews and non-Jews who endured the Holocaust.

Hurwitz, Johanna. *Anne Frank: A Life in Hiding*. Jewish Publication Society, PA, 1988.
     A perspective of the famous diarist that allows a glimpse of both her dreams and the tensions brought on by life in the Secret Annexe.

Landau, Elaine. *The Warsaw Ghetto Uprising.* The Millbrook Press, Bookfield, CT, 1993.
Describes life in the section of Warsaw where Polish Jews were confined by the Nazis in the early 1940s, focusing on the final days of fighting prior to the destruction of the Ghetto in 1943.

Leitner, Isabella. *The Big Lie: True Story.* Scholastic, Inc., N.Y. 1992.
The author describes her experiences as a survivor of the Nazi death camp at Auschwitz during World War II.

Meltzer, Milton. *Rescue: The Story of How Gentiles Saved the Jews in the Holocaust.* Harper & Row, N.Y. 1988.
A recounting drawn from historic source material of the many individual acts of heroism performed by Righteous Gentiles, who sought to thwart the extermination of Jews during the Holocaust.

Pettit, Jayne. *A Place to Hide.* Scholastic, Inc., N.Y. 1993.
True stories of Holocaust rescuers, including Oskar Schindler and Le Chambon.

Rossel, Seymour. *The Holocaust: The Fire That Raged.* Franklin Watts, N.Y. 1989.
Discusses the historical background, from the Treaty of Versailles through Hitler's rise to power, that lead to the horrible and systematic slaughter of millions of Jews by the Nazis during World War II.

Schuman, Michael A. *Elie Wiesel, Voice from the Holocaust.* Enslow Publishers, Inc., Hillside, N.J. 1994.
Biography of survivor awarded the Nobel Peace Prize in 1986 and his lifelong dedication to remembering the Holocaust.

Shirer, William L. *The Rise and Fall of Adolf Hitler.* Random House, N.Y. 1961.
A young reader's version of Shirer's landmark work, *The Rise and Fall of the Third Reich.*

Stadtler, Bea. *The Holocaust: A History of Courage and Resistance.* Behrman House, Inc., N.Y. 1973.
Well-written text with chapter questions covering the period from World War I through the War Tribunals at Nuremberg and describing the Jewish experience under the Third Reich.

_____. *Warsaw Ghetto.* Children's Press, Chicago, 1985
An in-depth account of life behind the ghetto walls from their erection through the Warsaw Ghetto Uprising, featuring large black-and-white photographs.

Tatelbaum, Itzhak. *Through Our Eyes: Children Witness the Holocaust.* I. B. T. Publications, Chicago, 1985.
Children's diary excerpts and poems combine with historical photographs to provide a chronology of the Holocaust in this text.

Tridenti, Lina. *Anne Frank.* Silver Burdett Co., Morristown, NJ 1985.
Biography of the famous diarist and her life in hiding.

Volavkova, Hana. *I Never Saw Another Butterfly.* McGraw-Hill, Inc., N.Y. 1964. Schocken Books, N.Y. 1978.
The Holocaust as revealed through the drawings and poetry of children in Theresienstadt (Terezin) concentration camp.

_____. *I Never Saw Another Butterfly.* Expanded Second Edition by the United States Holocaust Memorial Museum. Schocken Books, N.Y. 1993. Revised edition includes additional material.

Articles For Teachers

"If education implies preparing the individual and group for a better future, one function should be to teach civic virtues so students can become responsible citizens of the world."
—Claire Gaudiani, educator and author

INTRODUCTION

Four articles presenting background information and context useful to the lesson plans in this Guide are reprinted here. The topics include teaching about values, human rights, prejudice, and the Holocaust.

Herbert Buschbaum's "Why Do People Hate?" analyzes hate crimes as rooted in prejudice learned early and reinforced throughout childhood, demonstrating what can happen to human rights if prejudice is not confronted. He urges us all to actively teach our children *not* to hate.

"History of the Holocaust," "Children's History in the Holocaust," and "Guidelines for Teaching the Holocaust" are from the U.S. Holocaust Memoral Museum, which produces a number of useful documents to assist teachers with Holocaust education. These articles give a quick but excellent overview of the Holocaust.

The United Nations Declaration on the Rights of the Child is also reprinted in this appendix.

WHY DO PEOPLE HATE?

Herbert Buschbaum

Shortly after school opened last fall, more than one hundred white-robed "Christian Knights" of the Ku Klux Klan marched down the main street of Lenoir, North Carolina, a small city nestled on the edge of the Blue Ridge Mountains. The next day, racial fighting erupted at Lenoir's West Caldwell High School. Two black teenagers, Terry Wayne Maxwell and Randall Moore, were stabbed and killed by two white teenagers.

Last April 20, the racist Christian Identity Church in Portland, Oregon, celebrated the birthday of the notorious former German dictator Adolf Hitler. While church members listened to sermons on white supremacy, forty young neo-Nazi skinheads linked with the church attacked two 15-year-old black youths in Portland's Oaks Park, knifing one of them near-fatally.

In recent months, presidential candidates and prominent business leaders have been blaming America's deepening recession and loss of jobs on Japan. In January a group of white teenagers in Modesto, California, attacked an Asian-American couple in a grocery store parking lot, smashing the couple's car window with a tire iron, and upending their baby carriage, pitching their infant onto the concrete.

Typical Pattern

Experts say these incidents typify many racially or ethnically motivated attacks. All of the crimes were committed by white male teenagers; in each case, large groups attacked relatively defenseless victims; and each act of violence closely followed verbal expressions of prejudice and hatred by adults.

At one time these crimes were viewed as the isolated acts of alienated teenagers. But in recent years experts have come to understand crimes as more than just acts of teen rebellion. They see a direct link between the crimes and values shared by the attackers' parents, friends, and community.

The ugliest and most extreme violence, they say, is grounded in common, everyday prejudice, learned in childhood and reinforced by society.

Distrust

"We live in a prejudiced society that teaches us to distrust anyone different from ourselves," says Kent Koppelman, professor of human relations at the University of Wisconsin LaCrosse. "It's built into the language, the advertising, the images we receive. It's impossible to grow up with all of that stuff and remain free of it."

From early childhood, experts say American culture spoon-feeds its children white cartoon characters, white angels, and good guys in white hats. These subtle but powerful cues teach children what sociologist Abraham Citron calls "the rightness of whiteness" and instills in them illusions of a white-centered world.

Children also learn these biases from their parents—practically from birth. According to research conducted by the Anti-Bias Task Force in Southern California, by age 2, babies begin to notice differences in sex and race. By age 3, they begin to develop prejudicial attitudes. And at age 4 or 5, they cite race or sex as reasons for not playing with other children.

Once these early prejudices set in, they tend to take firm root. "The first associations [children] make, they hold on to for a long time," says Bill Sparks, an Anti-Bias Task Force member. "If the first thing they learn is untrue, it takes quite a while and quite a lot of effort to work them out of that."

Most children do not act on their prejudices violently. But for a few, this early prejudice begins to grow more extreme. They take the next step by engaging in name-calling and verbal harassment, researchers say. This escalating level of prejudice almost always precedes a violent physical attack, writes Gordon Allport in his classic book, *The Nature of Prejudice*.

But what makes some people take the final step, beyond expressions of bigotry, into physical violence? The primary reason is extreme insecurity, psychologists say. That's why teenagers, who are struggling with questions of identity and adulthood, commit such a great share of hate crimes.

"They build themselves up by putting someone else down," says Steven Salmony, a North Carolina psychologist who has studied young members of the Ku Klux Klan. More often than not, teenage hate criminals suffered as children from a lack of love or money, feeding their feelings of insecurity.

Mostly Young

Ironically, the attackers tend to come from the most powerful social group in America—white males. But most young white men who commit hate crimes are the so-called losers of the group, those who can't seem to make it in society and feel alienated and humiliated by their own lack of success.

"They're faced with the realities that they're going to make less money than their fathers made; that they're not going to be able to find those kinds of jobs," says Christina Davis-McCoy, executive director of North Carolinians Against Racist and Religious Violence. "Their anger, their indignation, their hopelessness, their helplessness is the place out of which they act."

Combining the extremes of hatred and insecurity in a group produces an explosive mix. Thrown together, a group of insecure individuals can bolster their flagging self-esteem by attacking helpless victims; that gives them a sense of power, Salmony says. Participation in a group also provides safety in numbers and the cowardly shelter of anonymity. On occasion, the group dynamic can produce a primal frenzy akin to a hunting pack. In 1988 Oregon skinheads murdered an Ethiopian man with baseball bats, smashing his skull to bits, indicating that the beating continued well after his death.

Resort to Violence

The linkage between hatred and insecurity means that violence often rises during war and economic hard times, when people may live in fear and are inclined to seek scapegoats for their problems; young men in particular may resort to violence to affirm their threatened sense of manhood.

During the Persian Gulf war last year, which engulfed the Middle East and Israel, attacks against both Arab and Jewish Americans surged. During the current recession, hate crimes have risen sharply, as they did during the recession of the late 1970s. Many analysts believe the recent wave of "Japan bashing" by politicians and the media has led to a series of attacks on Japanese Americans. In one incident in February, a Japanese-American real estate consultant in Camarillo, California, was killed just days after two youths yelled racial epithets at him blaming Japan for the loss of American jobs.

When hatred becomes so pervasive, no one in the culture is undeserving of blame. "Who taught our children to hate so thoroughly and so mercilessly?" asked New York City Mayor David Dinkins after a spate of racial attacks in January. An easier question might be, "Who didn't?"

THE HOLOCAUST: AN HISTORICAL SUMMARY

The Holocaust was the systematic, bureaucratic annihilation of six million Jews by the Nazi regime and their collaborators as a central act of state during World War II. In 1933 approximately nine million Jews lived in the 21 countries of Europe that would be occupied by Germany during the war. By 1945 two out of every three European Jews had been killed. Although Jews were the primary victims, hundreds of thousands of Roma (Gypsies) and at least 250,000 mentally or physically disabled persons were also victims of Nazi genocide. As Nazi tyranny spread across Europe from 1933 to 1945, millions of other innocent people were persecuted and murdered. More than three million Soviet prisoners of war were killed because of their nationality. Poles, as well as other Slavs, were targeted for slave labor, and as a result tens of thousands perished. Homosexuals and others deemed "anti-social" were also persecuted and often murdered. In addition, thousands of political and religious dissidents such as communists, socialists, trade unionists, and Jehovah's Witnesses were persecuted for their beliefs and behavior and many of these individuals died as a result of maltreatment.

The concentration camp is most closely associated with the Holocaust and remains an enduring symbol of the Nazi regime. The first camps opened soon after the Nazis took power in January 1933; they continued as a basic part of Nazi rule until May 8, 1945, when the war, and the Nazi regime, ended. The events of the Holocaust occurred in two main phases: 1933–1939 and 1939–1945.

I. 1933–1939

On January 30, 1933, Adolf Hitler was named Chancellor, the most powerful position in the German government, by the aged President Hindenburg who hoped Hitler could lead the nation out of its grave political and economic crisis. Hitler was the leader of the right-wing National Socialist German Workers Party (called the Nazi Party for short); it was, by 1933, one of the strongest parties in Germany, even though—reflecting the country's multi-party system—the Nazis had only won a plurality of 33 percent of the votes in the 1932 elections to the German parliament (Reichstag).

Once in power, Hitler moved quickly to end German democracy. He convinced his cabinet to invoke emergency clauses of the Constitution which permitted the suspension of individual freedoms of the press, speech, and assembly. Special security forces—the Special State Police (the Gestapo), the Storm Troopers (S.A.), and the Security Police (S.S.)—murdered or arrested leaders of opposition political parties (communists, socialists, and liberals). The Enabling Act of March 23, 1933, forced through a Reichstag already purged of many political opponents, gave dictatorial powers to Hitler.

United States Holocaust Memorial Museum. "The Holocaust: An Historical Summary," *Daniel's Story Videotape Teacher Guide*, November 1993, pp. 2–7. Reprinted with permission of the U.S. Holocaust Memorial Museum.

Also in 1933, the Nazis began to put into practice their racial ideology. Echoing ideas popular in Germany as well as most other western nations well before the 1930s, the Nazis believed that the Germans were "racially superior" and that there was a struggle for survival between them and "inferior races." They saw Jews, Roma (Gypsies), and the handicapped as a serious biological threat to the purity of the "German (Aryan[1]) Race," what they called the "master race."

Jews, who numbered around 500,000 in Germany (less than one percent of the total population in 1933), were the principal target of Nazi hatred. The Nazis mistakenly identified Jews as a race and defined this race as "inferior." They also spewed hatemongering propaganda which unfairly blamed Jews for Germany's economic depression and the country's defeat in World War I (1914–1918).

In 1933 new German laws forced Jews to quit their civil service jobs, university and law court positions, and other areas of public life. In April 1933 a boycott of Jewish businesses was instituted. In 1935 laws proclaimed at Nuremberg stripped German Jews of their citizenship even though they retained limited rights. These "Nuremberg Laws" defined Jews not by their religion or by how they wanted to identify themselves but by the blood of their grandparents. Between 1937 and 1939, new anti-Jewish regulations segregated Jews further and made daily life very difficult for them: Jews could not attend public schools, go to theaters, cinemas, or vacation resorts, or reside, or even walk, in certain sections of German cities.

Also between 1937 and 1939, Jews were forced from Germany's economic life: the Nazis either seized Jewish businesses and properties outright or forced Jews to sell them at bargain prices. In November 1938 this economic attack against German and Austrian[2] Jews changed into the physical destruction of synagogues and Jewish-owned stores, the arrest of Jewish men, the destruction of homes, and the murder of individuals. This centrally organized riot (pogrom) became known as *Kristallnacht* (the "Night of Broken Glass").

Although Jews were the main target of Nazi hatred, the Nazis persecuted other groups they viewed as racially or genetically "inferior." Nazi racial ideology was buttressed by scientists who advocated "selective breeding" (eugenics) to "improve" the human race. Laws passed between 1933 and 1935 aimed to reduce the future number of genetic "inferiors" through involuntary sterilization programs: about 500 children of mixed (African/German) racial backgrounds[3] and 320,000 to 350,000 individuals judged physically or mentally handicapped were subjected to surgical or radiation procedures so they could not have children. Supporters of sterilization also argued that the handicapped burdened the community with the costs of their care. Many of Germany's 30,000 Gypsies were also eventually sterilized and prohibited, along with Blacks, from intermarrying with Germans. Reflecting traditional prejudices, new laws combined traditional prejudices with the new racism of the Nazis which defined Gypsies, by race, as "criminal and asocial."

Another consequence of Hitler's ruthless dictatorship in the 1930s was the arrest of political opponents and trade unionists and others the Nazis labeled "undesirables" and "enemies of the state." Many homosexuals, mostly male, were arrested and imprisoned in concentration camps; under the 1935 Nazi-revised criminal code, the mere denunciation of an individual as "homosexual" could result in arrest, trial, and conviction. Jehovah's Witnesses were banned as an organization as early as April 1933, since the beliefs of this religious group prohibited them from swearing any oath to the state or

---

[1] The term "Aryan" originally referred to peoples speaking Indo-European languages. The Nazis perverted its meaning to support racist ideas by viewing those of Germanic background as prime examples of Aryan stock, which they considered racially superior. For the Nazis, the typical Aryan was blond, blue-eyed, and tall.

[2] On March 11, 1938, Hitler sent his army into Austria and on March 13 the incorporation (*Anschluss*) of Austria with the German empire (*Reich*) was proclaimed in Vienna. Most of the population welcomed the Anschluss and expressed their fervor in widespread riots and attacks against the Austrian Jews numbering 180,000 (90 percent of whom lived in Vienna).

[3] These children, called "the Rhineland bastards" by Germans, were the offspring of German women and African soldiers from French colonies who were stationed in the 1920s in the Rhineland, a demilitarized zone the Allies established after World War I as a buffer between Germany and western Europe.

serving in the German military. Their literature was confiscated, and they lost jobs, unemployment benefits, pensions, and all social welfare benefits. Many Witnesses were sent to prisons and concentration camps in Nazi Germany and their children were sent to juvenile detention homes and orphanages.

Between 1933 and 1936, thousands of people, mostly political prisoners and Jehovah's Witnesses, were imprisoned in concentration camps while several thousand German Gypsies were confined in special municipal camps. The first systematic round-ups of German and Austrian Jews occurred after Kristallnacht, when approximately 30,000 Jewish men were deported to Dachau and other concentration camps and several hundred Jewish women were sent to local jails. At the end of 1938, the waves of arrests also included several thousand German and Austrian Gypsies.

Between 1933 and 1939, about half the German Jewish population and more than two-thirds of Austrian Jews (1938–1939) fled Nazi persecution. They emigrated mainly to Palestine, the United States, Latin America, China (which required no visa for entry), and eastern and western Europe (where many would be caught again in the Nazi net during the war). Jews who remained under Nazi rule were either unwilling to uproot themselves, or unable to obtain visas, sponsors in host countries, or funds for emigration. Most foreign countries, including the United States, Canada, Britain, and France, were unwilling to admit very large numbers of refugees.

II. 1939–1945

On September 1, 1939, Germany invaded Poland and World War II began. Within days, the Polish army was defeated and the Nazis began their campaign to destroy Polish culture and enslave the Polish people, whom they viewed as "subhuman." Killing Polish leaders was the first step: German soldiers carried out massacres of university professors, artists, writers, politicians, and many Catholic priests. To create new living space for the "superior Germanic race," large segments of the Polish population were resettled, and German families moved into the emptied lands. Thousands of other Poles, including Jews, were imprisoned in concentration camps. The Nazis also "kidnapped" as many as 50,000 "Aryan-looking" Polish children from their parents and took them to Germany to be adopted by German families. Many of these children were later rejected as not capable of Germanization and sent to special children's camps where some died of starvation, lethal injection, and disease.

As the war began in 1939, Hitler initialled an order to kill institutionalized, handicapped patients deemed "incurable." Special commissions of physicians reviewed questionnaires filled out by all state hospitals and then decided if a patient should be killed. The doomed were then transferred to six institutions in Germany and Austria, where specially constructed gas chambers were used to kill them. After public protests in 1941, the Nazi leadership continued this euphemistically termed "euthanasia" program in secret. Babies, small children, and other victims were thereafter killed by lethal injection and pills and by forced starvation.

The "euthanasia" program contained all the elements later required for mass murder of European Jews and Gypsies in Nazi death camps: an articulated decision to kill, specially trained personnel, the apparatus for killing by gas, and the use of euphemistic language like "euthanasia" which psychologically distanced the murderers from their victims and hid the criminal character of the killings from the public.

In 1940 German forces continued their conquest of much of Europe, easily defeating Denmark, Norway, Holland, Belgium, Luxembourg, and France. On June 22, 1941, the German army invaded the Soviet Union and by September, was approaching Moscow. In the meantime, Italy, Romania, and Hungary had joined the Axis powers led by Germany and opposed by the Allied Powers (British Commonwealth, Free France, the United States, and the Soviet Union).

In the months following Germany's invasion of the Soviet Union, Jews, political leaders, communists, and many Gypsies were killed in mass executions. The overwhelming majority of those killed were Jews. These murders were carried out at improvised sites throughout the Soviet Union by members of mobile killing squads (*Einsatzgruppen*) who followed in the wake of the invading German army. The most famous of these sites was Babi Yar, near Kiev, where an estimated 33,000 persons, mostly Jews, were murdered. German terror extended to institutionalized, handicapped, and psychiatric patients in the Soviet Union; it also resulted in the mass murder of more than three million Soviet prisoners of war.

World War II brought major changes to the concentration camp system. Large numbers of new prisoners, deported from all German-occupied countries, now flooded the camps. Often, entire groups were committed to the camps, such as members of underground resistance organizations who were rounded up in a sweep across western Europe under the 1941 "Night and Fog" decree. To accommodate the massive increase in the number of prisoners, hundreds of new camps were established in occupied territories of eastern and western Europe.

During the war, ghettos, transit camps, and forced labor camps, in addition to the concentration camps, were created by the Germans and their collaborators to imprison Jews, Gypsies, and other victims of racial and ethnic hatred, as well as political opponents and resistance fighters. Following the invasion of Poland, three million Polish Jews were forced into approximately four hundred newly established ghettos where they were segregated from the rest of the population. Large numbers of Jews were also deported from other cities and countries, including Germany, to ghettos in Poland and German-occupied territories further east.

In Polish cities under Nazi occupation, like Warsaw and Lodz, Jews were confined in sealed ghettos where starvation, overcrowding, exposure to cold, and contagious diseases killed tens of thousands of people. In Warsaw and elsewhere, ghettoized Jews made every effort, often at great risk, to maintain their cultural, communal, and religious lives. The ghettos also provided a forced labor pool for the Germans, and many forced laborers (who worked on road gangs, in construction, or other hard labor related to the German war effort) died from exhaustion or maltreatment.

Between 1942 and 1944, the Germans moved to eliminate the ghettos in occupied Poland and elsewhere, deporting ghetto residents to "extermination camps," killing centers equipped with gassing facilities, located in Poland. After the meeting of senior German government officials in late January, 1942, at a villa in the Berlin suburb of Wannsee, the decision to implement "the final solution of the Jewish question" became formal state policy and Jews from western Europe were also sent to killing centers in the East.

The six killing sites were chosen because of their closeness to rail lines and their location in semirural areas, at Belzec, Sobibor, Treblinka, Chelmno, Majdanek, and Auschwitz-Birkenau. Chelmno was the first camp in which mass executions were carried out by gas, piped into mobile gas vans; 320,000 persons were killed there between December 1941 and March 1943, and June to July 1944. A killing center using gas vans and later gas chambers operated at Belzec where more than 600,000 persons were killed between May, 1942 and August, 1943. Sobibor opened in May, 1942 and closed one day after a rebellion of the prisoners on October 14, 1943; up to 200,000 persons were killed by gassing. Treblinka opened in July 1942 and closed in November 1943; a revolt by the prisoners in early August 1943 destroyed much of the facility. At least 750,000 persons were killed at Treblinka, physically the largest of the killing centers. Almost all of the victims at Chelmno, Belzec, Sobibor, and Treblinka were Jews; a few were Gypsies. Very few individuals survived these four killing centers, where most victims were murdered immediately after arrival.

Auschwitz-Birkenau, which also served as a concentration camp and slave labor camp, became the killing center where the largest numbers of European Jews and Gypsies were killed. After an experimental gassing there in September 1941 of 250 malnourished and ill Polish prisoners and 600 Russian POWs, mass murder became a daily routine; more than 1.25 million were killed at Auschwitz-Birkenau, 9 out of 10 were Jews. In addition, Gypsies, Soviet POWs, and ill prisoners of all nationalities died in the gas chambers. Between May 14 and July 8, 1944, 437,402 Hungarian Jews were deported to Auschwitz in forty-eight trains. This was probably the largest single mass deportation during the Holocaust. A similar system was implemented at Majdanek, which also doubled as a concentration camp and where at least 275,000 persons were killed in the gas chambers or died from malnutrition, brutality, and disease.

The methods of murder were the same in all the killing centers, which were operated by the S.S. The victims arrived in railroad freight cars and passenger trains, mostly from Polish ghettos and camps, but also from almost every other eastern and western European country. On arrival, men were separated from women and children. Prisoners were forced to undress and hand over all valuables. They were then driven naked into the gas chambers, which were disguised as shower rooms, and either carbon monoxide or Zyklon B (a form of crystalline prussic acid, also used as an insecticide in some camps) was used to asphyxiate them. The minority selected for forced labor were, after initial quarantine, vulnerable to malnutrition, exposure, epidemics, medical experiments, and brutality; many perished as a result.

The Germans carried out their systematic murderous activities with the active help of local collaborators in many countries and the acquiescence or indifference of millions of bystanders. However, there were instances of organized resistance. For example, in the fall of 1943, the Danish resistance, with the support of the local population, rescued nearly the entire Jewish community in Denmark from the threat of deportation to the East, by smuggling them via a dramatic boatlift to safety in neutral Sweden. Individuals in many other countries also risked their lives to save Jews and other individuals subject to Nazi persecution. One of the most famous was Raoul Wallenberg, a Swedish diplomat who led the rescue effort which saved the lives of tens of thousands of Hungarian Jews in 1944.

Resistance movements existed in almost every concentration camp and ghetto of Europe. In addition to the armed revolts at Sobibor and Treblinka, Jewish resistance in the Warsaw Ghetto led to a courageous uprising in April-May, 1943, despite a predictable doomed outcome because of superior German force. In general, rescue or aid to Holocaust victims was not a priority of resistance organizations whose principal goal was to fight the war against the Germans. Nonetheless, such groups and Jewish partisans (resistance fighters) sometimes cooperated with each other to save Jews. On April 19, 1943, for instance, members of the National Committee for the Defense of Jews in cooperation with Christian railroad workers and the general underground in Belgium, attacked a train leaving the Belgian transit camp of Malines headed for Auschwitz and succeeded in assisting several hundred Jewish deportees to escape.

After the war turned against Germany and the Allied armies approached German soil in late 1944, the S.S. decided to evacuate outlying concentration camps. The Germans tried to cover up the evidence of genocide and deported prisoners to camps inside Germany to prevent their liberation. Many inmates died during the long journeys on foot known as "death marches." During the final days, in the spring of 1945, conditions in the remaining concentration camps exacted a terrible toll in human lives. Even concentration camps never intended for extermination, such as Bergen Belsen, became death traps for thousands (including Anne Frank who died there of typhus in March, 1945).

In May, 1945, Nazi Germany collapsed, the S.S. guards fled, and the camps ceased to exist as extermination, forced labor, or concentration camps. (However, some of the concentration camps were turned into camps for displaced persons (DPs), which included former Holocaust victims. Nutrition, sanitary conditions, and accommodations often were poor. DPs lived behind barbed wire, and were exposed to humiliating treatment, and, at times, to anti-Semitic attacks.)

The Nazi legacy was a vast empire of murder, pillage, and exploitation that had affected every country of occupied Europe. The toll in lives was enormous. The full magnitude, and the moral and ethical implications, of this tragic era are only now beginning to be understood more fully.

CHILDREN IN THE HOLOCAUST

Up to one and a half million children were murdered by the Nazis and their collaborators between 1943 and 1945. The overwhelming majority of them were Jewish. Thousands of Roma (Gypsy) children, disabled children, and Polish children were also among the victims.

The deaths of these children were not accidental: they were deliberate results of actions taken by the German government under the leadership of Chancellor Adolf Hitler. The children were killed in various ways. Many were shot; many more were asphyxiated with poisonous gas in concentration camps or subjected to lethal injections. Others perished from disease, starvation, exposure, torture, and/or severe physical exhaustion from slave labor. Still others died as a result of medical experiments conducted on them by German doctors in the camps.

During the Holocaust, children—ranging in age from infants to older teens—were, like their parents, persecuted and killed not for anything they had done. Rather, Hitler and the Nazi government believed that so-called "Aryan" Germans were a superior race. The Nazis labeled other people they considered inferior as "non-Aryans." People belonging to non-Aryan groups, including children, were targeted by the Nazis for elimination from German society. The Nazis killed children to create a biologically pure society.

Even children who fit the Aryan stereotype suffered at the hands of the Nazis during World War II. Non-Jewish children in occupied countries whose physical appearance fit the Nazi notion of a "Master Race" (fair skin, blond-haired, blue-eyed) were at times kidnapped from their homes and taken to Germany to be adopted by German families. As many as 50,000 Polish children alone may have been separated from their families in this manner. Some of these children were later rejected and sent to special children's camps where they died of starvation or as a result of the terrible living conditions within the camps. Others were killed by lethal injections at the concentration camps of Majdanek and Auschwitz.

The experiences of children who were victims of Nazi hatred varied widely. Factors such as age, gender, family wealth, and where a child lived affected their experiences under German domination. Generally, babies and younger children deported to ghettos and camps had almost no chance of surviving. Children in their teens, or younger children who looked more mature than their years, had a better chance of survival since they might be selected for slave labor rather than for death. Some teens participated in resistance activities as well.

Children who were victims of the Holocaust came from all over Europe. They had different languages, customs, and religious beliefs. Some came from wealthy families; others from poor homes. Many ended their schooling early to work in a craft or trade; others looked forward to continuing their education at the university level. Still, whatever their differences, they shared one commonality: by the 1930s, with the rise of the Nazis to power in Germany, they all became potential victims, and their lives were forever changed.

Nazi Germany, 1922–1939

Soon after the Nazis gained power in Germany, Jewish children found life increasingly difficult. Due to legislation prohibiting Jews from engaging in various professions, their parents lost their jobs and businesses. As a result, many families were left with little money. Jewish children were not allowed to participate in sports and social activities with their "Aryan" classmates and neighbors. They could not go to museums, movies, public playgrounds, or even swimming pools. Even when they were permitted to go to school, teachers often treated them with scorn and even encouraged their humiliation by other students. Frequently, Jewish students were subject to being taunted and teased, picked upon and beaten up. Eventually, Jewish and Gypsy children were expelled from German schools.

Gypsy children, like Jewish children, faced many hardships in Nazi Germany. Along with their

United States Holocaust Memorial Museum. "Children in the Holocaust," *Daniel's Story Videotape Teacher Guide*, November, 1993, pp. 18–21. Reprinted with permission of the U.S. Holocaust Memorial Museum.

parents, they were rounded up and forced to live behind barbed wire in special municipal internment camps under police guard. Beginning in 1938, Gypsy teenagers were arrested and sent to concentration camps.

Murder under Cover of War

With the outbreak of World War II in September 1939, life became much harder for children all over Europe. European children of all backgrounds suffered because of the war, experiencing displacement, inadequate diets, the absence of fathers and brothers, loss of family members, trauma, and confusion. However, only certain groups of children were singled out for "extinction."

Wartime, Hitler suggested, "was the best time for the elimination of the incurably ill." Among the first victims of the Nazis were disabled persons, and children were not exempt. Many Germans, influenced by Nazi ideas, did not want to be reminded of individuals who did not measure up to their idealized concept of a "master race." The physically and mentally handicapped were viewed by the Nazis as unproductive to society, a threat to Aryan genetic purity, and ultimately, unworthy of life. Beginning almost simultaneously with the start of World War II, a "euthanasia" program was authorized personally by Adolf Hitler to systematically murder disabled Germans. Like disabled adults, children with disabilities were either injected with lethal drugs or asphyxiated by inhaling carbon monoxide fumes pumped into sealed mobile vans and gas chambers. Medical doctors cooperated in these so-called "mercy killings" in six institutions, and secretly at other centers, in Germany. Though some were Jewish, most of the children murdered in this fashion were non-Jewish Germans.

With the onset of war, Jewish children in Germany suffered increasing deprivations. Nazi government officials confiscated many items of value from Jewish homes, including radios, telephones, cameras, and cars. Even more importantly, food rations were curtailed for Jews as were clothing ration cards. Jewish children felt more and more isolated. Similarly, as Germany conquered various European countries in their war effort—from Poland and parts of the Soviet Union in the east, to Denmark, Norway, Belgium, France, and Holland in the west—more and more Jewish children came under German control, and with their parents, experienced persecution, forced separations, and very often, murder.

Throughout eastern Europe, Jewish families were forced to give up their homes and relocate into ghettos—restricted areas set up by the Nazis as "Jewish residential districts." Most of the ghettos were located in Nazi-occupied Poland; most were established in the poorer, more dilapidated sections of towns and cities. Ghettos were fenced in, typically with barbed wire or brick walls. Entry and exit were by permit or pass only; like a prison, armed guards stood at the gates. Families inside the ghettos lived under horrid conditions. Typically, many families would be crowded into a few rooms where there was little if any heat, food, or privacy. It was difficult to keep clean. Many people in the ghettos perished from malnutrition, starvation, exposure, and epidemics. Typhus, a contagious disease spread by body lice, was common, as was typhoid, spread through contaminated drinking water.

Some children managed to escape deportation to ghettos by going into hiding with their families, or by hiding alone, aided by non-Jewish friends and neighbors. Children in hiding often took on a secret life, sometimes remaining in one room for months or even years. Some hid in woodpiles, attics, or barns; others were locked in cupboards or concealed closets, coming out infrequently and only at night. Boys had it more difficult, because they were circumcised and could, therefore, be identified.

Children were often forced to live lives independent of their families. Many children who found refuge with others outside the ghettos had to assume new identities and conform to local religious customs that were different from their own in order to survive. Some Jewish children managed to pass as Catholics and were hidden in Catholic schools, orphanages, and convents in countries across Europe.

Every day, children became orphaned, and many had to take care of even younger children. In the ghettos of Warsaw and other cities, many orphans lived on the streets, begging for bread and food from others in the ghetto who likewise had little or none to spare. Exposed to severe weather, frost-bite, disease, and starvation, these children did not survive for long. Many froze to death.

In order to survive, children had to be resourceful and make themselves useful. In Lodz, healthy children could survive by working. Small children in the largest ghetto in occupied Poland, Warsaw, sometimes helped smuggle food to their families and friends by crawling through narrow openings in the ghetto wall. They did so at considerable risk, as smugglers who were caught were severely punished.

Deportation to Concentration Camps

The Nazis started emptying the ghettos in 1942, and deporting the victims to concentration camps. Children were often the target of special round-ups for deportation to the camps. The victims were told they were being resettled in the "East." The journey to the camps was difficult for everyone. Jammed into rail cars until there was no room for anyone to move, young children were often thrown on top of other people. Suffocating heat in the summer and freezing cold in the winter made the deportation journey even more brutal. During the trip, which often lasted several days, there was no food, except for what people managed to bring along. There were also no water or bathroom facilities and parents were powerless to defend their children.

Two concentration camps (Auschwitz-Birkenau and Majdanek) and four other camps (Chelmno, Sobibor, Belzec, and Treblinka) functioned as "killing centers." All were located near railroad lines in occupied Poland, and poison gas—either carbon monoxide or Zyklon B—was the primary weapon of murder. Upon arrival at these "death camps," individuals were "selected" to live or to die. Stronger, healthier people were often selected for slave labor, forced to work eleven-hour shifts with minimum provisions for clothing, food, or shelter.

Arrival at a killing center usually meant immediate death for babies and younger children. Children aged thirteen or older were frequently spared immediate gassing, and used instead for forced labor. Some who survived the "selection" process were used for medical experiments by German physicians.

The great majority of people deported to killing centers did not survive. For those who did survive the selection process, children and adults alike, life in the camps presented new challenges, humiliations, and deprivations. One became a prisoner; clothing and all possessions were removed; hair was shaved off; ill-fitting prison uniforms were distributed; one's name was replaced with a number often tattooed on the arm. Many people scarcely recognized their own family members after they had been processed in the camps.

Camp "inmates" were crowded into barracks fitted with wooden bunk beds stacked three on top of each other, and several people had to fit per level on the bunk beds, which had neither mattresses nor blankets. Lice were everywhere and contributed to the spread of disease, which was an ever-present enemy. Standing in roll-calls for extended periods in all kinds of weather and working long hours took its toll on everyone. Daily rations of food consisted of a small piece of bread and coffee or soup. As a result of these brutal living conditions, many people died. Few lasted more than a month or two. And, even among those that survived, one's vulnerability to "selection" had not ended at the point of arrival. The sick, the feeble, and those too exhausted to work were periodically identified and selected for gassing.

Liberation

Near the end of the war in 1945, the German concentration camps were liberated by Allied soldiers. By this time, many of the children who had entered camps as teenagers were now young adults. For most, the food and gestures of kindness offered by liberating soldiers were the links to life itself. Children who had survived in hiding now searched the camps trying to locate family members who might also have survived. Returning to hometowns, they had hopes that a former neighbor might know of other survivors.

It was rare for an entire family to survive the Holocaust. One or both parents were likely to have been killed; brothers and sisters had been lost; grandparents were dead. Anticipated reunions with family members gave surviving children some hope, but for many, the terrible reality was that they were now alone. Many found themselves sole survivors of once large extended families. A few were eventually able to locate missing family members.

Life as it had been before the Holocaust was forever altered. Though some individual survivors attempted to return to their former places of residence, Jewish and Gypsy communities no longer existed in most of Europe. Family homes had, in many instances, been taken over by others; personal possessions had been plundered. Because returning to one's home in hopes of reclaiming what had been lost was fraught with extreme danger, many young survivors eventually ended up instead in children's centers or displaced persons camps.

The future was as uncertain as the present was unstable. Many young people had had their schooling interrupted and could not easily resume their studies. Merely surviving took precedence over other concerns. Owning nothing and belonging nowhere, many children left Europe and, with assistance provided by immigrant aid societies or sponsorship from relatives abroad, they emigrated, usually to the United States, South Africa, and/or Palestine which, after 1948, became the State of Israel. There, in these newly adopted countries, they slowly developed new lives.

GUIDELINES FOR TEACHING ABOUT THE HOLOCAUST

The primary mission of the United States Holocaust Memorial Museum is to promote education about the history of the Holocaust and its implications for our lives today. This pamphlet is intended to assist educators who are preparing to teach Holocaust studies and related subjects.

Why Teach Holocaust History?

The history of the Holocaust represents one of the most effective, and most extensively documented, subjects for a pedagogical examination of basic moral issues. A structured inquiry into Holocaust history yields critical lessons for an investigation of human behavior. A study of the Holocaust also addresses one of the central tenets of education in the United States which is to examine what it means to be a responsible citizen. Through a study of the Holocaust, students can come to realize that:

- Democratic institutions and values are not automatically sustained, but need to be appreciated, nurtured, and protected;
- Silence and indifference to the suffering of others, or to the infringement of civil rights in any society, can—however, unintentionally—serve to perpetuate the problems; and
- the Holocaust was not an accident in history—it occurred because individuals, organizations, and governments made choices which not only legalized discrimination, but which allowed prejudice, hatred, and ultimately, mass murder to occur.

Questions of Rationale

Because the objective of teaching any subject is to engage the intellectual curiosity of the student in order to inspire critical thought and personal growth, it is helpful to structure your lesson plan on the Holocaust by considering throughout, questions of rationale. Before addressing what and how to teach, we would recommend that you contemplate the following:

- Why should students learn this history?
- What are the most significant lessons students can learn about the Holocaust?
- Why is a particular reading, image, document, or film an appropriate medium for conveying the lessons about the Holocaust which you wish to teach?

Among the various rationales offered by educators who have incorporated a study of the Holocaust into their various courses and disciplines are these:

- The Holocaust was a watershed event, not only in the 20th century, but in the entire history of humanity.
- Study of the Holocaust assists students in developing understanding of the ramifications of prejudice, racism, and stereotyping in any society. It helps students develop an awareness of the value of pluralism, and encourages tolerance of diversity in a pluralistic society.
- The Holocaust provides a context for exploring the dangers of remaining silent, apathetic, and indifferent in the face of others' oppression.
- Holocaust history demonstrates how a modern nation can utilize its technological expertise and bureaucratic infrastructure to implement destructive policies ranging from social engineering to genocide.
- A study of the Holocaust helps students think about the use and abuse of power, and the role and responsibilities of individuals, organizations, and nations when confronted with civil rights violations and/or policies of genocide.
- As students gain insight into the many historical, social, religious, political, and economic factors which cumulatively resulted in the Holocaust, they gain a perspective on how history happens, and how a convergence of factors can contribute to the disintegration of civilized values. Part of one's responsibility as a citizen in a democracy is to learn to identify the danger signals, and to know when to react.

When you, as an educator, take the time to consider the rationale for your lesson on the Holocaust, you will be more likely to select content that speaks to your students' interests and which provides them with a clearer understanding of the history. Most students demonstrate a high level of interest in studying the Holocaust precisely because the subject raises questions of fairness, justice, individual identity, peer pressure, conformity, indifference, and obedience—issues which adolescents confront in their daily lives. Students are also struck by the magnitude of the Holocaust, and the fact that so many people acting as collaborators, perpetrators, and bystanders allowed this genocide to occur by failing to protest or resist.

Methodological Considerations

1. Define What You Mean by "Holocaust"

The Holocaust refers to a specific event in 20th-century history: the systematic, bureaucratic annihilation of six million Jews by the Nazi regime and their collaborators as a central act of state during World War II. Although Jews were the primary victims, up to one half million Gypsies and at least 250,000 mentally or physically disabled persons were also victims of genocide. As Nazi tyranny spread across Europe from 1933 to 1945, millions of other innocent people were persecuted and murdered. More than three million Soviet prisoners of war were killed because of their nationality. Poles, as well as other Slavs, were targeted for slave labor, and as a result tens of thousands perished. Homosexuals and others deemed "anti-social" were also persecuted and often murdered. In addition, thousands of political and religious dissidents such as communists, socialists, trade unionists, and Jehovah's Witnesses were persecuted for their beliefs and behavior and many of these individuals died as a result of maltreatment.

2. Avoid Comparisons of Pain

A study of the Holocaust should always highlight the different policies carried out by the Nazi regime towards various groups of people; however, these distinctions should not be presented as a basis for comparison of suffering between them. Avoid generalizations which suggest exclusivity, such as "the victims of the Holocaust suffered the most cruelty ever faced by a people in the history of humanity." One cannot presume that the horror of an individual, family, or community destroyed by the Nazis was any greater than that experienced by victims of other genocides.

3. Avoid Simple Answers to Complex History

A study of the Holocaust raises difficult questions about human behavior, and it often involves complicated answers as to why events occurred. Be wary of oversimplifications. Allow students to contemplate the various factors which contributed to the Holocaust; do not attempt to reduce Holocaust history to one or two catalysts in isolation from the other factors which came into play. For example, the Holocaust was not simply the logical and inevitable consequence of unbridled racism. Rather, racism, combined with centuries-old bigotry, renewed by a nationalistic fervor which emerged in Europe in the latter half of the 19th century, fueled by Germany's defeat in World War I and its national humiliation following the Treaty of Versailles, exacerbated by worldwide economic hard times, the ineffectiveness of the Weimar Republic, and international indifference, and catalyzed by the political charisma, militaristic inclusiveness, and manipulative propaganda of Adolf Hitler's Nazi regime, contributed to the eventuality of the Holocaust.

4. Just Because It Happened, Doesn't Mean It Was Inevitable

Too often, students have the simplistic impression that the Holocaust was inevitable. Just because an historical event took place, and it was documented in textbooks and on film, does not mean that it had to happen. This seemingly obvious concept is often overlooked by students and teachers alike. The Holocaust took place because individuals, groups, and nations made decisions to act or not to act. By focusing on those decisions, we gain insight into history and human nature, and we can better help our students to become critical thinkers.

5. Strive for Precision of Language

Any study of the Holocaust touches upon nuances of human behavior. Because of the complexity of the history, there is a temptation to overgeneralize and thus to distort the facts (e.g., "all concentration camps were killing centers" or "all Germans were collaborators"). Rather, teachers must strive to help students distinguish between prejudice and discrimination, collaborators and bystanders, armed and spiritual resistance, direct orders and assumed orders, concentration camps and killing centers, and guilt and responsibility.

Words that describe human behavior often have multiple meanings. Resistance, for example, usually refers to a physical act of armed revolt. During the Holocaust, it also meant partisan activism that ranged from smuggling messages, food, and weapons to actual military engagement. But, resistance also embraced willful disobedience: continuing to practice religious and cultural traditions in defiance of the rules; creating fine art, music and poetry inside ghettos and concentration camps. For many, simply maintaining the will to remain alive in the face of abject brutality was the surest act of spiritual resistance.

6. Make Careful Distinctions about Sources of Information

Students need practice in distinguishing between fact, opinion, and fiction; between primary and secondary sources; and between types of evidence such as court testimonies, oral histories, and other written documents. Hermeneutics—the science of interpretation—should be called into play to help guide your students in their analysis of sources. Students should be encouraged to consider why a particular text was written, who the intended audience was, whether there were any biases inherent in the information, any gaps in discussion, whether gaps in certain passages were inadvertent or not, and how the information has been used to interpret various events.

Because scholars often base their research on different bodies of information, varying interpretations of history can emerge. Consequently, all interpretations are subject to analytical evaluation. Only by refining their own "hermeneutic of suspicion" can students mature into readers who discern the difference between legitimate scholars who present competing historical interpretations, and those who distort or deny historical fact for personal political gain.

7. Try to Avoid Stereotypical Descriptions

Though all Jews were targeted for destruction by the Nazis, the experiences of all Jews were not the same. Simplistic views and stereotyping take place when groups of people are viewed as monolithic in attitudes and actions. How ethnic groups or social clusters are labeled and portrayed in school curricula has a direct impact on how students perceive groups in their daily lives. Remind your students that although members of a group may share common experiences and beliefs, generalizations about them, without benefit of modifying or qualifying terms (e.g., "sometimes," "usually," "in many cases but not all"), tend to stereotype group behavior and distort historical reality. Thus, all Germans cannot be characterized as Nazis, nor should any nationality be reduced to a singular or one-dimensional description.

8. Do Not Romanticize History to Engage Students' Interest

One of the great risks of Holocaust education is the danger of fostering cynicism in our students by exposing them to the worst of human nature. Regardless, accuracy of fact must be a teacher's priority. People who risked their lives to rescue victims of Nazi oppression provide useful and important role models for students, yet an overemphasis on heroic tales in a unit on the Holocaust results in an inaccurate and unbalanced account of the history. It is important to bear in mind that "at best, less than one-half of one percent of the total population [of non-Jews] under Nazi occupation helped to rescue Jews" [Oliner and Oliner, p. 363].

9. Contextualize the History You Are Teaching

Events of the Holocaust, and particularly how individuals and organizations behaved at that time, must be placed in an historical context so that students can begin to comprehend the circumstances that encouraged or discouraged these acts. Frame your approach to specific events and acts of complicity or defiance by considering when and where an act took place; the immediate consequences to oneself and one's family of assisting victims; the impact of contemporaneous events; the degree of control the Nazis had on a country or local population; the cultural attitudes of particular native populations historically toward different victim groups; and the availability, effectiveness, and risk of potential hiding places.

Students should be reminded that individuals and groups do not always fit neatly into the same categories of behavior. The very same people did not always act consistently as "bystanders," "collaborators," "perpetrators," or "rescuers." Individuals and groups often behaved differently depending upon changing events and circumstances. The same person who in 1933 might have stood by and remained uninvolved while witnessing social discrimination of Jews, might later have joined up with the S.A. and become a collaborator or have been moved to dissent vocally or act in defense of Jewish friends and neighbors.

Encourage your students not to categorize groups of people only on the basis of their experiences during the Holocaust; contextualization is critical so that victims are not perceived only as victims. Although Jews were the central victims of the Nazi regime, they had a vibrant culture and long history in Europe prior to the Nazi era. By exposing students to some of the cultural contributions and achievements of two thousand years of European Jewish life, you help students to balance their perception of Jews as victims and to better appreciate the traumatic disruption in Jewish history caused by the Holocaust.

Similarly, students may know very little about Gypsies, except for the negative images and derogatory descriptions promulgated by the Nazis. Students would benefit from a broader viewpoint, learning something about Gypsy history and culture, and understanding the diverse ways of life among different Gypsy groups.

10. Translate Statistics into People

In any study of the Holocaust, the sheer number of victims challenges easy comprehension. Teachers need to show that individual people are behind the statistics, comprised of families of grandparents, parents, and children. First-person accounts and memoir literature provide students with a way of making meaning out of collective numbers. Although students should be careful about over-generalizing from first-person accounts such as those from survivors, journalists, relief workers, bystanders, and liberators, personal accounts can supplement a study of genocide by moving it "from a welter of statistics, remote places and events, to one that is immersed in the 'personal' and 'particular'" [Totten, p. 63].

11. Be Sensitive to Appropriate Written and Audio-Visual Content

One of the primary concerns of educators is how to introduce students to the horrors of the Holocaust. Graphic material should be used in a judicious manner and only to the extent necessary to achieve the objective of the lesson. Teachers should remind themselves that each student and each class is different, and that what seems appropriate for one may not be for all.

Students are essentially a "captive audience." When we assault them with images of horror for which they are unprepared, we violate a basic trust: the obligation of a teacher to provide a "safe" learning environment. The assumption that all students will seek to understand human behavior after being exposed to horrible images is fallacious. Some students may be so appalled by images of brutality and mass murder that they are discouraged from studying the subject further; others may become fascinated in a more voyeuristic fashion, subordinating further critical analysis of the history to the superficial titillation of looking at images of starvation, disfigurement, and death. Many events and deeds that occurred within the context of the Holocaust do not rely for their depiction directly on the graphic horror of mass killings or other barbarisms. It is recommended that images and texts that do not exploit either the victims' memories or the students' emotional vulnerability form the centerpiece of Holocaust curricula.

12. Strive for Balance in Establishing Whose Perspective Informs Your Study of the Holocaust

Often, too great an emphasis is placed on the victims of Nazi aggression, rather than on the victimizers who forced people to make impossible choices or simply left them with no choice to make. Most students express empathy for victims of mass murder. But, it is not uncommon for students to assume that the victims may have done something to justify the actions against them, and thus to place inappropriate blame on the victims themselves.

There is also a tendency among students to glorify power, even when it is used to kill innocent people. Many teachers indicate that their students are intrigued and in some cases, intellectually seduced, by the symbols of power which pervaded Nazi propaganda (e.g., the swastika, Nazi flags and regalia, Nazi slogans, rituals, and music). Rather than highlight the trappings of Nazi power, teachers should ask students to evaluate how such elements are used by governments (including our own) to build, protect, and mobilize a society. Students should be encouraged to contemplate as well how such elements can be abused and manipulated by governments to implement and legitimize acts of terror and even genocide.

In any review of the propaganda used to promote Nazi ideology, Nazi stereotypes of targeted victim groups, and the Hitler regime's justifications for persecution and murder, teachers need to remind students that just because such policies and beliefs are under discussion in class does not mean they are acceptable. It would be a terrible irony if students arrived at such a conclusion.

Furthermore, any study of the Holocaust should address both the victims and the perpetrators of violence, and attempt to portray each as human beings, capable of moral judgment and independent decision-making but challenged by circumstances which made both self-defense and independent thought not merely difficult but perilous and potentially lethal.

13. Select Appropriate Learning Activities

Just because students favor a certain learning activity does not necessarily mean that it should be used. For example, such activities as word scrambles, crossword puzzles, and other gimmicky exercises tend not to encourage critical analysis, but lead instead to low level types of thinking and, in the case of Holocaust curricula, trivialize the importance of studying this history. When the effects of a particular activity run counter to the rationale for studying the history, then that activity should not be used.

Similarly, activities that encourage students to construct models of killing camps should also be reconsidered since any assignment along this line will almost inevitably end up being simplistic, time-consuming, and tangential to the educational objectives for studying the history of the Holocaust.

Thought-provoking learning activities are preferred, but even here, there are pitfalls to avoid. In studying complex human behavior, many teachers rely upon simulation exercises meant to help students "experience" unfamiliar situations. Even when teachers take great care to prepare a class for such an activity, simulating experiences from the Holocaust remains pedagogically unsound. The activity may engage students, but they often forget the purpose of the lesson, and even worse, they are left with the impression at the conclusion of the activity that they now know what it was like during the Holocaust.

Holocaust survivors and eyewitnesses are among the first to indicate the grave difficulty of finding words to describe their experiences. Even more revealing, they argue the virtual impossibility of trying to simulate accurately what it was like to live on a daily basis with fear, hunger, disease, unfathomable loss, and the unrelenting threat of abject brutality and death.

The problem with trying to simulate situations from the Holocaust is that complex events and actions are oversimplified, and students are left with a skewed view of history. Since there are numerous primary source accounts, both written and visual, as well as survivors and eyewitnesses who can describe actual choices faced and made by individuals, groups, and nations during this period, teachers should draw upon these resources and refrain from simulation games that lead to a trivialization of the subject matter.

If they are not attempting to recreate situations from the Holocaust, simulation activities can be used effectively, especially when they have been designed to explore varying aspects of human behavior such as fear, scapegoating, conflict resolution, and difficult decision-making. Asking students in the course of a discussion, or as part of a writing assignment, to consider various perspectives on a particular event or historical experience is fundamentally different from involving a class in a simulation game.

14. Reinforce the Objectives of Your Lesson Plan

As in all teaching situations, the opening and closing lessons are critically important. A strong opening should serve to dispel misinformation students may have prior to studying the Holocaust. It should set a reflective tone, move students from passive to active learners, indicate to students that their ideas and opinions matter, and establish that this history has multiple ramifications for themselves as individuals and as members of society as a whole.

A strong closing should emphasize synthesis by encouraging students to connect this history to other world events as well as the world they live in today. Students should be encouraged to reflect on what they have learned and to consider what this study means to them personally and as citizens of a democracy. Most importantly, your closing lesson should encourage further examination of Holocaust history, literature, and art.

Incorporating a Study of the Holocaust into Existing Courses

The Holocaust can be effectively integrated into various existing courses within the school curriculum. This section presents sample rationale statements and methodological approaches for incorporating a study of the Holocaust in seven different courses. Each course synopsis constitutes a mere fraction of the various rationales and approaches currently used by educators. Often, the rationales and methods listed under one course can be applied as well to other courses.

United States History

Although the history of the United States is introduced at various grade levels throughout most school curricula, all states require students to take a course in United States history at the high school level. Including a study of the Holocaust in U.S. history courses can encourage students to:

- examine the dilemmas that arise when foreign policy goals are narrowly defined, as solely in terms of the national interest, thus denying the validity of universal moral and human priorities;
- understand what happens when parliamentary democratic institutions fail;
- examine the responses of governmental and non-governmental organizations in the United States to the plight of Holocaust victims (e.g., the Evian Conference, the debate over the Wagner-Rogers bill to assist refugee children, the ill-fated voyage of the S.S. St. Louis, the Emergency Rescue Committee, the rallies and efforts of Rabbi Stephen S. Wise, and the decision by the U.S. not to bomb the railroad lines leading into Auschwitz);
- explore the role of American and Allied soldiers in liberating victims from Nazi concentration camps and killing centers, using, for example, first-person accounts of liberators to ascertain their initial responses to, and subsequent reflections about, what they witnessed; and
- examine the key role played by the U.S. in bringing Nazi perpetrators to trial at Nuremberg and in other war crimes trials.

Since most history and social studies teachers in the United States rely upon standard textbooks, they can incorporate the Holocaust into regular units of study such as the Great Depression, World War II, and the Cold War. Questions that introduce Holocaust studies into these subject areas include:

1. The Great Depression: How did the U.S. respond to the Depression? How were U.S. electoral politics influenced by the Depression? What were the immediate consequences of the Depression on the European economic and political system established by the Versailles Treaty of 1919? What was the impact of the Depression upon the electoral strength of the Nazi party in Germany? Was the Depression a contributing factor to the Nazis' rise to power?
2. World War II: What was the relationship between the U.S. and Nazi Germany from 1933 to 1939? How did the actions of Nazi Germany influence U.S. foreign policy? What was the response of the U.S. Government and non-governmental organizations to the unfolding events of the Holocaust? What was the role of the U.S. in the war crimes trials?
3. The Cold War: How did the rivalries between the World War II allies influence American attitudes toward former Nazis? What was the position of America's European allies toward members of the former Nazi regime?

World History

Although various aspects of world history are incorporated throughout school curricula, most students are not required to take World History courses. It is in the context of world history courses, however, that the Holocaust is generally taught. Inclusion of the Holocaust in a world history course helps students to:

- examine events, deeds, and ideas in European history that contributed to the Holocaust, such as the history of anti-Semitism in Europe, 19th-century race science, the rise of German nationalism, the defeat of Germany in World War I, and the failure of the Weimar Republic to govern successfully;
- reflect upon the idea that civilization has been progressing (one possible exercise might be to have students develop a definition of "civilization" in class, and then have them compare and contrast Nazi claims for the "1000 Year Reich" with the actual policies they employed to realize that vision; the dissonance raised in such a lesson helps students to see that government policies can encompass evil, particularly when terror and brute force crush dissent).

Once again, since most teachers of European history rely upon standard textbooks and a chronological approach, teachers may wish to incorporate the Holocaust into the following, standardized units of study in European history: the aftermath of World War I; the rise of dictators; the world at war, 1939–1945; and the consequences of war. Questions which introduce Holocaust studies into these subject areas include:

1. The aftermath of World War I: What role did the Versailles Treaty play in the restructuring of European and world politics? How did the reconfiguration of Europe following World War I influence German national politics in the period 1919-1933?
2. The rise of the dictators: What factors led to the rise of totalitarian regimes in Europe in the period between the two world wars? How was anti-Semitism used by the Nazis and other regimes (Hungary, Romania, U.S.S.R.) to justify totalitarian measures?
3. The world at war, 1939-1945: Why has the Holocaust often been called a "war within the war?" How did the Holocaust affect Nazi military decisions? Why might it be "easier" to commit genocidal acts during wartime than during a period of relative peace?
4. The consequences of war: What was the connection between World War II and the formation of the State of Israel? Was a new strain of international morality introduced with the convening of the Nuremberg Tribunals? How did the Cold War impact the fate of former Nazis?

World Cultures

A course of world cultures incorporates knowledge from both the humanities and the social sciences into a study of cultural patterns and social institutions of various societies. A study of the Holocaust in a world cultures course helps students:

* examine conflicts arising between majority and minority groups in a specific cultural sphere (Europe between 1933-45);
* further their understanding of how a government can use concepts such as culture, ethnicity, race, diversity, and nationality as weapons to persecute, murder, and annihilate people;
* analyze the extent to which cultures are able to survive and maintain their traditions and institutions, when faced with threats to their very existence (e.g., retaining religious practices, recording eyewitness accounts, and hiding cultural symbols and artifacts); and
* apply understandings gleaned from an examination of the Holocaust to genocides that have occurred in other cultural spheres.

Government

Government courses at the high school level usually focus on understanding the U.S. political system, comparative studies of various governments, and the international relationship of nations. The Holocaust can be incorporated into a study of government in order to demonstrate how the development of public policy can become directed to genocidal ends when dissent and debate are silenced. Inclusion of Holocaust studies in government courses helps students:

* compare governmental systems (e.g., by investigating how the Weimar Constitution in Germany prior to the Nazi seizure of power was similar to, or different from, the Constitution of the United States; by comparing the Nazi system of governance with that of the United States);
* study the process of how a state can degenerate from a (parliamentary) democracy into a totalitarian state (e.g., by examining the processes by which the Nazis gained absolute control of the German government and how the Nazi government then controlled virtually all segments of German society);
* examine how the development of public policy can lead to genocidal ends, especially when people remain silent in the face of discriminatory practices (e.g., the development of Nazi racial and genocide policies towards Jews and other victim groups beginning with the philosophical platform elaborated in Hitler's Mein Kampf, continuing through the state-imposed Nuremberg Laws, and culminating with governmental policies of murder and extermination after 1941);
* examine the role of Nazi bureaucracy in implementing policies of murder and annihilation (e.g.,

the development and maintenance of a system to identify, isolate, deport, enslave, and kill targeted people, and then redistribute their remaining belongings);

- examine the role of various individuals in the rise and fall of a totalitarian government (e.g., those who supported Nazi Germany, those who were passive, and those who resisted both internally, such as partisans and others who carried out revolts, and externally, such as the Allies); and
- recognize that among the legacies of the Holocaust have been the creation of the United Nations in 1945, and its ongoing efforts to develop and adopt numerous, significant human rights bills (e.g., the U.N. Declaration of Human Rights and the U.N. Convention on Genocide).

Contemporary World Problems

Many schools include a Contemporary World Problems course at the senior high level which allows students to conduct an in-depth study of a topic such as genocide. The focus is usually on what constitutes genocide, and areas of investigation include various preconditions, patterns, consequences, and methods of intervention and prevention of genocide. A study of the Holocaust in a contemporary world problems curricula can help students to:

- comprehend the similarities and differences between governmental policies during the Holocaust and contemporary policies that create the potential for ethnocide or genocide (e.g., comparing and contrasting the philosophy and/or policies of the Nazi regime with that of the Khmer Rouge in Cambodia);
- compare and contrast the world response of governments and non-governmental organizations to the Holocaust with the responses of governments and non-governmental organizations to mass killings today (e.g., comparing the decisions made at the Evian Conference in 1938 to the U.S. response to the Cambodian genocide between 1974–1979, or the response of non-governmental organizations like the International Red Cross to the Nazi genocide of Jews during the Holocaust with that of Amnesty International to political killings in Argentina, Guatemala, Indonesia, and Cambodia in contemporary times); and
- analyze the relationship of the Holocaust and its legacy to the formation of the State of Israel.

Literature

Literature is read in English classes across grade levels and is also used to enhance and strengthen social studies and science courses. The literature curriculum is generally organized thematically or around categories such as American Literature, British Literature, European Literature, and world literature. Literature is capable of providing thought-provoking perspectives on a myriad of subjects and concerns that can engage students in ways that standard textbooks and essays do not.

Holocaust literature encompasses a variety of literary genres including novels, short stories, drama, poetry, diaries, and memoirs. This broad spectrum gives teachers a wide range of curriculum choices. Because Holocaust literature derives from a true-to-life epic in human history, its stories reveal basic truths about human nature, and provide adolescent readers with credible models of heroism and dignity. At the same time, it compels them to confront the reality of the human capacity for evil.

Because so many of the stories intersect with issues in students' own lives, Holocaust literature can inspire a commitment to reject indifference to human suffering, and can instruct them about relevant social issues such as the effects of intolerance and elitism. Studying literary responses to the Holocaust helps students:

- develop a deeper respect for human decency by asking them to confront the moral depravity and the extent of Nazi evil (e.g., the abject cruelty of the Nazi treatment of victims even prior to the round-ups and deportations; the event of *Kristallnacht*; the deportations in boxcars; the mass killings; and the so-called medical experiments of Nazi doctors);
- recognize the deeds of heroism demonstrated by teenagers and adults in ghettos and concentration

camps (e.g., the couriers who smuggled messages, goods, and weapons in and out of the Warsaw Ghetto; the partisans who used arms to resist the Nazis; the uprisings and revolts in various ghettos including Warsaw and in killing centers such as Treblinka);

- explore the spiritual resistance evidenced in literary responses which portray the irrepressible dignity of people who transcended the evil of their murderers, as found, for example, in the clandestine writing of diaries, poetry, and plays;
- recognize the different roles which were assumed or thrust upon people during the Holocaust, such as victim, oppressor, bystander, and rescuer;
- examine the moral choices, or absence of choices, which were confronted by both young and old, victim and perpetrator; and
- analyze the corruption of language cultivated by the Nazis, particularly in the use of euphemisms to mask their evil intent (e.g., their use of the terms "emigration" for expulsion, "evacuation" for deportation, "deportation" for transportation to concentration camps and killing centers, "police actions" for round-ups that typically led to mass murder, and "final solution" for the planned annihilation of every Jew in Europe).

Art and Art History
One of the goals for studying art history is to enable students to understand the role of art in society. The Holocaust can be incorporated into a study of art and art history to illuminate how the Nazis used art for propagandistic purposes, and how victims used artistic expression to communicate their protest, despair, and/or hope. A study of art during the Holocaust helps students:

- analyze the motivations for, and implications of, the Nazis' censorship activities in the fine and literary arts, theater, and music (e.g., the banning of books and certain styles of painting; the May 1933 book burnings);
- examine the values and beliefs of the Nazis and how the regime perceived the world by, for example, examining Nazi symbols of power, Nazi propaganda posters, paintings, and drawings deemed "acceptable" rather than "degenerate";
- study how people living under Nazi control used art as a form of resistance (e.g., examining the extent to which the victims created art; the dangers they faced in doing so; the various forms of art that were created and the settings in which they were created, and the diversity of themes and content in this artistic expression);
- examine art created by Holocaust victims and survivors and explore its capacity to document diverse experiences including life prior to the Holocaust, life inside the ghettos, the deportations, and the myriad of experiences in the concentration camp system; and
- examine interpretations of the Holocaust as expressed in contemporary art, art exhibitions, and memorials.

Conclusion
A study of the Holocaust can be effectively integrated into any number of subject areas. Sample curricula and lesson plans currently in use around the country have been collected by the United States Holocaust Memorial Museum and are available for reference purposes. For further information on the range of materials available and how to acquire copies of these materials for your own use in developing or enhancing study units on the Holocaust, please contact the Education Department: Schools and Children Division, United States Holocaust Memorial Museum, 100 Raoul Wallenberg Place, SW, Washington, DC 20024-2150; telephone: (202) 488-0400.

References
Oliner, Pearl M. and Samuel P. Oliner. "Righteous People in the Holocaust." *Genocide: A Critical Bibliographic Review*. Edited by Israel Charny. London and New York: Mansell Publishing and

Facts on File, respectively, 1991.

Totten, Samuel. "The Personal Face of Genocide: Words of Witnesses in the Classroom." Special Issue of the *Social Science Record* ("Genocide: Issues, Approaches, Resources") 24, 2 (1987):63-67.

Acknowledgments

Primary authors are William S. Parsons, Director of Education, Schools and Children, U.S. Holocaust Memorial Museum (U.S.H.M.M.); Samuel Totten, Assistant Professor of Curriculum and Instruction, University of Arkansas, Fayetteville.

Editorial suggestions were made by: Helen Fagin, Chair, U.S. Holocaust Memorial Council Education Committee; Sara J. Bloomfield, Executive Director, U.S. Holocaust Memorial Council; Alice M. Greenwald, Consultant (U.S.H.M.M.); Stephen Feinberg, Social Studies Department Chairman, Wayland Middle School, Wayland, MA; William R. Fernekes, Social Studies Supervisor, Hunterdon Central Regional High School, Flemington, NJ; Grace M. Caporino, Advanced Placement English Teacher, Carmel High School, Carmel, NY; and Kristy L. Brosius, Resource Center Coordinator (U.S.H.M.M.).

THE UNITED NATIONS DECLARATION ON THE RIGHTS OF THE CHILD, 1959

Another set of ideas that can help guide discussions of human rights issues, including concepts such as cultural diversity, prejudice, and ethical decision making, is the U.N. Declaration on the Rights of the Child, which was drafted in 1959:

1. All children have the right to what follows, no matter what their race, color, sex, language, religion, political or other opinion, or where they were born or whom they were born to.

2. You have the right to grow up in a healthy and normal way, free and with dignity.

3. You have a right to a name and to be a member of a country.

4. You have the right to good food, housing, and medical care.

5. You have the right to special care if handicapped in any way.

6. You have the right to love and understanding, preferably from parents, but from the government when you have no parent.

7. You have the right to go to school for free, to play, and to have an equal chance to be what you are and to learn to be responsible and useful.

8. You have the right always to be among the first to get help.

9. You have the right not to be harmed and not to be hired for work until old enough.

After a discussion of the history of the United Nations, teachers might want to post the above list prominently in the classroom. During discussion of the books featured in the Guide, when appropriate, teachers and students might refer to the Declaration. What rights were being violated for a particular character? Did these rights have anything to do with why immigrants to this country left their native lands? What rights did Hitler violate for the Jews, the Gypsies, and others such as the disabled? The U.N. Declaration on the Rights of the Child can help to ground discussion and provide a common thread between lessons.

Resources For Teachers

But for learning, heaven and earth would not endure.
—The Talmud

INTRODUCTION

"Resources for Teachers" offers four documents: an annotated bibliography, a videography, a list of organizations, and a list by author of the children's books featured in *The Spirit That Moves Us*, Volume I.

As you look through the bibliography, you will note that there is a wealth of information on some topics but almost nothing on others. We believe this phenomenon points to future worthwhile endeavors. We hope that as teachers use this Guide and note the deficiency of supplemental materials in certain areas, they will develop their own, sharing them with their colleagues.

The "Videography" is an annotated list of videos, many of which are not suitable for young children, but do offer much information for teachers preparing Holocaust lessons. Several of the videos on prejudice were produced for elementary school students.

Many national organizations offer information and educational programs on the concepts and issues presented in *The Spirit That Moves Us*. The "Organizations" section lists their addresses and telephone numbers.

PART ONE: ETHNIC STUDIES BIBLIOGRAPHY
GENERAL
Background:

Banks, James A. *Teaching Strategies for Ethnic Studies.* 5th ed. Boston: Allyn & Bacon, 1991.
Banks presents information, concepts, strategies, and resources for integrating content about ethnic groups into mainstream curricula. The majority of the book consists of chapters on the larger minority ethnic groups in the United States. Each chapter contains a chronology of key events; an historical overview; demographic data; key concepts and teaching strategies for primary, middle, and high schools; and annotated bibliographies for teachers and students. 538 pp., bibliographies, chronologies.

Banks, James A. and Cherry A. McGee Banks. *Multicultural Education*: Issues and Perspectives, 3rd ed. Seattle: University of Washington, 1997.

Gollnick, Donna M. and Philip C. Chinn. *Multicultural Education in a Pluralistic Society.* 2nd ed. Columbus, OH: Merrill, 1986.
Taking a different approach from most books on multicultural education, these authors present cultural overviews from the perspectives of socioeconomic status, ethnicity, religion, gender, exceptionality, and age. Additional chapters explore the pervasive influence of culture; why teachers need to understand their own cultural background as well as that of their students; and ideas for implementing multicultural education. Important concepts, such as the difference between race and ethnicity, are explained throughout the book. 291 pp., bibliography.

Miller-Lachmann, Lyn, ed. *Our Family, Our Friends, Our World: An Annotated Guide to Significant Multicultural Books for Children and Teenagers.* New Providence, NJ: R.R. Bowker, 1992.
As a reference work for teachers and librarians who want to explore multicultural children's literature, this book is invaluable. It contains detailed annotations, identified by grade level, of approximately one thousand books published between 1970 and 1990. It has chapters on the four largest minority ethnic groups in the United States—Native Americans, African Americans,

Asian Americans, and Latino Americans—as well as chapters on every region of the world. Each chapter has an introduction on contextual themes, publishing trends, criteria for selecting and evaluating books, and comparisons of book series, about groups or regions. Children's books that have shortcomings are identified and critiqued, with reasons why a popular book or book series should not be taught or should be taught only with reservations. 710 pp.

Perry, Theresa and James W. Fraser, eds. *Freedom's Plow*. New York: Routledge, 1993.

In a series of essays combining theory and practice, the authors set forth their belief that multicultural education is not a fad; rather, it is "the fundamental question to be addressed if schools are to be agents of democracy in an increasingly diverse United States." Part I advances the theoretical framework for reconstructing schools as multicultural democracies. Part II, written by teachers from diverse ethnic backgrounds, describes their experiences in creating multicultural classrooms. Several of these essays share a vision of early elementary education as a place for authentic intellectual work. Part III explores how a variety of cultures can contribute to the development of a new common culture and intellectual canon. Part IV advances a structure that includes the voices of peoples traditionally excluded from school curricula. 309 pp.

Resources for the classroom:

Anderson, William M. *Teaching Music with a Multicultural Approach*. Reston, VA: Music Educators National Conference, 1991.

The music of four cultures—African American, American Indian, Asian American (principally Chinese), and Latino American—is featured in this resource guide. Each section begins with the history, musical traditions, and musical instruments of the relevant culture. Lesson plans follow, most of which have examples of music for children to learn. The sections conclude with annotated bibliographies of books, filmographies, and discographies. 91 pp., bibliographies.

Blackaby, Susan. *One World: Multicultural Projects and Activities*. Mahway, NJ: Troll Associates, 1992.

Taking the same approach as *The Spirit That Moves Us*, this resource guide focuses on African-American, Native-American, Latino-American, and Asian-American cultures. Each section has a brief introduction to the relevant culture, activities for students, and detailed annotations of children's books. 96 pp.

Hayden, Carla D., ed. *Venture into Cultures*. Chicago: American Library Association, 1992.

This book offers information on the following cultures: African American, Arabic, Asian, Latino, Jewish, Native American, and Russian. Each chapter has a section on the identified culture; an annotated bibliography of children's books (principally K–8); and program ideas. The activities are easily adaptable to different grades, and expose children to aspects of culture such as festivals, food, poetry, games, and art. 165 pp., bibliography.

Heltshe, Mary Ann and Audrey Burie Kirchner. *Multicultural Explorations*. Englewood, CO: Teacher Idea Press, 1991.

This workbook of background information, lesson plans, classroom activities, vocabulary lists, and bibliographies on six areas around the world—Hawaii, Australia, Japan, Italy, Kenya, and Brazil—is designed to develop geographical skills and multicultural understanding. The activity-based lessons emphasize whole language, literary development, and experiential learning. 275 pp., bibliographies.

Knight, Margy Burns and Thomas V. Chan. *Talking Walls Teacher's Guide*. Gardiner, ME: Tilbury House, 1992. Also, *Talking Walls: The Stories Continue Teacher's Guide*, 1995.

The companions to *Talking Walls* and *Talking Walls: The Stories Continue* (annotated in Chapter 2), these guides feature activity-based lessons to teach geography, language, poetry, world culture, ethnic heritage, religion, science, math, art, architecture, and basic concepts related to numbers, color, shapes, and sizes. In Part 1, "Over the Walls," activities help students see ways in which walls are similar the world over. In Part 2, "Within the Walls," activities relate specifically to each wall. 65 pp. and 144 pp. respectively, bibliographies.

Teaching Tolerance Project. *Starting Small*. Montgomery, AL: Southern Poverty Law Center, 1997.

Supplemental children's books:

Aliki. *Corn Is Maize.* New York: Crowell, 1976.

> The story of corn—how it grows, how it was discovered and cultivated by Native Americans, its history, and its multiple uses today—is told for young readers. The author discusses the interdependence of people and corn, "the gift of the Indians," over many hundreds of years. 34 pp.

Brown, Ruth. *Alphabet Times Four.* New York: Dutton Children's Books, 1991.

> In this international ABC book, each letter is illustrated and given a representative word in English, Spanish, French, and German. A simple pronunciation guide explains how to say the words aloud. 28 pp.

Chermayeff, Ivan and Jane Clark. *First Words.* New York: Harry N. Abrams, Inc., 1990.

> The authors have compiled a list of "first words" for young children to spell in English and to repeat in French, Spanish, German, and Italian. Each word is illustrated with several different works of art collected from five Parisian museums. 32 pp., pronunciation guide.

Goodrum, Don. *Lettres Acadiennes: A Cajun ABC.* Gretna, LA: Pelican Publishing Co., Inc., 1992.

> The author has illustrated each letter of the alphabet with French and English words. The drawings for each letter show aspects of Cajun culture. A glossary gives the pronunciation and translation for each French word. 32 pp.

Provensen, Alice and Martin Provensen. *A Peaceable Kingdom: The Shaker Abecedarius.* New York: Puffin Books, 1981.

> A book of an animal alphabet, with more than one hundred real and imagined animals, was used by the Shakers to teach young children how to read. A brief afterword explains Shaker education and history. 36 pp.

AFRICANS AND AFRICAN AMERICANS

Background:

Murphy, E. Jefferson and Harry Stein. *Teaching Africa Today: A Handbook for Teachers and Curriculum Planners.* New York: Citation Press, 1973.

> Written principally for teachers of grades 5 through 12 but with much that is useful for teachers of the early elementary grades, this book provides condensed, practical information on African studies. The book presents Africa from an African rather than a European perspective. Chapters on geography, history, and the development of African nation states offer good background material for teaching African children's literature. Because it is twenty years old, however, teachers may need to update the information. 285 pp., bibliography, filmography.

Resources for the classroom:

Sullivan, Charles. *Children of Promise: African-American Literature and Art for Young People.* New York: Harry N. Abrams, Inc., 1991.

> In this anthology of poems, folk songs, literary pieces, paintings, and photographs, African-American history and art are explored for children of all ages. African-American history is traced from slavery to the twentieth-century Civil Rights movement. Published in an accessible format of short excerpts interspersed among many beautifully reproduced paintings and photographs, the book conveys the depth and breadth of African-American culture. 126 pp.

ASIANS AND ASIAN AMERICANS

Resources for the classroom:

Heinz, Elgin. *Stepping Stones: Teaching About Japan in Elementary Grades.* Mill Valley, CA: The U.S.-Japan Education Group, 1991.

> Since 1977 North American teachers have received fellowships to learn firsthand about contemporary Japan. This teacher's resource guide gathers lesson plans created by these "Japan Alumni."

The lesson plans cover a wide variety of topics, such as land and people, economic interdependence, and culture and customs. Although principally written for older elementary students, many of the plans can be adapted easily for younger students. Other lesson plans— learning simple games, identifying cultural values, practicing Japanese manners—are ideal for young students. A concluding outline of Japan's history puts contemporary Japan in perspective. 97 pp.

Japanese American Day of Remembrance Resource Guide. San Francisco: Day of Remembrance Curriculum Committee, 1991.

This teacher's resource guide gives a concise history of the internment of Japanese Americans during World War II and their postwar fight for redress by the government. A summary of the constitutional rights violated by the internment and a chronology of important dates in Japanese-American history are included. 38 pp., bibliography.

Li, Marjorie H. and Peter Li, eds. *Understanding Asian Americans: A Curriculum Resource Guide.* New York: Neal-Schuman Publishers, Inc., 1990.

This comprehensive book analyzes misperceptions and stereotypes about Asian Americans, offers classroom activities, advice on incorporating Asian-American studies into curricula, an extensive annotated bibliography, and chronologies of events and legislation pertinent to Asian Americans. Activities and annotated book entries are identified by grade level. Throughout, the authors recognize that Asian Americans represent a wide variety of cultures, so activities and bibliography entries identify specific countries or cultures. 186 pp., bibliography, chronologies.

Supplemental children's books:

Goldstein, Peggy. *Long Is a Dragon.* San Francisco: China Books and Periodicals, 1991.

Subtitled *Chinese Writing for Children*, the author shows how to make the basic strokes used in Chinese writing, how characters evolved from pictures, how characters combine to form new words, and how the Chinese language is pronounced. 30 pp.

Humanaka, Sheila. *The Journey: Japanese Americans, Racism, and Renewal.* New York: Orchard Books, 1990.

With a text illustrated by the author's paintings, this book describes discrimination against Japanese Americans in the 1930s, the incarceration of Japanese Americans during World War II, the simultaneous service of Japanese Americans in the military, and the struggle during the 1960s and 1970s to win reparations from the United States Government. The book is written for students in grades 5 and up, but teachers can simplify the story without losing its historicity and impact. 39 pp.

Kem, Peng and Diana Rudloe. *Cambodian Folktales.* Portland, ME: Portland Public Schools, 1987.

This is a series of eight short folktales written in Khmer and English. Most of them feature Judge Rabbit, a famous figure in Cambodian folklore. For children who want to further explore Khmer culture, these stories can be used to supplement *Judge Rabbit and the Tree Spirit*, annotated in Chapter 2, "Learning from Many Cultures."

JEWS AND JUDAISM

Background:

Greenberg, Irving. *The Jewish Way: Living the Holidays.* New York: Summit Books, 1988.

For teachers who want an in-depth study of Jewish holidays, this book is an excellent reference. Greenberg explains each holiday's background, ceremonial rituals, and religious significance. Taking into consideration the different branches within Judaism, he gives instructions for observance, stressing how the rituals, prayers, foods, and songs used to celebrate the holidays reflect and reinforce their central message. Of particular interest to Holocaust study is a chapter on Yom Hashoah, the Holocaust Day of Remembrance. 463 pp., bibliography, glossary.

Kushner, Harold S. *To Life! A Celebration of Jewish Being and Thinking.* Boston: Little, Brown and Company, 1993.

In an acclaimed book that is both a practical and a spiritual guide to Jewish traditions, *To Life!*

explores Judaism for Jews and Gentiles alike. Kushner explains prayer, holiday observances and life-cycle events, dietary laws, how Jews view Christianity, and why the world needs committed Jews. 304 pp.

Trepp, Leo. *The Complete Guide of Jewish Observance*. New York: Behrman House/Summit Books, 1980.

Subtitled *A Practical Manual for the Modern Jew* but equally accessible to non-Jews, this book presents Jewish observance as part of the cycle of the year and of life. Jewish customs are described from the standpoint of the major branches of Judaism: Orthodox, Conservative, Reform, and Reconstructionist. The book's comprehensiveness and readability make it both a practical guide and a general reference work for those who want to know more about Judaism. 370 pp., bibliography.

Resources for the classroom:

Ben-Asher, Naomi and Hayim Leaf, eds. *The Junior Jewish Encyclopedia*. 11th ed. New York: Sheingold, 1991.

This is a comprehensive, one-volume reference book of Jewish history, custom, communal life, biography, and religion written for middle and secondary students. It is, however, also useful for teachers and librarians. The articles are short but thorough, and do not oversimplify the complexity and richness of Jewish life. Teachers can use the encyclopedia to quickly fill gaps in their knowledge, and to encourage third and fourth graders to look up answers to questions about Judaism. 352 pp.

Chaikin, Miriam. *Menorahs, Mezuzas, and Other Jewish Symbols*. New York: Clarion Books, 1990.

Written for older elementary and middle school students but easily adapted for younger students, the author explains the meaning of a variety of Jewish symbols. Symbols such as angels, numbers, and the *Mikveh* (ritual bath) are described and connected to Jewish traditions. 102 pp., bibliography.

Supplemental children's books:

Edwards, Michelle. *Blessed Are You: Traditional Everyday Hebrew Prayers*. New York: Lothrop, Lee & Shepard Books, 1993.

This book presents thirteen prayers ideal for young children to learn and ponder. Each prayer is written in Hebrew, in a transliteration of the Hebrew, and in an English translation. Each prayer is also accompanied by a picture of three children and their everyday activities. The pictures tell stories without words, helping to explain when the prayers might be said. 30 pp.

Gross, Judith. *Celebrate: A Book of Jewish Holidays*. New York: Platt & Munk, 1992.

Told in simple language with colorful illustrations, this book explains the tradition, history, and celebration of ten important Jewish holidays. A pronunciation guide for Hebrew words important to the holidays is included. 30 pp.

Patterson, Jose. *Stories of the Jewish People*. New York: Peter Bedrick Books, Inc., 1991.

These stories supplement the history and traditions of the Jewish people. Some stories are legends from biblical times. Some are tales of folk heroes from the time of the Roman occupation of Israel. Others come from the Middle Ages, when stories were told of the many figures who defended Jews and of the evil viziers and demons who symbolized their enemies. 142 pp.

Poskanzer, Susan Cornell. *What Can It Be? Riddles about Passover*. Englewood Cliffs, NJ: Silver Press, 1991.

By asking and answering riddles, this book explores the history and customs of Passover for young children. Color photographs of a Passover seder help explain this important holiday. 30 pp.

Schnur, Steven. *The Tie Man's Miracle: A Chanukah Story*. New York: William Morrow & Co., 1995.

During Chanukah, Mr. Hoffman, who sells ties from a cardboard box, tells seven-year-old Seth a miracle story from his village in the old country. Mr. Hoffman ends up telling Seth about his family and about the Holocaust. *The Tie Man's Miracle: A Chanukah Story* is beautifully written with stunning watercolor illustrations.

NATIVE AMERICANS

Background:

Smith, Carter, ed. *Native Americans of the West: A Source Book on the American West.* Brookfield, CT: The Millbrook Press Inc., 1992.

Concentrating on Native peoples of the West but including brief histories of eastern Native American nations, this source book relies on prints and photographs from the Library of Congress to illustrate Native American life from the arrival of Europeans to the massacre at Wounded Knee. The text and pictures are supplemented by timelines of major events. 94 pp.

Resources for the classroom:

Caduto, Michael J. and Joseph Bruchac. *Keepers of the Earth: Native American Stories and Environmental Activities for Children.* Golden, CO: Fulcrum Publishing, Inc., 1989.

This book uses stories from a variety of North American Indian nations to teach children about their environment and Native American culture. Each story is followed by discussion questions and hands-on activities. The multidisciplinary activities are especially strong on science, ecology, and natural history lessons. The activities, emphasizing Native American relationships with nature, focus on four themes: sensory awareness of Earth, understanding of Earth, caring for Earth, and caring for people. 209 pp.

_____. *Keepers of the Animals: Native American Stories and Wildlife Activities for Children.* Golden, CO: Fulcrum Publishing, Inc., 1991.

This book continues the methods established in *Keepers of the Earth*. Here, the purpose is to help children understand, live with, and care for animals. It combines stories from North America's Native American nations with teacher background information, discussion questions, and multi-disciplinary activities about animals, ecology, and conservation. The activities are particularly strong in the sciences. As with *Keepers of the Earth*, this activity book encourages learning through direct, hands-on experience with animals and their environments. 226 pp., glossary.

_____. *Keepers of the Animals: Teacher's Guide.* Golden, CO: Fulcrum Publishing, 1992.

This guide supplements the information in the Introduction and Part 1 of *Keepers of the Animals*. It also provides additional text and readings keyed to the chapters of its parent book. For teachers who want more information about Native Americans, Chapter 2, "Native North American Stories: Window for Cultural and Environmental Understanding," offers a concise history and cultural study of the major North American Native American nations. 56 pp., bibliography.

Civilizations of the Americas. Austin, TX: Raintree/Steck-Vaughn Publishers, 1992.

Using text, maps, illustrations, and photographs of artifacts, this book tells the history of Native peoples in North, Central, and South America prior to European colonization. 80 pp., glossary.

Harvey, Karen D., Lisa D. Harjo and Jane K. Jackson. *Teaching About Native Americans.* Washington, DC: National Council for the Social Studies, 1990.

Organized around four concepts—environment and resources, culture and diversity, change and adaptation, conflict and discrimination—this resource for grades K–12 provides teachers with information and lesson plans. The authors offer practical guides for teaching about Native Americans that stress historical and cultural accuracy and warn about perpetuating negative stereotypes. For example, they offer advice on respectful terminology and methods for celebrating Thanksgiving that emphasize the true role of the Wampanoag people. 80 pp., chronology.

Kuipers, Barbara J. *American Indian Reference Books for Children and Young Adults.* Englewood, CO: Libraries Unlimited, Inc., 1991.

Of particular use for libraries, this book clearly explains evaluation criteria for choosing books about Native Americans. It also has suggestions for incorporating resource materials into the curriculum. It concludes with an extensive annotated bibliography of reference books for children. 176 pp., bibliography.

Slapin, Beverly and Doris Seale, eds. *Through Indian Eyes: The Native Experience in Books for Children.* 3rd ed. Philadelphia: New Society Publishers, 1992.

This is an indispensable resource guide for teachers who use children's literature about Native Americans. To begin, the book offers short articles by Native Americans on the experience of living in a culture that routinely denigrates and trivializes Native people's experience. Poetry by Native Americans supplements the lessons in these articles. The major portion consists of critiques of books about Native peoples, explaining why each children's book is or is not an accurate portrayal of Native American culture. The authors conclude with a section on how to review books for stereotypes. 312 pp., bibliography.

The Wabanakis of Maine and the Maritimes, by the American Friends Service Committee, 1989.
This guide contains a multiplicity of options and supportive materials for the classroom. Particularly impressive are the strong, vibrant, and well-documented contemporary sections and sections dealing with the broader picture of prejudice and discrimination.

LATINO AMERICANS

Resources for the classroom:

Beilke, Patricia F. and Frank J. Sciara. *Selecting Materials for and about Hispanic and East Asian Children and Young People.* Hamden, CT: Library Professional Publications, 1986.
Useful for both libraries and teachers, this book advances criteria for assessing community needs, selecting multicultural books, and preparing in-service training. Of particular interest to teachers are the chapters giving concise background information on subgroups comprising Latino and East Asian peoples (e.g., Cuban Americans, Vietnamese Americans). 178 pp., bibliographies.

PEOPLE WITH DISABILITIES

Background

Batshan, Mark L. *Your Child Has a Disability: A Complete Source Book of Daily and Medical Care.* Boston: Little, Brown and Company, 1991.
This book's title is somewhat misleading. Written for parents, it includes answers to many common questions about the education as well as the diagnosis and care of children with disabilities. This is a good teacher's resource for basic information on the definitions of, limitations imposed by, and methods for adapting and accommodating developmental disabilities. 344 pp., bibliography.

Biklen, Douglas, Diane Ferguson and Alison Ford, eds. *Schooling and Disability.* Chicago: The National Society for the Study of Education, 1989.
For teachers who want to investigate the theory and practice of integrating students with disabilities in the schools, the editors offer a series of articles by educators involved in this work. Of particular interest are articles on schools based on successful integration models, a look at what true integration entails, and parental and student perspectives on disability and education. 281 pp.

Resources for the classroom:

ACTION Office of Equal Opportunity. *Handicap Accessibility: A Self-Evaluation Guidebook for ACTION and its Grantees.* Washington, D.C.: U.S. Government Printing Office, 1992.
Teachers can use this short, straightforward publication to help students design an accessibility evaluation for their school. Part B of the Appendix, which is a checklist for building and site accessibility, is particularly handy. 43 pp.

Sygall, Susan and Cindy Lewis. *Global Perspectives on Disability: A Curriculum.* Eugene, OR: Mobility International USA, 1992.
The curriculum presents five detailed lesson plans, supplemental readings, and annotations of disability-related resources. The readings provide excellent background on specific disabilities, use of appropriate language to describe people with disabilities, human and legal rights, and accessibility. The lesson plan activities are written for secondary students but many are adaptable for elementary students. 170 pp.

PART 2: PREJUDICE AND DISCRIMINATION BIBLIOGRAPHY

Background:

Allport, Gordon W. *ABC's of Scapegoating.* 9th ed. New York: Anti-Defamation League, 1983.
    Allport outlines definitions of scapegoating, motives for and types of scapegoaters, forms of scapegoating and its effects upon its victims, and methods for combating scapegoating. 36 pp., bibliography.

_____. *The Nature of Prejudice.* 2nd ed. Reading, MA: Addison-Wesley, 1979.
    This is a landmark study on the nature of prejudice. The book examines all aspects of prejudice: its roots in individual and social psychology, its impact on individuals and communities, and varieties of its expression. Allport explores different kinds of prejudice, including racial, religious, ethnic, economic, and social. The book concludes with suggestions for prejudice reduction. 537 pp.

Baird, Robert M. and Stuart E. Rosenbaum, eds. *Bigotry, Prejudice and Hatred: Definitions, Causes and Solutions.* Buffalo, NY: Prometheus Books, 1992.
    Through case studies and analysis, the essays in this compilation present theories of prejudice and suggest methods for combating it by working towards solutions of the social problems arising from bigotry. 236 pp., bibliography.

Perlmutter, Philip. *Divided We Fall.* Ames, IA: Iowa State University Press, 1992.
    Subtitled *A History of Ethnic, Religious, and Racial Prejudice in America*, the author traces the development of American minority group relations from pre-Revolutionary to contemporary times. Chapters examine the nature of group identity; the social, psychological, and political dynamics of bigotry; the history of ethnicity; the relationship between education and prejudice; and the implications of majority and minority group relations for democracy. 402 pp.

Pettigrew, Thomas F., et al. *Prejudice: Dimensions of Ethnicity.* Cambridge, MA: Harvard University Press, 1982.
    In 1980 Harvard University Press published the *Harvard Encyclopedia of American Ethnic Groups*, a synthesis of literature on ethnic groups and ethnicity. This book reprints three articles from the *Encyclopedia*. The articles describe the nature of prejudice, historical discrimination, and governmental action against discrimination. 127 pp., bibliography.

Resources for the classroom:

Anti-Defamation League. *The Wonderful World of Difference: A Human Relations Program for Grades K-8.* New York: Anti-Defamation League, 1986.
    Twenty classroom activities, organized into seven primary objectives, are provided to help students learn through experience. The objectives focus on helping students to understand individual and group similarities and differences, to appreciate diversity, and to recognize the consequences of prejudice and discrimination. 23 pp., glossary.

Derman-Sparks, Louise. *Anti-Bias Curriculum.* Washington, D.C.: National Association for the Education of Young Children, 1989.
    Subtitled *Tools for Empowering Young Children*, this curriculum addresses bias issues related to race, gender, ethnicity, and disability. It gives suggestions for creating an anti-bias classroom environment, teaching children how to recognize and resist stereotyping, working with parents, and raising teacher consciousness. The curriculum contains numerous teaching strategies and classroom activities for children ages 2–5 which can be adapted for older elementary students. 148 pp., bibliography.

Japanese American Day of Remembrance Resource Guide. San Francisco: Day of Remembrance Curriculum Committee, 1991.
    This teacher's resource guide gives a concise history of the internment of Japanese Americans during World War II and their postwar fight for redress by the government. A summary of the constitutional rights violated by the internment and a chronology of important dates in Japanese-American history are included. 38 pp., bibliography.

Teaching Tolerance. *Starting Small: Teaching Tolerance in Preschool and the Early Grades.* Montgomery, AL: Southern Poverty Law Center, 1997.
    Five equity education programs are explored; designed to promote staff discussion and personal reflection on effecive ways of fostering respect for differences. Video and teacher's guide.

Supplemental children's books:

Humanaka, Sheila. *The Journey: Japanese Americans, Racism, and Renewal.* New York: Orchard Books, 1990.
    With a text illustrated by the author's paintings, this book describes discrimination against Japanese Americans in the 1930s, the incarceration of Japanese Americans during World War II, the simultaneous service of Japanese Americans in the military, and the struggle during the 1960s and 1970s to win reparations from the United States Government. The book is written for students in grades 5 and up, but teachers can simplify the story without losing its historicity and impact. 39 pp.

PART 3: HUMAN RIGHTS BIBLIOGRAPHY

Resources for the classroom:

United Nations. *Human Rights: Questions and Answers.* New York: United Nations Department of Public Information, 1987.
    Presented in an accessible question and answer format, this pamphlet explains the substance of U.N. human rights documents, the process for filing human rights complaints with the U.N., the status of enforcement mechanisms, and U.N. positions on current human rights problems. 54 pp.

Supplemental children's books:

Durrell, Ann and Marily Sachs, eds. *The Big Book for Peace.* New York: Dutton Children's Books, 1990.
    This is an anthology of selections celebrating peace. Different approaches—fantasy tales, true incidents, poems, pictures, songs— are used to explore the concept of peace. 120 pp.

Lucas, Eileen. *Peace on the Playground: Nonviolent Ways of Problem Solving.* New York: Franklin Watts, Inc., 1991.
    Exploring methods for resolving conflicts between individuals, groups, and nations, this book defines and gives examples of peace, violence, and methods of nonviolent conflict resolution. The author also includes examples of activities to promote peace. A list with addresses of children's peace organizations is helpful for children who want more information or want to become activists for peace. 63 pp., bibliography.

Scholes, Katherine. *Peace Begins With You.* Boston: Little, Brown and Company, 1989.
    Presenting a clear, simple explanation of the concept of peace, the book begins at the personal level, explaining how different people's needs and wants can become a source of conflict. It then explores the many ways in which conflicts can be resolved. From this starting point, the scope broadens, considering national and international issues. The book suggests that the best way to protect peace is to ensure that everyone is treated fairly. 38 pp.

PART 4: HOLOCAUST BIBLIOGRAPHY

Holocaust history:

Bauer, Yehuda and Nili Keren. *A History of the Holocaust.* New York: Franklin Watts, Inc., 1982.
    Bauer begins with a history of the Jewish people and of anti-Semitism, proceeds through a clearly written account of all phases of the Holocaust, and concludes with the Holocaust's immediate aftermath, the story of displaced persons, and the creation of the state of Israel. For readers grappling with the enormity of the Holocaust, Bauer offers a brief summary of his historical conclusions related to causes of the Holocaust, the difference between genocide and Holocaust, and his answers to theological questions. 398 pp., bibliography.

Berenbaum, Michael. *The World Must Know: The History of the Holocaust as Told in the United States Holocaust Memorial Museum*. Boston: Little, Brown and Company, 1993.
The three parts of the book address the Nazis' rise to power; ghettos and camps; and rescue, resistance, and the postwar period. Over two hundred photographs and many eyewitness accounts supplement the text. As it combines history, biography, and visual images in an easily readable style, this is a good introductory book to the Holocaust. 240 pp.

Wyman, David S. *The Abandonment of the Jews*. New York: Pantheon Books, 1984.
Wyman documents the degree to which all segments of the American population, including churches and the Jewish community, failed to act as quickly as needed, and in some cases obstructed efforts to rescue Jews from the Holocaust. The book's first part proves that by 1942 the "final solution" was well publicized in the United States. The second part deals with the struggle to move the government to action. Finally, Wyman examines the War Refugee Board, whose substantial efforts were nonetheless hampered by tardiness and the United States government's lack of commitment to rescue operations. 444 pp., bibliography.

The following are appropriate for secondary students but contain useful background for elementary age students:

Adler, David A. *We Remember the Holocaust*. New York: Henry Holt & Co., 1995.
This book uses the stories of survivors who were children or adolescents during the Holocaust to present a compelling history. Survivor accounts and photographs are woven together to explain European Jewish life before the 1930s, the violence of Hitler's rise to power, the struggle to survive in the ghettos and camps, and the Nuremberg trials. 147 pp., bibliography, chronology, glossary.

Altshuler, David A. and Lucy Dawidowicz. *Hitler's War Against the Jews. The Holocaust: A Young Reader's Version of the War Against the Jews*. West Orange, NJ: Behrman House, Inc., 1978.
Altshuler follows the text of Dawidowicz's classic history but simplifies it for younger readers. He also includes many photographs. Part One, "The Final Solution," describes German anti-Semitism, the life of Adolf Hitler, and the Nazi persecution of the Jews. Part Two, "The Holocaust," describes European Jewish experience: ghetto life, armed and spiritual resistance, and the ultimate fate of the Jews. The book does not emphasize the death camps or mass murder, so it may be used, carefully, with third- and fourth-grade children. 190 pp.

Rogasky, Barbara. *Smoke and Ashes: The Story of the Holocaust*. New York: Holiday House, Inc., 1988.
Rogasky's thorough history begins with the Holocaust's roots in European anti-Semitism, and proceeds to examine the process of the "final solution," the concentration and death camps, and armed resistance and rescue. Of additional interest are discussions of the roles of the United States and Great Britain, the Holocaust's uniqueness, and the Nuremberg trials. Maps, illustrations, photographs, and lists of numbers of persons murdered supplement the text. 187 pp., bibliography, glossary.

Rossel, Seymour. *The Holocaust: The World and the Jews, 1933–1945*. West Orange, NJ: Behrman House, 1992.
This history is supplemented throughout by firsthand evidence of the Holocaust: official documents, memoirs, diaries, journals, maps, and photographs. The book also is designed as a teaching text, with review and discussion questions at the end of each chapter. It touches on all of the major events and issues raised by the Holocaust: anti-Semitism, the Nazi rise to power, life in the ghettos and camps, resistance, and the Nuremberg trials. 191 pp., bibliography, chronology.

Stadtler, Bea. *The Holocaust: A History of Courage and Resistance*. West Orange, NJ: Behrman House, Inc., 1995.
An enduring question, why did the Jews not resist genocide, is answered in this book. Jews did resist. A second enduring question, why did governments and individuals not try to stop the killing, also is answered. The answer is a few, but only a few, did try. Stadtler addresses these two

questions by describing armed and spiritual resistance by Jews, and attempts by "Righteous Gentiles" to rescue Jews targeted for destruction. 210 pp., bibliography.

Resources for the classroom:

Margolis, Peppy. *Caring Makes a Difference. Responding to Prejudice, Genocide and the Holocaust: A K-8 Curriculum.* Lincroft, NJ: Center for Holocaust Studies, Brookdale Community College, 1990. Using many of the same books as those in *The Spirit That Moves Us*, this work references objectives, instructional activities, and instructional materials for building a curriculum. The curriculum for grades K–2 focuses on prejudice. For grades 3 and 4, it builds on prejudice lessons to teach children's Holocaust literature. 36 pp., bibliography.

Volavkova, Hana, ed. *I Never Saw Another Butterfly: Children's Drawings and Poems from Terezin Concentration Camp, 1942–1944.* New York: Schocken Books, 1978. This book of poems and drawings made by children in the "model ghetto" at Terezin, Czechoslovakia, shows how children experienced life in a concentration camp. Their art, a testament to the children who died, can be used to help children understand what life was like in a camp and to inspire children to create artwork based on their own feelings about the Holocaust. 80 pp.

Personal accounts:

Delbo, Charlotte. *None of Us Will Return.* Boston: Beacon Press, 1968. Delbo, a Gentile and member of the French Resistance until 1942, was captured and sent to Auschwitz. In powerful and poetic prose, her memoir helps readers to imagine the unimaginable. She takes readers to the world of Auschwitz's slave laborers: interminable roll calls, starvation and thirst, beatings, backbreaking and often senseless labor, and the daily death of her compatriots. She tells as well of friends who helped each other survive in the face of almost certain death. 128 pp.

Haas, Gerda. *These I Do Remember: Fragments from the Holocaust.* Freeport, ME: Cumberland Press, 1982. Haas is a Holocaust survivor, incarcerated in the Theresienstadt concentration camp, who until recently lived in Maine. In this book, she tells her story and those of seven other Holocaust survivors who experienced the Holocaust in different ways. The excerpts include recollections from a member of the underground, the diary of a "hidden child," and a memoir by a non-Jew who suffered under Nazi rule. Each account is preceded by an overview of its historical context. 283 pp., bibliography, glossary.

_____. *Tracking the Holocaust.* Minneapolis, MN: Lerner, 1995. This history of the Holocaust is unique in that it tells the author's own story of survival while explaining historical events. The book is enhanced by maps, photographs, and explanations of events taking place in the world at different points during the Holocaust.

Isaacson, Judith Magyar. *Seed of Sarah.* 2nd ed. Urbana, IL: University of Illinois Press, 1991. Isaacson, a frequent speaker on the Holocaust, lives in Auburn, Maine. In her widely acclaimed memoir, she describes a happy childhood in Hungary, brief internment in the "Mexico" section of Birkenau-Auschwitz, and a year as a slave laborer at a munitions factory in Germany. Unlike many memoirs, hers continues to the present. She recounts meeting her soldier husband in Europe after the war, and many years later, reunions with surviving friends in Hungary and Germany. 192 pp.

Wiesel, Elie. *Night.* New York: Bantam Books, 1960. One of the most-read books about the Holocaust, this "fictional autobiography" describes the protagonist's adolescence in Transylvania and his deep faith in God. His family is transported to Auschwitz, where his mother and sister die. He and his father survive, to be sent to the Buna concentration camp, and after a terrible journey, to Buchenwald. Wiesel confronts his readers not only with a literate, deeply moving account of camp life but also with questions about whether innocence and good survived Auschwitz. 109 pp.

Bibliographies and reference works:

Arad, Yitzhak. *The Pictorial History of the Holocaust.* New York: Macmillan Publishing USA, 1990. Prepared by Yad Vashem, Israel's Holocaust Remembrance Authority, this reference work features over four hundred photographs and maps accompanied by a concisely written history. The history proceeds chronologically, covering each phase of the Holocaust. Other information of interest is the fate of Jews in each Nazi-occupied country, the world's reaction, and post-liberation survivor efforts to reach Israel. 396 pp.

Drew, Margaret A. *Annotated Bibliography.* Washington, D.C: United States Holocaust Memorial Council, 1993. Designed to help teachers choose appropriate books for themselves and their students, the bibliography identifies books appropriate to middle school students, high school students, and adults. Each section is further divided into general and specialized history, biography, fiction, and art and literary criticism, making it easy to locate books that meet teachers' specific needs. 31 pp.

Gilbert, Martin. *Atlas of the Holocaust.* London: Michael Joseph/Board of Deputies of British Jews, 1982. Gilbert uses 316 original maps, supplemented by brief explanatory text, to trace each phase of the Holocaust. The maps document early random killings; mass expulsion of Jews from thousands of towns; the establishment of concentration, slave labor, and death camps; deportations; sites of resistance; and forced death marches. To personalize the movement and death of millions of Jews, Gilbert includes maps tracing the fate of individuals caught in the Holocaust. 256 pp., bibliography.

PART 5: ECOLOGY BIBLIOGRAPHY

Resources for the classroom:

Caduto, Michael J. and Joseph Bruchac. *Keepers of the Earth: Native American Stories and Environmental Activities for Children.* Golden, CO: Fulcrum Publishing, Inc., 1989. This book uses stories from a variety of North American Indian nations to teach children about their environment and Native American culture. Each story is followed by discussion questions and hands-on activities. The multidisciplinary activities are especially strong on science, ecology, and natural history lessons. The activities, emphasizing Native American relationships with nature, focus on four themes: sensory awareness of Earth, understanding of Earth, caring for Earth, and caring for people. 209 pp.

Supplemental children's books:

Foster, Joanna. *Cartons, Cans, and Orange Peels: Where Does Your Garbage Go?* New York: Clarion Books, 1991. Written for older children but easily adapted for the early elementary grades, this book explains why garbage has become a serious problem. It explores ways people can make better use of waste products. Chapters explain landfills, incinerators, recycling, and new ways to think about garbage. 64 pp., bibliography, glossary.

Kalbacken, Joan and Emilie U. Lepthion. *Recycling.* Chicago: Children's Press, 1991. The authors explain why recycling is important, what materials can be recycled, how they are recycled, and recycling's benefits to the community. 48 pp., glossary.

Stille, Darlene R. *Ozone Hole.* Chicago: Children's Press, 1991. Stille explains different types of ozone, how ozone is produced, the consequences of the ozone hole in the atmosphere, and ways to get rid of "bad" ozone. 47 pp., glossary.

PART 6: TEACHING STRATEGIES BIBLIOGRAPHY

Byrnes, Dr. Deborah. *Teacher, They Call Me A_____!* Utah State Department of Education. This book by Byrnes and the Utah State Department of Education is a collection of sixty-nine classroom activities for the elementary school student. Teachers have found this book very useful in raising children's levels of awareness, understanding, and tolerance of difference.

Egan, Kieran. *Teaching as Storytelling: An Alternative Approach to Teaching and Curriculum in the Elementary School.* Chicago: University of Chicago Press, 1989.
  Egan explains how to use the power of the story form to teach content more engagingly and meaningfully. He develops an alternative model to the usual procedures for planning lessons, giving examples of how to apply this model to content in social studies, history, language arts, science, and math by stimulating children's imaginations. 122 pp.

Johnson, Lauri and Sally Smith. *Dealing with Diversity through Multicultural Fiction: Library-Classroom Partnerships.* Chicago: American Library Association, 1993.
  This practical guide shows how to design a multicultural literature-based program to develop critical reading skills and awareness of stereotyping. Although designed for adolescents, the program's concept—multicultural literature selection, a thematic approach to literature, and models for collaboration among teachers, librarians, and administrators—is equally applicable to programs in the early elementary grades. 106 pp.

Meagher, Laura. *Teaching Children about Global Awareness.* New York: The Crossroad Publishing Co., Inc., 1991.
  Meagher defines global awareness education as an appreciation of the common humanity and diversity of people and cultures. She argues that children need awareness of the tensions between self-interest and responsibility, of basic facts about geography and economic development, of human rights and justice, and of advocacy skills for an enhanced quality of human life. She offers educational theory, practical applications, and specific activities for infusing the school curriculum with global awareness. Of particular interest are ideas for creating or modifying traditional disciplines to reflect the experience of people from diverse cultures. 144 pp., bibliography, glossary.

Paul, Richard, et al. *Critical Thinking Handbook: Grades K-3rd.* Sonoma State University, CA: Foundation for Critical Thinking, 1990.
  Subtitled *A Guide for Remodeling Lesson Plans in Language Arts, Social Studies, and Science,* these handbooks offer theory and application for teaching critical thinking skills. Part 1 includes examples of grade-specific revised lesson plans for different disciplines. Each plan shows the traditional didactic method, a critique of what is not learned by students, and a revised plan with discussion questions, activities, and techniques for developing critical thinking skills. Part 2 explains the theory of teaching critical thinking, giving ideas for staff development, curriculum change, and multicultural education. 396 pp., bibliography, glossary.

Teaching Tolerance. *Starting Small: Teaching Tolerance in Preschool and the Early Grades.* Montgomery, AL: Southern Poverty Law Center, 1997.
  Five equity education programs are explored; designed to promote staff discussion and personal reflection on effective ways of fostering respect for differences. Video and teacher's guide.

PART 7: VIDEOGRAPHY

VIDEOS FOR STUDENTS

(Teachers: Please preview the videos to make sure they are appropriate for your students.)

Appreciating others:

African Story Magic, 27 minutes.
  Kwaku visits his roots and sees the wisdom of his ancestors. He returns home with new self-confidence and strength.

Behind the Mask, 8 minutes.

Using artwork created by children and a script based on their perceptions of the world around them, this imaginative video is an exploration of the uniqueness of each individual and the similarities that unite us all. The video develops an understanding of the manifestations of prejudice while it teaches an appreciation of difference.

Brushstrokes, 7 minutes.

This short animated film demonstrates how prejudice affects the way we behave toward one another.

Doctor in the Sky, 8 minutes.

This animated video presents a doctor in space who is faced with a very ill patient—the Earth. Symptoms of illness include weapons, war and poverty. The doctor diagnoses the trouble, gives the right medicine (basic freedoms and rights of man) and sends Earth to recuperate.

Henry's Decision, 26 minutes.

The universal problem of acceptance, rejection, and peer pressure is explored in *Henry's Decision*. Henry, an awkward fifth grader, faces a dilemma when Brian, a small, shy newcomer replaces him as the object of ridicule. Despite the temptation to join the group and bully the newcomer, Henry resolves to treat Brian with kindness, drawing the group together in an atmosphere of mutual trust and appreciation.

How We're Different and Alike, 10 minutes.

This short film features four children of diverse ethnic backgrounds exploring the things they all have in common and those that make them different from each other.

Molly's Pilgrim, 24 minutes.

Winner of an Academy Award for Best Short Feature, this is the story of a nine-year-old Russian-Jewish girl who is the object of her classmates taunts because of her foreign accent, strange ways, and peculiar clothes. When each child makes a doll for a class display of the first Thanksgiving, Molly brings a very different looking doll: a Russian-Jewish doll. This leads the children to understand Molly and her family's search for religious freedom.

Neighbors, 8 minutes.

A gentle, humorous, imaginative fiction on the theme of "nimby" (not in my backyard), this short video demonstrates the value of diversity and human differences. A family of mimes moves into an invisible house in a typical middle class neighborhood; and, despite the open, warm attempts by the father, mother, and son at neighborliness, the neighbors are scandalized by their difference—differences that are amusing and delightful to the audience.

Positively Native, 15 minutes, with teacher's guide.

A Native American boy makes a video about his life to try to counter the stereotypes he must contend with; he tries to come up with other ways to educate people about Native American life.

Rapsody in Orange, 10 minutes.

An award-winning musical documentary of Boston's historic Orange Line, one of the nation's oldest elevated railway stations. Set to original rap music, it is a video journey between six elevated stations. As the train travels through various ethnic neighborhoods, the video shows the lack of tolerance and understanding among the riders.

Set Straight on Bullies, 18 minutes.

This drama shows how responsible teachers and parents can remedy the injustice and modify the behavior of students who ostracize their classmates. It brings to light the damaging effect bullying has on all concerned.

Shalom Sesame, 30 minutes.

The culture, history, values, and traditions of the Jewish people and Israel are presented in an adaptation of the well-beloved American TV program *Sesame Street*. Produced in five videocassettes—The Land of Israel; Tel Aviv; Kibbutz; The People of Israel; Jerusalem—this program is performed in English and introduces children to the Hebrew language. A great teaching aid for Jewish grade schools.

Sound of Sunshine, Sound of Rain, 14 minutes.

This animated production brings viewers into the intimate world of sound and touch of a blind seven-year-old black child. His world of fantasy and imagination contrasts sharply with the world of reality—a harsh one, which limits the horizons of the handicapped, the poor, and people of color.

Vandalism: It's a Dog's Life, 12 minutes.

This animated film shows how a really "nice kid," Paul, becomes a vandal. Told from the point of view of his pet dog Tiger, we see how easily a person's irresponsible behavior can lead to vandalizing; and how damaging someone's property affects the instigator as well as others. Eventually, Paul learns his lesson.

The World at My Door, 15 minutes, with teacher's guide.

When her classmates make fun of her new haircut, a young girl learns that prejudice is an important issue in her life even though the town she lives in is ethnically homogeneous.

The Holocaust:

Just a Diary, 30 minutes.

The story of Anne Frank is told by a young Dutch woman who is going to act the part of Anne Frank in a play. Through studying Anne's diary and immersing herself in the environment of Anne's hiding place, she is able to more fully understand the child-woman she is to portray. Excerpts from the diary, documentary film, and dramatizations are used. Some subtitles.

Life of Anne Frank, 26 minutes.

Using photos and Anne's diary, the video shows the family's home life in Germany, their lives in Holland before and during World War II, their being discovered and shipped to the concentration camps, and their final destiny. There is much historical background on the life and destruction of Jewish communities in Germany and Holland.

The Holocaust: rescue and resistance:

Miracle at Moreaux: Wonderworks, 58 minutes.

Based on the book *Twenty and Ten*, by Clair Huchet Bishop, (See Annotated Bibliography for a description), this film tells the fictional story of a group of Catholic children who shelter a group of Jewish children and go to great lengths to hide them when the Nazis visit their school.

VIDEOS FOR TEACHERS

Prejudice and anti-Semitism:

The Longest Hatred: The History of Anti-Semitism, 2hr. 30 minutes.

This PBS documentary traces anti-Semitism through art, cartoons, and film, with commentary from scholars, journalists, clerics, and politicians, to demonstrate the religious and historic origins and course of anti-Semitism.

Prejudice: Answering Children's Questions, 75 minutes.

This 1992 ABC News special features an audience of diverse young people, scientists, and reporters who investigate the roots and effects of prejudice. The program is a good discussion of, and challenge to, stereotypes based on ethnicity, sex, religion, and disability.

The Shadow of Hate: A History of Intolerance in America, 40 minutes.

"He didn't look like one of us." To many residents of Atlanta in 1913, this was reason enough to suspect Leo Frank of murder. For some, it was reason enough to hang him. It's a story as old as humanity—pointing the finger at those who don't look or act or think like we do.

Starting Small: Teaching Tolerance in Preschool and the Early Grades, 58 minutes, closed-captioned.

Five equity education programs are explored; designed to promote staff discussion and personal reflection on effective ways of fostering respect for differences. Teacher's guide included.

Video Vignettes: A World of Difference Training Program, 11 minutes, with discussion guide.

Three reenactments of real-life situations, each designed to illustrate how stereotyping can lead to biased treatment, provide educators with an effective teaching tool for sensitizing participants to the subtleties of prejudice. The vignettes include "Ethnic Humor" and how it perpetuates stereotypes; "The Art Exhibit" which explores freedom of expression and social responsibility; and "Routine Check" which examines how group generalizations influence everyday life. The discussion guide provides group leaders with "how-to's" for generating honest, open discussion and includes detailed questions and suggested follow-up activities.

The Holocaust:

Courage to Care, 28 minutes, with discussion guide.

This video is an unforgettable encounter with ordinary people who refused to succumb to Nazi tyranny. While others "followed orders," these people followed their consciences, risking their lives to save Jews. The deeds they recall refute allegations that individuals were powerless against the might of the Third Reich. Their acts were exceptional in an era marked by apathy and complicity.

Genocide, 121 minutes.

Narrated by Orson Welles and Elizabeth Taylor and winner of a Best Documentary Academy Award, this excellent film explains the Nazi attempt to destroy European Jews. It contains graphic footage of mass murder and the death camps.

Ghetto Life, 19 minutes.

The ghetto was one vehicle used by the Nazis to reduce the Jewish population through starvation and disease. This film describes ghetto conditions, Jewish efforts to survive, and the rule of the *Judenrat*, the Jewish council.

Maine Survivors Remember the Holocaust, 43 minutes.

This documentary presents a clear compelling introduction to the Holocaust for general audiences. Interviews with eight Maine survivors and an American liberator propel the viewer through this tragic history.

Persecuted and Forgotten: The Gypsies of Auschwitz, 54 minutes.

A group of German Gypsies, many of them Holocaust survivors, return to Auschwitz, offering testimony on the attempted annihilation of their people. Many also reveal the discrimination they still face today.

Purple Triangles, 25 minutes.

A story of courage and faith as told by the Kusserow family who, because they were Jehovah's Witnesses, were hunted and persecuted by the Nazis.

Triumph of Memory, 30 minutes.

Among the inmates of concentration camps in World War II, there were men and women "non-Jews" who were interned for their resistance to the Nazis. Four of these who fought and survived testify to the suffering of millions in the camps and bear witness to the uniqueness of the Holocaust. Though each speaks from a different perspective, collectively they provide testimony to a historical reality: "Not all victims of the Nazis were Jews, but all Jews were victims."

RESOURCES FOR TEACHERS: HOLOCAUST AND HUMAN RIGHTS RESOURCE ORGANIZATIONS

Holocaust Human Rights Center of Maine
P.O. Box 4645
Augusta, ME 04330-1644
(207) 993-2620

U.S. Holocaust Memorial Museum
100 Raoul Wallenberg Place, SW
Washington, DC 20024
(202) 488-0400

Anti-Defamation League of B'nai B'rith
823 United Nations Plaza
New York, NY 10017
(212) 867-0779

Facing History and Ourselves
16 Hurd Road
Brookline, MA 02146-6919
(617) 232-1595

Southern Poverty Law Center
400 Washington Avenue
Montgomery, AL 36195
(205) 264-0286

The Wiesenthal Center
Museum of Tolerance
9786 West Pico Blvd.
Los Angeles, CA. 90035
(800) 900-9036

RESOURCES FOR TEACHERS: RECOMMENDED CHILDREN'S BOOKS

Aardema, Verna. *Bringing the Rain to Kapiti Plain*. New York: Dial Books for Young Readers, 1981.
_____. *Why Mosquitoes Buzz in People's Ears*. New York: Dial Books for Young Readers, 1975.
Ackerman, Karen. *The Night Crossing*. New York: Random House, Inc., 1995.
Adler, David A. *The Number on My Grandfather's Arm*. New York: Union of American Hebrew Congregations (UAHC) Press, 1987.
_____. *A Picture Book of Anne Frank*. New York: Holiday House, Inc., 1993.
Adoff, Arnold. *Black Is Brown Is Tan*. New York: Harper Trophy, 1973.
Ancona, George. *POWWOW*. San Diego: Harcourt Brace & Company, 1993.
Baylor, Byrd. *Hawk, I'm Your Brother*. New York: Aladdin Books, 1976.
_____. *The Way to Start a Day*. New York: Charles Scribner's Sons, 1977.

_____. *When Clay Sings*. New York: Charles Scribner's Sons, 1972.

Bloom, Suzanne. *A Family for Jamie*. New York: Clarkson Potter Publishers, 1991.

Bond, Ruskin. *Cherry Tree*. Honesdale, PA: Caroline House, 1988.

Bonners, Susan. *The Wooden Doll*. New York: Lothrop, Lee & Shepard Books, 1991.

Booth, Barbara D. *Mandy*. New York: Lothrop, Lee & Shepard Books, 1991.

Brown, Tricia. *Lee Ann*. New York: G. P. Putnam's Sons, 1991.

Browne, Anthony. *Willy and Hugh*. New York: Alfred A. Knopf, Inc., 1991.

Bruchac, Joseph. *The Wind Eagle and Other Abenaki Stories*. Greenfield Center, NY: Bowman Books, 1985.

Bryan, Ashley. *The Cat's Purr*. New York: Atheneum, 1985.

_____. *The Dancing Granny*. New York: Aladdin Books, 1977.

Bunting, Eve. *How Many Days to America?* New York: Clarion Books, 1988.

_____. *Terrible Things*. Philadelphia: The Jewish Publication Society, 1989.

Cech, John. *My Grandmother's Journey*. New York: Bradbury Press, 1991.

Cherry, Lynne. *The Great Kapok Tree*. San Diego: Gulliver Books, 1990.

_____. *A River Ran Wild*. San Diego: Harcourt Brace and Company, 1992.

Chief Seattle. *Brother Eagle, Sister Sky*. New York: Dial Books, 1991.

Cohen, Barbara. *Molly's Pilgrim*. New York: Bantam Skylark, 1983.

Cooney, Barbara. *Miss Rumphius*. New York: Puffin Books, 1982.

Cowcher, Helen. *Tigress*. New York: Farrar, Straus & Giroux, Inc., 1991.

De Gerez, Toni. *Louhi, Witch of North Farm*. New York: Puffin Books, 1986.

DePaola, Tomie. *The Legend of the Bluebonnet*. New York: G. P. Putnam's Sons, 1983.

DiSalvo-Ryan, DyAnne. *Uncle Willie and the Soup Kitchen*. New York: Morrow Junior Books, 1991.

Dooley, Norah. *Everybody Cooks Rice*. Minneapolis: Carolrhoda Books, 1991.

Drucker, Malka. *Jacob's Rescue: A Holocaust Story*. New York: Bantam Skylark, 1993.

Dwight, Laura. *We Can Do It!* New York: Checkerboard Press, Inc., 1992.

Ernst, Lisa Campbell. *Sam Johnson and the Blue Ribbon Quilt*. New York: Lothrop, Lee & Shepard Books, 1983.

Estes, Eleanor. *The Hundred Dresses*. New York: Harcourt Brace Jovanovich, 1944, 1971.

Feder, Paula K. *The Feather-Bed Journey*. Morton Grove, IL: Albert Whitman & Company, 1995.

Fife, Dale H. *The Empty Lot*. San Francisco: Sierra Club Books, 1991.

Fluek, Toby Knobel. *Memories of My Life in a Polish Village 1930–1949*. New York: Alfred A. Knopf, Inc., 1990.

Fradin, Dennis Brindell. *Hanukkah*. Hillside, NJ: Enslow Publishers, Inc., 1990.

Friedman, Ina R. *How My Parents Learned to Eat*. Boston: Houghton Mifflin Co., 1984.

Garcia, Maria. *The Adventures of Connie and Diego*. Rev. ed. San Francisco: Children's Book Press, 1987.

Geras, Adele. *My Grandmother's Stories*. New York: Alfred A. Knopf, Inc., 1990.

Ginsburg, Marvell. *The Tattooed Torah*. New York: Union of American Hebrew Congregations, 1983.

Girard, Linda Walvoord. *At Daddy's on Saturdays*. Morton Grove, IL: Albert Whitman, 1987.

Gordon, Erica. *The Rabbi's Wisdom*. New York: Peter Bedrick Books, Inc., 1991.

Gray, Nigel. *A Country Far Away*. New York: Orchard Books, 1988.

Hamilton, Virginia. *The People Could Fly: American Black Folktales*. New York: Alfred A. Knopf, Inc., 1985.

Haskins, Jim. *Amazing Grace: The Story Behind the Song*. Brookfield, CT: The Millbrook Press, Inc., 1992.

Hautzig, Esther. *Riches*. New York: HarperCollins, Publishers, 1992.

Haviland, Virginia. *The Talking Pot*. Boston: Little, Brown and Company, 1971.

Heide, Florence Parry and Judith Heide Gilliland. *The Day of Ahmed's Secret*. New York: Lothrop, Lee & Shepard Books, 1990.

Hendry, Diana. *Christmas on Exeter Street*. New York: Alfred A. Knopf, Inc., 1989.

Herman, Erwin and Agnes Herman. *The Yanov Torah*. Rockville, MD: KAR-BEN Copies, 1985.

Hest, Amy. *The Ring and the Window Seat*. New York: Scholastic, Inc., 1990.

Hoestlandt, Jo. *Star of Fear, Star of Hope*. New York: Walker and Company, 1995.

Innocenti, Roberto. *Rose Blanche*. Minneapolis: Creative Education, Inc., 1995.

Isadora, Rachel. *Ben's Trumpet*. New York: Mulberry Books, 1979.

Jules, Jacqueline. *The Grey Striped Shirt, How Grandma and Grandpa Survived the Holocaust*. Los Angeles: Alef Design Group, 1993.

Kerr, Judith. *When Hitler Stole Pink Rabbit*. New York: Dell, 1987.

Klein, Gerda Weissmann. *Promise of a New Spring*. Chappaqua, NY: Rossel Books, 1981.

Knight, Margy Burns. *Talking Walls*. Gardiner, ME: Tilbury House, 1992.

_____. *Talking Walls: The Stories Continue*. Gardiner, ME: Tilbury House, 1995.

_____. *Who Belongs Here?* Gardiner, ME: Tilbury House, 1993.

Kraus, Robert. *Owliver*. New York: Prentice-Hall Books for Young Readers, 1974.

Kuklin, Susan. *How My Family Lives in America*. New York: Bradbury Press, 1992.

Kurelek, William. *Lumberjack*. Montreal: Tundra Books, Inc., 1974.

Lakin, Patricia. *Don't Forget*. New York: William Morrow & Company, Inc., 1994.

Lamorisse, Albert. *The Red Balloon*. New York: Doubleday, 1956.

Lester, Julius. *The Knee-High Man and Other Tales*. New York: Dial Books for Young Readers, 1972.

Levinson, Riki. *Watch the Stars Come Out*. New York: E. P. Dutton, 1985.

Levitin, Sonia. *The Man Who Kept His Heart in a Bucket*. New York: Dial Books for Young Readers, 1991.

Lionni, Leo. *The Biggest House in the World*. New York: Alfred A. Knopf, 1968.

_____. *Swimmy*. New York: Pantheon Books, 1968.

_____. *Tillie and the Wall*. New York: Alfred A. Knopf, Inc., 1989.

Lowry, Lois. *Number the Stars*. Boston: Houghton Mifflin Co., 1989.

Ludwig, Warren. *Old Noah's Elephants*. New York: G. P. Putnam's Sons, 1991.

Mani-Leib. *Yingl Tsingl Khvat*. Mt. Kisco, NY: Moyer Bell, 1918, 1986.

Martinez, Alejandro Cruz, et al. *The Woman Who Outshone the Sun*. San Francisco: Children's Book Press, 1991.

Matas, Carol. *Daniel's Story*. New York: Scholastic, 1993.

Mayo, Gretchen Will. *Earth Maker's Tales: North American Indian Stories*. New York: Walker & Co., 1989.

McCloskey, Robert. *Blueberries for Sal*. New York: Puffin Books, 1948, 1976.

McSwigan, Marie. *Snow Treasure*. New York: E. P. Dutton & Company, 1942.

Mendez, Phil. *The Black Snowman*. New York: Scholastic Trade, 1989.

Mills, Lauren. *The Rag Coat*. Boston: Little, Brown and Company, 1991.

Morpurgo, Michael. *Waiting for Anya*. New York: Viking, 1991.

Munsch, Robert. *The Paper Bag Princess*. Toronto: Annick Press, 1980.

Munsch, Robert and Michael Kusugak. *A Promise is a Promise*. Willowdale, Ont.: Firefly Books, 1988.

Nerlove, Miriam. *Flowers on the Wall*. New York: McEldry Books, 1996.

Oppenheim, Shulamith Levey. *The Lily Cupboard*. New York: Harper Collins, 1992.

Ortiz, Simon. *The People Shall Continue*. Rev. ed. San Francisco: Children's Book Press, 1988.

Osofsky, Audrey. *My Buddy*. New York: Henry Holt & Co., Inc., 1992.

Parker, Carol. *Why Do You Call Me Chocolate Boy?* Boothbay Harbor, ME: Gull Crest, 1993.

Passen, Lisa. *Fat, Fat Rose Marie*. New York: Henry Holt, 1991.

Pellegrini, Nina. *Families Are Different*. New York: Holiday House, Inc., 1991.

Peterson, Jeanne Whitehouse. *I Have a Sister—My Sister is Deaf*. New York: Harper Trophy, 1977.

Phillips, Mildred. *The Sign in Mendel's Window*. New York: Macmillan Publishing, 1985.

Polacco, Patricia. *Mrs. Katz and Tush.* New York: Bantam Books, 1992.

Pushker, Gloria Teles. *Toby Belfer Never Had a Christmas Tree.* Gretna, LA: Pelican Publishing Co., Inc., 1991.

Rabe, Berniece. *Where's Chimpy?* Niles, IL: Albert Whitman & Co., 1988.

Reuter, Elisabeth. *Best Friends.* New York: Pitspopany Press, 1994.

Ringgold, Faith. *Tar Beach.* New York: CrownPublishing Group, 1991.

Rohmer, Harriet, Octavio Chow and Morris Vidaure. *The Invisible Hunters.* San Francisco: Children's Book Press, 1987.

Rohmer, Harriet and Dorminster Wilson. *Mother Scorpion Country.* San Francisco: Children's Book Press, 1987.

Rose, Deborah Lee. *The People Who Hugged the Trees.* Niwot, CO: Roberts Rinehart Publishers, 1990.

Ross, Lillian Hammer. *Buba Leah and Her Paper Children.* Philadelphia: The Jewish Publication Society, 1991.

Russo, Marisabina. *A Visit to Oma.* New York: Greenwillow Books, 1991.

Sachs, Marily. *A Pocket Full of Seeds.* New York: (Scholastic Inc., 1973) Puffin Books, 1994.

Say, Allen. *Tree of Cranes.* Boston: Houghton Mifflin Co., 1991.

Schwartz, Amy. *Bea and Mr. Jones.* New York: Puffin Books, 1982.

Sewall, Marcia. *People of the Breaking Day.* New York: Atheneum, 1990.

Shetterly, Susan Hand. *Raven's Light.* New York: Atheneum, 1991.

Sim, Dorrith M. *In My Pocket.* San Diego: Harcourt Brace, 1996.

Simon, Norma. *Why Am I Different?* Niles, IL.: Albert Whitman & Co., 1976.

Spier, Peter. *People.* New York: Delacorte Press, 1980.

Spinelli, Eileen. *Somebody Loves You, Mr. Hatch.* New York: Bradbury Press, 1991.

Steptoe, John. *Mufaro's Beautiful Daughters.* New York: Lothrop, Lee & Shepard Books, 1987.

_____. *Stevie.* New York: Harper Trophy, 1986.

_____. *The Story of Jumping Mouse.* New York: Lothrop, Lee & Shepard Books, 1984.

Surat, Michele Maria. *Angel Child, Dragon Child.* New York: Scholastic, Inc., 1983.

Tran-Khanh-Tuyet. *The Little Weaver of Thai-Yen Village.* Rev. ed. San Francisco: Children's Book Press, 1987.

Treseder, Terry W. *Hear O Israel: A Story of the Warsaw Ghetto.* New York: Atheneum, 1990.

Tresselt, Alvin. *The Mitten.* New York: Mulberry Books, 1964.

Va, Leong. *A Letter to the King.* New York: HarperCollins, Publishers, 1988.

Volkmer, Jane Anne. *Song of the Chirimia.* Minneapolis: Carolrhoda Books, 1990.

Vos, Ida. *Anna Is Still Here.* Boston: Houghton Mifflin, 1993.

_____. *Hide and Seek.* Boston: Houghton Mifflin, 1991.

Wall, Lina Mao and Cathy Spagnoli. *Judge Rabbit and the Tree Spirit.* San Francisco: Children's Book Press, 1991.

White Deer of Autumn. *Ceremony—In the Circle of Life.* Milwaukee: Raintree/Steck-Vaughn Publishers, 1983.

Wild, Margaret. *Let the Celebrations Begin!* New York: Orchard Books, 1991.

Williams, Karen Lynn. *Galimoto.* New York: Mulberry Books, 1990.

Williams, Vera B. *A Chair for My Mother.* New York: Mulberry Books, 1982.

Winter, Jeanette. *Follow the Drinking Gourd.* New York: Alfred A. Knopf, Inc., 1988.

Young, Ed. *Lon Po Po.* New York: Philomel Books, 1989.

Ziefert, Harriet. *A New Coat for Anna.* New York: Alfred A. Knopf, Inc., 1986.